THE ULTIMATE
Christmas
COOKBOOK

THE ULTIMATE
Christmas
COOKBOOK

C O N T

Sugar-free pudding, page 74

Salmon and fennel frittata, page 137

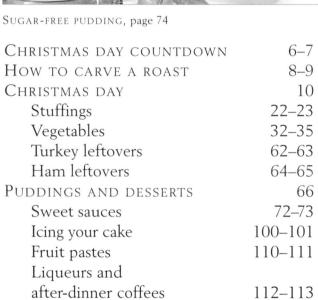

Berries in Champagne jelly, page 82

Pickled prawns, page 52

E N T S

Honey-glazed ham, page 14

Pineapple and mango jam, page 166

The Publisher thanks the following for their assistance: Chief Australia, Sunbeam Corporation, Kambrook, Sheldon & Hammond, Southcorp Appliances, Bertoli Olive Oil, Waterford Wedgewood, Christoflé, Villeroy & Boch, Hale Imports, Ruby Star Traders, Camarge.

Pork with apple and prune stuffing, page 20

All recipes are double-tested by our team of home economists. When we test our recipes, we rate them for ease of preparation. The following cookery ratings are on the recipes in this book, making them easy to use and understand.

A single Cooking with Confidence symbol indicates a recipe that is simple and generally quick to make—perfect for beginners.

Two symbols indicate the need for just a little more care and a little more time.

Three symbols indicate special dishes that need more investment in time, care and patience—but the results are worth it.

IMPORTANT

Those who might be at risk from the effects of salmonella food poisoning (the elderly, pregnant women, young children and those suffering from immune deficiency diseases) should consult their GP with any concerns about eating raw eggs.

CHRISTMAS DAY COUNTDOWN

CHRISTMAS is a time of relaxing with family and friends, of giving and receiving, and indulging in the better things in life. However, if you're the one doing all the organising, it can all seem a bit overwhelming. We are trying to take some of the pressure off, to help you plan ahead and save time and worry, whether your event be quiet pre-Christmas drinks or a fully fledged Christmas day extravaganza. After all, you should be able to relax and enjoy the spirit of the season with everyone else. The key to success is organisation, so here's a schedule to help you along.

1 YEAR AHEAD	✳ Of course, it sounds ridiculous to start planning this early, but the post-Christmas sales are an ideal time to stock up on budget-priced decorations and place settings.
3 MONTHS AHEAD 	✳ Work out your budget, a rough guest list and plan your menu. ✳ If you need to hire equipment—anything from a marquee to cutlery—do so. ✳ Christmas cakes and puddings can be made well ahead of time if stored properly. Wrap securely in greaseproof paper, then in plastic wrap and store in an airtight container in the refrigerator or a cool, dark place. Indeed, a long storage time is actually beneficial as it allows the flavours to develop. As a general rule, Christmas cake can be stored for up to 3 months and puddings for up to 6 weeks. Both can also be frozen for up to 12 months. ✳ Make your liqueur fruits so they are ready for Christmas day or for giving as gifts. If you can, buy fruits in season when they are cheaper and full of flavour as they will keep bottled for up to 6 months.
1 MONTH AHEAD	✳ If you have storage space, purchase wine, beer and soft drinks now. Or, if you have planned a large party, order drinks now and have them delivered on the day. ✳ Order turkeys and hams. As a general guide a 7 kg ham will serve around 20 people and a 4.5 kg turkey will feed 6–8 people when served as a main course with vegetables and all the trimmings.
1 WEEK AHEAD	✳ Ensure you have a carving knife and fork on hand—it is a good idea to have your knives professionally sharpened. Some sturdy chopping boards will come in handy too! Make sure your baking dish is large enough for your ham or turkey. ✳ Prepare your shopping list and buy most of your non-perishable ingredients. Pick up items like napkins, tablecloths, candles and toothpicks while you are shopping. ✳ Make your gingerbread house, mince pies, shortbread, biscotti, panettone, panforte, stollen, etc and keep them well sealed in an airtight container.

* Ice the Christmas cake, if required (see page 100).
* Make your jams, curds, chocolates and fudges.
* Freeze ahead—the great thing about many Christmas goodies is that they can be made ahead and either frozen or left, well sealed, at either room temperature or in the refrigerator until ready to use.

2 DAYS AHEAD

* Try to choose a dessert, starter or side dish that can be made, at least partially, beforehand and will keep refrigerated.
* If you are having a buffet, wrap the cutlery in napkins and place in an attractive, decorated basket.
* Think about the food you are serving and select your serving dishes, platters and utensils. Make sure they are all clean, polished and a suitable size.
* Fill up your salt and pepper shakers, sugar bowls, etc.
* Defrost anything that needs defrosting. A large turkey can take up to 3 days— take it out of the original packaging and sit it on a rack in a baking tray in the refrigerator. Make sure it is not sitting in the liquid while thawing. Cover with clean plastic wrap.

1 DAY AHEAD

* Set your table—iron the tablecloth, put the candles in holders, fold the napkins and lay out any decorations.
* Polish glasses and cutlery, and then put a light cloth over the whole setting to ensure no dust or greasy fingers spoil your hard work.
* Buy all your last-minute fresh produce, seafood and fresh flowers.
* Make stuffings and refrigerate them in a covered bowl.
* Make your pavlova, or any dessert sauces or custards that will keep overnight.
* Prepare the glaze for your ham and score and stud the ham with cloves.
* Refrigerate all your drinks now unless you are purchasing ice tomorrow.
* Don't forget the little things like butter, coffee, milk and garbage bags.
* Calculate how long things will take to cook and plan what to cook when.

Christmas Day

* Preheat your oven. Just prior to cooking, prepare your roast by trimming, trussing, tying or stuffing as required. Do not stuff a turkey ahead of time as bacteria can develop in the cavity even when refrigerated and no-one wants to be responsible for giving their entire family food poisoning—especially on Christmas day!!
* Put the ham, turkey or other roast on to cook.
* Vegetables to be roasted should go on an hour before the meat is cooked.
* Other vegetables should be peeled and chopped when you first put your roast on and finished off just toward the end of cooking. Vegetables that don't take long to cook, such as peas, beans or asparagus, should be cooked while your roast is resting.
* Gravy can also be made while the meat is resting.
* If you are having pudding, it will take 2 hours to reheat.
* Remember to chill the drinks, warm the plates, put on some music, fill your glass and, above all, enjoy yourself!

HOW TO CARVE A ROAST

Carving a roast can be tricky, so follow these instructions and even the most inexperienced carver will be able to serve a perfect Christmas roast in a quick and fuss-free manner.

TURKEY AND ham are the most popular Christmas roasts—and the most daunting. They are rarely eaten at other times of the year and can easily confound even the most confident of cooks when it comes to carving and presenting them.

Before carving any roast, it is important to let the meat 'rest' for 15 minutes or so. Remove the roast from the oven and cover it with foil so the heat does not escape too quickly and the juices can settle and distribute evenly, moistening and tenderising the flesh.

Also, make sure your carving knife is sharp and try to slice rather than saw—the more you hack into the meat, tearing the flesh, the more juices are lost, making the meat dry and tasteless. An electric knife can make life much easier. A carving fork is also important for holding the meat steady. Do not pierce the meat if possible—try to use the back or the flat of the fork to get a good hold. When carving a bird, however, a sharp-pronged fork is usually needed to dig deep into the carcass (not the flesh) to keep it still.

Always carve on a carving board, not a serving platter. China and metal surfaces can scratch easily and can be quite slippery, causing you to lose control of the knife.

It is preferable to use a carving board with a rim around the edges to catch any excess juices—this not only stops the juices from spilling over onto the table but it also means they can be strained off and used in your gravy for an extra boost of flavour. It is also a good idea to place a damp cloth underneath your board to keep it steady while carving.

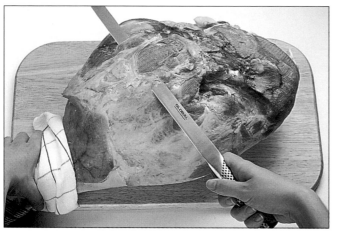

Cut a slice from the underside of the ham to steady it while carving.

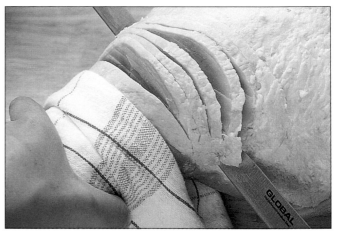

Cut thin slices, working away from the knuckle.

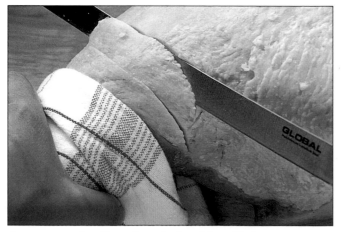

Remove a wedge of ham from the knuckle end before you carve.

Cut the slices away from the bone and serve.

Remove the leg and thigh section from the body of the turkey.

Similarly, remove the turkey wing by cutting through the joint.

With larger birds it is possible to separate the leg and thigh.

Carve the turkey breast, using the fork to keep the bird steady.

HAM

1 After resting, place the ham on a cutting board with the bone to the left. Use a clean tea towel to hold the bone firmly while carving. Remember to keep your fingers away from the blade! Slice a piece from the underside of the leg so that it sits flat on the board. Remove this slice and set aside.

2 Slice into the meat about 10 cm from the knuckle. Make another cut at an angle to the first so that it forms a wedge, then remove. Continue cutting to the right, cutting several thin slices right down to the bone. The meat will still be attached to the bone so to release the pieces you must run the knife along the bone, under the meat. Lift off the slices with the flat of the knife. Cut enough slices for serving, covering the slices with foil as you go if the ham is to be served warm.

TURKEY

1 After resting, place the turkey on a cutting board, breast-side-up and with the legs facing you.

2 Use a carving fork to steady the bird and cut downward into the skin and meat where the leg meets the breast. Bend the leg outwards with the carving knife until you can see the joint where the thighbone and the backbone connect. Keep cutting at a slight angle towards the joint, then cut down and through it until the leg section (the thigh and drumstick) can be easily removed. Depending on the size of the turkey, you can also cut through the leg at the joint to remove the thigh and have two separate pieces. Set the meat aside on a warm serving dish and keep covered with foil while you are carving the rest of the turkey. This will keep it warm and stop it from drying out.

3 On the same side of the bird, find where the wing meets the body and cut down, again until you meet the joint. You may need to pull the wing out with your left hand while you are cutting with your right hand to loosen the wing from the bird. Set aside and cover to keep warm.

4 Continuing on the same side, begin to carve the breast. Start at the top of the breast where it attaches to the ridge of bone and carve downwards in even slices, at a slight angle, towards the cutting board. Add to the rest of the meat and cover. Now repeat this process on the other side of the turkey. To remove the wishbone, snip the sinews on either side.

5 Remove the stuffing from the opening of the carcass with a spoon and, depending on the texture of the stuffing, serve it either in slices or in spoonfuls.

CHRISTMAS DAY

CHRISTMAS DAY is a time of family and friends, of indulging in fine foods and celebrating all there is to be grateful for. It's also a chance to get out your best tableware. . . Fine china plates, crystal glassware and thick damask tablecloths— a traditional Christmas table setting can't help but invoke the holiday spirit. How could you eat roast turkey any other way?

ROAST TURKEY

Christmas dinner would hardly seem complete without an enormous turkey, with stuffing and roast vegetables, weighing down the centre of the table. Make gravy to accompany it, and why not try bread sauce or some cranberry relish as well.

Preparation time: 45 minutes
Total cooking time: 2 hours +
    15 minutes resting
Serves 6–8

4.5 kg turkey
stuffing (see pages 22–23)
2 tablespoons oil
½ cup (125 ml) chicken stock

1 Preheat the oven to moderate 180°C (350°F/Gas 4).

2 Remove the neck and giblets from inside the turkey. Wash the turkey well and pat the cavity and the skin dry with paper towels.

3 Spoon the stuffing loosely into the turkey cavity. Tuck the wings underneath and join the cavity with a skewer. Tie the legs together. Place on a rack in a baking dish. Roast for 2 hours, basting with the combined oil and the chicken stock. Cover the breast and legs with foil after 1 hour if the turkey is overbrowning. Test by inserting a skewer between the drumstick and thigh. If the turkey is cooked, the juices will run clear. Reserve any pan juices for making the gravy. Cover and leave to rest for 15 minutes before carving.

NUTRITION PER SERVE (8)
Protein 125 g; Fat 22 g; Carbohydrate 0 g; Dietary Fibre 0 g; Cholesterol 275 mg; 2931 kJ (701 cal)

NOTE: It is always a good idea to salt the turkey as a precaution against the growth of harmful bacteria. To do this, pour 2 tablespoons salt into the turkey carcass. Use your hand, or a clean tea towel, to rub the salt into the carcass, making sure it covers all of the inside. Rinse the carcass with water, making sure all the salt is removed. Pat dry with another clean tea towel and proceed with stuffing and baking the turkey.

Remove the neck and the giblets from inside the turkey before you roast it.

After stuffing the turkey, tuck the wings underneath the body.

TURKEY GRAVY

Once the turkey is cooked, drain off all except 2 tablespoons of the pan juices from the baking dish. Place the dish on the stove over low heat, add 2 tablespoons plain flour and stir over medium heat until well browned. Gradually add 1½ cups (375 ml) hot chicken stock, stirring until the gravy boils and thickens. *Makes 1¼ cups (315 ml)*

BREAD SAUCE

Push 2 whole cloves into an onion and place it in a pan with 1 cup (250 ml) milk and a bay leaf. Bring to the boil, watching carefully so that it does not boil over, then remove from the heat, and leave for 10 minutes. Remove the onion and bay leaf and discard. Add 50 g breadcrumbs (made with about 3 slices of day-old bread in a food processor) to the pan and season with salt and freshly ground black pepper. Return to the heat, cover and simmer gently for 10 minutes, stirring occasionally. Stir in 3 tablespoons cream. *Makes 1 cup (250 ml)*

CRANBERRY RELISH

Put 4 cups (500 g) fresh or frozen cranberries, ½ cup (125 g) sugar, ½ cup (125 ml) fresh or bottled orange juice, the rind of 1 medium orange, 1 cinnamon stick and 2 tablespoons port in a heavy-based pan. Bring to the boil, then reduce the heat and simmer for 5 minutes. Remove the cinnamon stick, making sure you remove any small pieces that have broken away from the stick, and orange rind and cool before serving. Store, covered, in the refrigerator for up to a week. *Makes 2 cups (500 ml)*

Join the cavity with a skewer and tie the legs together to seal the stuffing in.

Place the turkey on a rack in a baking dish to roast.

HONEY-GLAZED HAM

A mustard and redcurrant glaze is a delicious alternative to this honey glaze, and either can be accompanied by cumberland or mustard sauce.

Preparation time: 30 minutes
Total cooking time: 65 minutes +
   15 minutes resting
Serves 20

7 kg leg ham
cloves, to garnish

GLAZE
2/3 cup (125 g) soft brown sugar
1/4 cup (90 g) honey
1 tablespoon English mustard

1 Preheat the oven to moderate 180°C (350°F/Gas 4). Using a sharp knife, cut through the rind 6 cm from the shank end. To remove the rind from the ham, run a thumb around the edge, under the rind and carefully pull back. Using a sharp knife, remove and discard some of the excess fat from the ham.

2 Using a sharp knife, score the fat with cuts crossways and then diagonally to form a diamond pattern. Do not cut all the way through to the ham or the fat will fall off during cooking. Press a clove into the centre of each diamond.

3 To make the glaze, combine all the ingredients in a bowl and spread carefully over the ham with a palette knife or the back of a spoon.

4 Place the ham on a rack in a deep baking dish. Add 2 cups (500 ml) water to the dish. Cover the ham and dish securely with foil, and cook for 45 minutes.

5 Remove the ham from the oven. Increase the heat to hot 210°C (415°F/Gas 6–7). Return the ham to the oven and bake for 20 minutes, or until the surface is slightly caramelised. Rest for 15 minutes before carving.

NUTRITION PER SERVE
Protein 53 g; Fat 10 g; Carbohydrate 10 g; Dietary Fibre 0 g; Cholesterol 144 mg; 1439 kJ (345 cal)

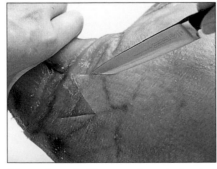

Use a sharp knife to cut through the rind at the shank end of the ham.

Run your thumb under the rind and carefully pull it back.

CUMBERLAND SAUCE

Boil the shredded rind of 2 oranges and 1 lemon with 1 cup (250 ml) water for 5 minutes, then drain and set aside. Squeeze the juice from the oranges and lemon and place in a pan. Add a 225 g jar redcurrant jelly, 2 teaspoons Dijon mustard, 2 tablespoons red wine vinegar, 1 cup (250 ml) port and the reserved rind. Slowly bring to the boil, stirring as the jelly melts. Reduce the heat and simmer for 15 minutes. Season and serve at room temperature. Cover and refrigerate for up to 1 week. *Makes 2 cups (500 ml)*

MUSTARD CREAM

Combine 1/3 cup (90 g) French or grain mustard, 2 crushed garlic cloves, 1 cup (250 g) sour cream and 1/2 cup (125 ml) cream. Leave, covered, in the refrigerator for 1 hour then season well before serving. This sauce can be served warm by placing it in a small pan and stirring over low heat until heated through. Take care not to boil the sauce or it will split. *Makes 2 cups (500 ml)*

MUSTARD AND REDCURRANT GLAZE

Combine 1/3 cup (90 g) Dijon mustard, 1 cup (315 g) redcurrant jelly, 4 crushed garlic cloves, 2 tablespoons oil and 2 tablespoons soy sauce in a pan. Stir over medium heat until the jelly has melted. Take care that the glaze does not catch on the bottom of the pan. Use to glaze ham in the same way as the honey glaze is used. *Makes 1 1/3 cups (330 ml)*

Score the ham in a diamond pattern using a sharp knife.

Press cloves into the diamonds and cover the ham with the glaze.

ROAST BEEF WITH YORKSHIRE PUDDINGS

Cooking times for roast beef vary, but as a general rule, for a rare result, cook for 20 minutes per 500 g, for a medium result, cook for 30 minutes per 500 g, and for a well-done result, cook for 35 minutes per 500 g.

Preparation time: 15 minutes +
　1 hour standing
Total cooking time:
　1 hour 40 minutes +
　15 minutes resting
Serves 6

2 kg piece roasting beef
　(Scotch fillet, rump or sirloin)
2 cloves garlic, crushed

YORKSHIRE PUDDINGS
¾ cup (90 g) plain flour
½ cup (125 ml) milk
2 eggs

1 Preheat the oven to very hot 240°C (475°F/Gas 9). Rub the beef with the garlic and some freshly cracked black pepper and drizzle with a little oil. Place on a rack in a baking dish and roast for 20 minutes.

2 Meanwhile, to make the Yorkshire puddings, sift the flour and ½ teaspoon salt into a large bowl, make a well in the centre and whisk in the milk. In a separate bowl, whisk the eggs until fluffy, then add them to the batter and mix well. Add ½ cup (125 ml) water and whisk until large bubbles form on the surface. Cover the bowl with plastic wrap and refrigerate for 1 hour.

3 Reduce the heat to moderate 180°C (350°F/Gas 4) and roast the meat for 1 hour for a rare result, or longer for well done. Cover loosely with foil and leave in a warm place for 20 minutes before carving. Increase the oven to hot 220°C (425°F/Gas 7).

4 Pour off all the pan juices into a jug and reserve for making gravy. Put ½ teaspoon of the juices into 12 ⅓ cup (80 ml) muffin tins. Heat the tins in the oven until the fat is almost smoking. Take the batter out of

the refrigerator and whisk again until bubbles form on the surface. Pour the batter into each muffin tin to three-quarters full. Bake for 20 minutes,

then reduce the oven to moderate 180°C (350°F/Gas 4) and cook for a further 10 minutes, or until puffed and lightly golden. Make the gravy

Rub the beef with crushed garlic and freshly cracked black pepper.

Whisk the ingredients for the Yorkshire puddings to a smooth batter.

CREAMY HORSERADISH
Combine 175 g horseradish cream, 1 finely chopped spring onion bulb and 1/4 cup (60 g) sour cream in a small bowl. Fold in 1/2 cup (125 ml) softly whipped cream. Season. *Makes about 1 1/2 cups (375 ml)*

RED WINE GRAVY
Place 2 tablespoons of reserved pan juices in the baking dish on the stove over low heat. Add 2 tablespoons plain flour and stir well, ensuring that you scrape the bottom of the dish to incorporate all the sediment. Cook over medium heat for 1–2 minutes, stirring constantly, until the flour is well browned. Combine 1/3 cup (80 ml) red wine and 2 1/2 cups (600 ml) beef stock, and gradually stir into the flour mixture, making sure the liquid is well absorbed before each addition. Heat, stirring constantly, until the gravy boils and thickens. Simmer for 3 minutes, then season to taste with salt and black pepper. *Makes 3 cups (750 ml)*

BEARNAISE SAUCE
Put 3 chopped spring onions, 1/2 cup (125 ml) dry white wine, 2 tablespoons tarragon vinegar and 1 tablespoon chopped fresh tarragon (or 1 teaspoon dried tarragon) in a pan and boil rapidly until only 2 tablespoons of liquid is left. Strain with a fine sieve, put in a food processor with 4 egg yolks and process for 30 seconds. With the motor running, slowly add 125 g melted butter in a thin stream. Process until the sauce has thickened and is a smooth consistency. Add 1 tablespoon lemon juice, and season with salt and white pepper. *Makes 1 cup (250 ml)*

and carve the roast while the puddings are baking.

5 Serve the roast beef with the hot Yorkshire puddings and gravy.

NUTRITION PER SERVE
Protein 100 g; Fat 33 g; Carbohydrate 35 g; Dietary Fibre 2 g; Cholesterol 430 mg; 3510 kJ (840 cal)

Put 1 teaspoon of pan juices in each patty pan before adding the batter.

Bake the puddings for 10 minutes, or until they are risen, crisp and golden.

ROAST DUCK

Roast duck is a delicious alternative to turkey. Make sure the duck is sitting on a roasting rack in the baking dish while cooking to drain off excess fat.

Preparation time: 40 minutes
Total cooking time:
    2 hours 15 minutes +
    15 minutes resting
Serves 4

2 kg duck, with neck
2 chicken wings, chopped
1/2 cup (125 ml) white wine
1 onion, chopped
1 small carrot, sliced
1 tomato, chopped
bouquet garni (a bay leaf and
    small sprigs of parsley,
    thyme and marjoram,
    in muslin tied with string)

1 Place the duck neck, chicken wings and wine in a pan. Simmer over medium heat for 5 minutes, or until the wine has reduced by half. Add the onion, carrot, tomato, bouquet garni and 2 cups (500 ml) water. Bring to the boil and simmer gently for 40 minutes. Strain and set aside about 1 cup (250 ml) of the stock. Discard the vegetables and the bouquet garni.

2 Preheat the oven to moderate 180°C (350°F/Gas 4). Place the duck in a large pan, cover with boiling water, and then drain. Dry with paper towels. Using a fine skewer, prick all over the outside of the duck, piercing only the skin, not the flesh. Place the duck breast-side-down on a roasting rack in a baking dish and roast for 50 minutes.

3 Drain off any fat, turn the duck over and add the stock to the pan. Roast for 40 minutes, or until the breast is golden brown. Pour off and reserve the stock. Remove the duck from the pan and leave in a warm place for 15 minutes before carving. Reserve any pan juices for making gravy or orange sauce.

NUTRITION PER SERVE
Protein 90 g; Fat 30 g; Carbohydrate 3 g; Dietary Fibre 1.5 g; Cholesterol 550 mg; 2689 kJ (640 cal)

Make a bouquet garni with a bay leaf and sprigs of parsley, thyme and marjoram.

After simmering the stock ingredients, strain and reserve 1 cup of the liquid.

ORANGE SAUCE

Skim any extra fat off the reserved stock from the duck. Add 2 tablespoons shredded orange rind, 2/3 cup (170 ml) orange juice and 1/3 cup (80 ml) Cointreau. Bring to the boil, then reduce the heat and simmer gently for 5 minutes. Blend 2 teaspoons cornflour with 1 tablespoon water, and stir into the sauce until it boils and thickens. *Makes 2/3 cup (170 ml)*

CHERRY SAUCE

Drain 350 g morello (sour) cherries, reserving the syrup. Measure the syrup and add red wine to make 1 cup (250 ml). Combine the syrup and wine in a pan with 1 strip orange rind, 1 tablespoon sugar, 1/2 small chicken stock cube, and 1/4 teaspoon ground cinnamon. Bring to the boil, then reduce the heat and simmer for 4 minutes. Blend 2 teaspoons cornflour with 1 tablespoon water and stir into the sauce. Return to the boil, stirring, until thickened. Add the cherries and simmer for 5 minutes. Remove the rind, add 15 g butter, stir until melted and serve. *Makes 1 1/2 cups (375 ml)*

DUCK GRAVY

Strain the juices from the baking dish into a small jug. Discard all but 1 tablespoon of the fat from the surface of the juices. Place the reserved fat in a pan over medium heat, add 2 tablespoons plain flour and stir until smooth. Cook over moderate heat for 3–4 minutes, or until lightly golden. Remove from the heat and add the remaining pan juices and 1 cup (250 ml) chicken stock, stirring until combined. Return to the heat and cook, stirring, until the gravy thickens. *Makes 1 cup (250 ml)*

Use a fine skewer to prick the skin of the duck, being careful not to pierce the flesh.

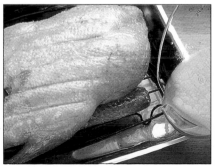

Remove any fat from the pan, turn the duck over and pour the stock into the pan.

PORK WITH APPLE AND PRUNE STUFFING

Pork rind must be scored before cooking for it to crisp up properly. Ask your butcher to do this for you.

Preparation time: 35 minutes
Total cooking time:
    2 hours 15 minutes +
    15 minutes resting
Serves 8

2 kg piece boned pork loin
1 small green apple, chopped
¹/₃ cup (90 g) pitted chopped
    prunes
2 tablespoons port
1 tablespoon chopped fresh parsley
olive oil and salt, to rub on pork

1 Preheat the oven to very hot 240°C (475°F/Gas 9). Score the pork rind (if the butcher hasn't already done so). To make the stuffing, combine the apple, prunes, port and parsley. Lay the pork loin fat-side-down on a board. Spread the stuffing over the meat side, roll up and secure with skewers or string at regular intervals. If some of the filling falls out while tying, carefully push back in with a flat-bladed knife. Rub generously with oil and salt.

2 Place on a rack in a baking dish. Bake the pork for 15 minutes, then reduce the heat to moderate 180°C (350°F/Gas 4). Bake for a further 1¹/₂–2 hours, or until the pork is cooked through. Cover and leave for 15 minutes before carving. Reserve any pan juices for gravy.

NUTRITION PER SERVE
Protein 57 g; Fat 6.5 g; Carbohydrate 7.5 g; Dietary Fibre 1 g; Cholesterol 120 mg; 1350 kJ (320 cal)

NOTE: If you prefer your rind really crackly, carefully remove it from the meat, cutting between the fat layer and the meat. Scrape off any excess fat and put the rind on a piece of aluminium foil. Place under a moderate grill, and grill until the rind has crackled.

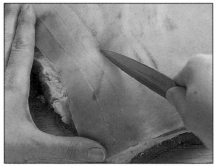

If your butcher has not scored the pork rind, you must do this before cooking.

Spread the apple and prune stuffing over the meat side of the loin.

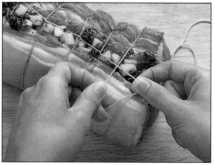

Roll up the pork loin, securing with string or skewers at regular intervals.

Rub the pork loin with oil and salt before cooking to ensure a crisp rind.

CHAMPAGNE APPLE SAUCE

Boil 3/4 cup (185 ml) Champagne or sparkling wine in a pan for 1 minute. Add 4 green apples, peeled, cored and chopped, and 1/2 teaspoon finely grated lemon rind. Cover and simmer until the apple is tender. Stir in 1 tablespoon finely chopped fresh thyme and leave to cool for 5 minutes. Purée in a food processor. Gradually add 45 g chopped butter, processing between additions. Season to taste and serve warm. *Makes 2 cups (500 ml)*

PRUNE AND COINTREAU SAUCE

Place 250 g pitted prunes, 1 cup (250 ml) white wine, 1/2 cup (125 ml) orange juice, 1/4 cup (60 ml) water and 1 tablespoon Cointreau in a pan. Bring to the boil, then reduce the heat and simmer for 10 minutes. Remove from the heat and add 1/4 cup (60 ml) orange juice, 1/4 cup (60 ml) water and 1 tablespoon Cointreau, and cool slightly. Pass through a fine sieve into a clean pan. Heat before serving and add 20 g chilled and chopped butter, a little at a time, whisking to thicken slightly. *Makes 1 1/4 cups (315 ml)*

CALVADOS GRAVY

Drain off all but 2 tablespoons of the pan juices from the baking dish. Place on the stove over moderate heat, add 1 tablespoon Calvados and stir. Cook for 1 minute. Remove from the heat, stir in 2 tablespoons plain flour and mix well. Return to the heat and cook for 2 minutes, stirring. Gradually add 1 1/2 cups (375 ml) chicken stock and 1/2 cup (125 ml) unsweetened apple juice, and cook, stirring, until the gravy thickens. Season to taste. *Makes 2 cups (500 ml)*

STUFFINGS

The wonderful, fresh ingredients in stuffings add colour, flavour and texture to your roast. They also help turn everyday meals into special occasion feasts. All stuffings make enough to stuff a 4.5 kg turkey.

Citrus stuffing

Heat 1 tablespoon oil in a small pan. Add 2 finely chopped onions and cook until soft, then transfer to a large bowl and cool. Add 400 g sausage mince, 4 cups (320 g) fresh white breadcrumbs, 2 crushed garlic cloves, 1 tablespoon each grated lemon and orange rind, and 1 cup (120 g) finely chopped pecans and mix to combine. Season with salt and pepper and mix well. Suitable for roast turkey or pork.

Cashew and herb stuffing

Heat 60 g butter in a pan, add 1 chopped onion and 2 crushed garlic cloves and cook until golden. Transfer to a large bowl and allow to cool. Add 2½ cups (465 g) cooked brown rice, 1 cup (185 g) chopped dried apricots, ½ cup (80 g) chopped unsalted cashews, ¼ cup (15 g) chopped fresh parsley, 2 tablespoons chopped fresh mint, 1 tablespoon lemon juice and salt and pepper to taste. Suitable for roast turkey, pork or duck.

Rice and fruit stuffing

Place 3 cups (600 g) cooked long-grain rice, ½ cup (80 g) toasted pine nuts, 1½ cups (280 g) chopped dried apricots, 1½ cups (375 g) chopped pitted prunes, 4 sliced spring onions, 1 tablespoon finely grated orange rind, ⅓ cup (80 ml) orange juice, ½ teaspoon salt, a pinch of white pepper and 1 lightly beaten egg in a large bowl and mix to combine. Suitable for roast turkey, pork or duck.

Pistachio stuffing

Heat 2 tablespoons oil in a small pan and cook 5 finely chopped spring onions and 2 teaspoons grated fresh ginger for 2 minutes. Add 6 chopped bacon rashers and cook for 3–4 minutes. Transfer to a large bowl and allow to cool. Add 350 g pork and veal mince, 2 cups (160 g) fresh breadcrumbs, ⅓ cup (105 g) marmalade, ½ cup (30 g) chopped fresh parsley, 1 lightly beaten egg and 1 cup (150 g) pistachio kernels, season with salt and pepper and mix to combine. Suitable for roast turkey or pork.

Mushroom and tomato stuffing

Heat 2 tablespoons oil in a pan. Add 1 finely chopped onion, 3 crushed garlic cloves, 3 cups (270 g) finely sliced button mushrooms and 2 chopped tomatoes and cook for 5 minutes. Remove from the heat. Combine the mushroom mixture with 2 cups (370 g) cooked white or brown rice, ⅓ cup (50 g) finely chopped sundried tomatoes, 2 tablespoons shredded fresh basil, ⅓ cup (35 g) freshly grated Parmesan, 2 lightly beaten eggs, salt and pepper in a bowl and mix to combine. Suitable for roast turkey, pork or duck.

Ricotta and bacon stuffing

Finely chop 4 bacon rashers. Fry in a dry pan until crisp. Remove and set aside. In the same pan, heat 1 tablespoon oil and fry 2 chopped onions and 2 crushed garlic cloves until golden. Combine 2 cups (500 g) ricotta cheese, 1 lightly beaten egg, ⅓ cup (35 g) freshly grated Parmesan, 2 cups (160 g) fresh breadcrumbs, ½ cup (30 g) chopped fresh parsley, 2 tablespoons chopped fresh chives, 2 tablespoons chopped fresh tarragon, a pinch of nutmeg and the onion and bacon in a large bowl and mix to combine. Suitable for roast turkey or pork.

BAKED SALMON

Baked salmon is a perfect light alternative to traditional roast turkey or ham. Add a creamy cucumber, a hollandaise or dill mayonnaise sauce.

Preparation time: 10 minutes
Total cooking time: 30 minutes +
    45 minutes standing
Serves 8

2 kg whole salmon, cleaned,
    gutted and scaled
2 spring onions, roughly
    chopped
3 sprigs fresh dill
1/2 lemon, thinly sliced
6 black peppercorns
1/4 cup (60 ml) dry white wine
3 bay leaves

1 Preheat the oven to moderate 180°C (350°F/Gas 4). Rinse the salmon under cold running water and pat dry inside and out with paper towels. Stuff the salmon cavity with the spring onion, dill, lemon and peppercorns.

2 Brush a large double-layered piece of foil with oil and lay the salmon on the foil. Sprinkle on the wine and arrange the bay leaves over the top. Fold the foil over and wrap up, covering the salmon tightly.

3 Place the salmon in a shallow baking dish in the oven and cook for 30 minutes. Turn the oven off and leave the salmon in the oven for 45 minutes with the door closed.

4 Undo the foil and carefully peel away the skin of the salmon on the top side. Carefully flip the salmon onto the serving plate and remove the skin from the other side. Pull out the fins and any visible bones. Serve at room temperature with lemon slices.

NUTRITION PER SERVE
Protein 45 g; Fat 30 g; Carbohydrate 0 g; Dietary Fibre 0 g; Cholesterol 175 mg; 1930 kJ (459 cal)

NOTE: Do not open or remove the foil during the cooking or standing time. If the salmon is too long for your baking tray, remove the head before baking.

Stuff the fish with spring onion, dill, lemon and peppercorns.

Arrange the bay leaves over the top of the fish before wrapping it in foil.

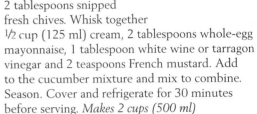

CUCUMBER SAUCE

Cut 4 large Lebanese cucumbers in half lengthways and scoop out the seeds. Chop into 5 mm cubes and mix with 2 tablespoons chopped capers, 2 tablespoons chopped pickled gherkins and 2 tablespoons snipped fresh chives. Whisk together 1/2 cup (125 ml) cream, 2 tablespoons whole-egg mayonnaise, 1 tablespoon white wine or tarragon vinegar and 2 teaspoons French mustard. Add to the cucumber mixture and mix to combine. Season. Cover and refrigerate for 30 minutes before serving. *Makes 2 cups (500 ml)*

HOLLANDAISE

Melt 175 g butter, skim any froth from the surface and cool. Mix 4 egg yolks with 2 tablespoons water and whisk for 30 seconds, or until the mixture is pale and foamy. Place over very low heat and whisk for about 2–3 minutes, or until thick and the whisk leaves a trail—do not let the pan get too hot or the eggs will scramble. Remove from the heat. Add the cooled butter, a little at a time, whisking well between each addition. Do not use the milky butter whey in the bottom of the pan. Stir in 1 tablespoon lemon juice or vinegar, season and serve immediately. *Makes 1 cup (250 ml)*

DILL MAYONNAISE

Mix 3/4 cup (185 g) whole-egg mayonnaise, 1/4 cup (60 g) plain yoghurt, 1/4 teaspoon finely grated lemon rind, 1 1/2 tablespoons chopped fresh dill, 1 teaspoon lemon juice and a pinch of caster sugar. Season. Refrigerate for 1 hour before serving. *Makes 1 cup (250 ml)*

Tightly wrap the fish in foil, making sure it is completely covered.

Unwrap the fish, then peel away the skin on both sides before serving.

MUSHROOM NUT ROAST

Vegetarians need no longer miss out on a Christmas roast. Accompany this delicious roast with tomato, apricot or roasted pumpkin sauce.

Preparation time: 30 minutes
Total cooking time: 50 minutes
Serves 4–6

2 tablespoons olive oil
1 large onion, diced
2 cloves garlic, crushed
300 g cap mushrooms,
    finely chopped
1½ cups (235 g) brazil nuts
1⅓ cups (200 g) raw cashews
1 cup (125 g) grated Cheddar
¼ cup (25 g) freshly grated
    Parmesan
1 egg, lightly beaten
2 tablespoons chopped fresh chives
1 cup (80 g) fresh wholemeal
    breadcrumbs

1 Preheat the oven to moderate 180°C (350°F/Gas 4). Grease an 11 x 21 cm loaf tin and line the base with baking paper. Heat the oil in a frying pan and add the onion, garlic and mushrooms. Cook over medium heat for 5 minutes, or until soft. Transfer to a large bowl and cool.

2 Place the brazil nuts on a baking tray in the oven for 2–3 minutes. Remove the tray from the oven, add the cashews to the brazil nuts and return to the oven for 3–5 minutes, or until the nuts are toasted but not burnt. Allow to cool slightly. Process the nuts in a food processor until finely chopped, but be careful not to overprocess.

3 Combine the nuts, mushroom mixture, cheeses, egg, chives and breadcrumbs. Mix well. Press firmly into the loaf tin and bake for 45 minutes, or until firm. Leave for 5 minutes, then turn out. Cut into slices and serve warm with tomato, roasted pumpkin or apricot sauce.

NUTRITION PER SERVE (6)
Protein 22 g; Fat 55 g; Carbohydrate 17 g; Dietary Fibre 7 g; Cholesterol 55 mg; 2725 kJ (650 cal)

Using a sharp knife, finely chop the cap mushrooms into small cubes.

Fry the onion, garlic and mushrooms in oil until they are soft.

TOMATO SAUCE
Heat 30 ml olive oil in a pan and add 1 finely chopped onion and 1 crushed garlic clove. Fry for 5 minutes, or until the onion is soft, but not brown. Add a 400 g can chopped tomatoes, 1 teaspoon caster sugar, 1 tablespoon tomato paste and

⅓ cup (80 ml) water. Boil for 3–5 minutes, or until slightly thickened. Season to taste.
Makes 2 cups (500 ml)

ROASTED
PUMPKIN SAUCE
Preheat the oven to moderately hot 200°C (400°F/ Gas 6). Cut 500 g unpeeled pumpkin into wedges and place in a baking dish. Combine 2 tablespoons olive oil with 2 crushed garlic cloves and drizzle over the

pumpkin. Season. Cook for 1 hour, or until the pumpkin is tender. Cool slightly. Dry-fry 2 teaspoons cumin seeds and 2 teaspoons coriander seeds for 5 minutes. Grind in a food processor or mortar and pestle. Remove the skin from the pumpkin and put the flesh, ground spices and 1 cup (250 ml) vegetable stock in a food processor. Purée until smooth, then transfer to a pan and heat through gently.
Makes 2 cups (500 ml)

APRICOT SAUCE
Place 250 g dried apricots in a pan with 1 cinnamon stick and 1 cardamom pod and enough cold water to cover. Bring to the boil, then reduce the heat and simmer for 15 minutes, or until the apricots are very soft. Cool, remove the spices and purée until smooth, adding

more water if needed. Cool completely and then stir in ⅓ cup (80 g) thick plain yoghurt.
Makes 2 cups (500 ml)

Process the brazil nuts and cashews in a food processor until finely chopped.

Combine the ingredients well and press firmly into the prepared tin.

COUSCOUS VEGETABLE LOAF

Preparation time: 20 minutes
+ cooling time
+ overnight refrigeration
Total cooking time: 10 minutes
Serves 6

1 litre vegetable stock
500 g instant couscous
30 g butter
3 tablespoons olive oil
2 cloves garlic, crushed
1 onion, finely chopped
1 tablespoon ground coriander
1 teaspoon ground cinnamon
1 teaspoon garam masala
250 g cherry tomatoes, quartered
1 zucchini, diced
130 g can corn kernels, drained
8 large fresh basil leaves
150 g sun-dried capsicums in oil
1 cup (60 g) chopped fresh basil,
    extra
1/3 cup (80 ml) orange juice
1 tablespoon lemon juice
3 tablespoons chopped fresh flat-leaf
    parsley
1 teaspoon honey
1 teaspoon ground cumin

1 Bring the stock to the boil in a saucepan. Place the couscous and butter into a bowl, cover with the stock and leave aside for 10 minutes.
2 Meanwhile, heat 1 tablespoon of the oil in a large frying pan and cook the garlic and onion over low heat for 5 minutes, or until the onion is soft. Add the spices and cook for 1 minute, or until fragrant. Remove from the pan.

3 Add the remaining oil to the pan and cook the tomatoes, zucchini and corn over high heat until soft.
4 Line a 3 litre loaf tin with plastic wrap, letting it overhang the sides. Form the basil into two flowers on the base of the tin. Drain the capsicums, reserving 2 tablespoons of the oil, then roughly chop. Add the onion mixture, tomato mixture, capsicum and extra basil to the couscous and mix. Cool.

5 Press the mixture into the tin and fold the plastic wrap over. Weigh down with cans and chill overnight.
6 To make the dressing, place the remaining ingredients and oil in a jar. Turn out the loaf, cut into slices and serve with the dressing.

NUTRITION PER SERVE
Protein 8.5 g; Fat 19 g; Carbohydrate 67 g; Dietary Fibre 5 g; Cholesterol 13 mg; 1985 kJ (474 cal)

Cook the tomatoes, zucchini and corn until softened.

Arrange the basil leaves in the shape of two flowers in the base of the loaf tin.

Mix together the onion mixture, vegetables, capsicum, basil and couscous.

EGGPLANT AND SPINACH TERRINE

Preparation time: 1 hour + overnight refrigeration
Total cooking time: 55 minutes
Serves 6

3 large red capsicums
1 large old potato, halved
40 g butter
2 cloves garlic, crushed
800 g English spinach leaves, shredded
¼ cup (60 ml) cream
1 egg yolk
⅓ cup (80 ml) olive oil
2 eggplants, cut into 5 mm slices lengthways
1 cup (30 g) fresh basil
350 g ricotta
2 cloves garlic, crushed, extra

1 Cut the capsicums into large pieces, removing all seeds and membranes. Cook, skin-side-up, under a hot grill until the skin blisters. Cool, then peel.

2 Preheat the oven to 180°C (350°F/Gas 4). Grease a 1.5 litre terrine and line with baking paper. Boil a saucepan of salted water and cook the potato for 10 minutes. Drain and cool. Cut into 5 mm slices.

3 Melt the butter and cook the garlic for 30 seconds. Add the spinach and toss. Steam, covered, for 2–3 minutes, or until wilted. Cool slightly and place in a food processor or blender until smooth. Squeeze out any excess liquid, place in a bowl and stir the cream and egg in well.

4 Heat a chargrill plate over high heat and brush with some of the oil. Cook the eggplant on each side for 2–3 minutes, or until golden, brushing with the oil while cooking.

5 To assemble, arrange one third of the eggplant neatly in the base of the terrine, cutting to fit. Top with a layer of half the capsicum, spinach mixture, basil, all the potato, and all the combined ricotta and garlic. Repeat with the rest of the ingredients, finishing with eggplant. Oil a piece of foil and cover the terrine. Place in a baking dish and half fill with water. Bake for 25–30 minutes. Remove from the oven, put a piece of cardboard on top and weigh it down with food cans. Chill overnight.

6 When you are ready to serve, turn out the terrine and cut into slices.

NUTRITION PER SERVE
Protein 12 g; Fat 30 g; Carbohydrate 8 g; Dietary Fibre 5 g; Cholesterol 88 mg; 1457 kJ (348 cal)

Grill the capsicum pieces until the skin blackens, cool in a plastic bag, then peel.

Blend the spinach mixture in a food processor until smooth.

Spread a layer of the spinach mixture over the second layer of capsicum.

VEGETABLE TART WITH SALSA VERDE

Preparation time: 30 minutes + 30 minutes refrigeration
Total cooking time: 50 minutes
Serves 6

PASTRY
1¾ cups (220 g) plain flour
120 g butter, chilled and cubed
¼ cup (60 ml) cream
1–2 tablespoons iced water

SALSA VERDE
1 clove garlic
2 cups (40 g) firmly packed fresh flat-leaf parsley
⅓ cup (80 ml) extra virgin olive oil
¼ cup (15 g) chopped fresh dill
1½ tablespoons Dijon mustard
1 tablespoon red wine vinegar
1 tablespoon baby capers, drained

FILLING
1 large (250 g) Desiree potato, chopped into 2 cm cubes
1 tablespoon olive oil
2 cloves garlic, crushed
1 red capsicum, chopped into 3 cm squares
1 red onion, sliced into rings
2 zucchini, sliced
2 tablespoons chopped fresh dill
1 tablespoon chopped fresh thyme
1 tablespoon baby capers, drained
150 g marinated artichoke hearts, drained
⅔ cup (30 g) baby English spinach leaves

1 Sift the flour and ½ teaspoon salt into a large bowl and rub in the butter with your fingers until the mixture resembles fine breadcrumbs. Add the cream and water and mix with a flat-bladed knife until the mixture just comes together in small beads. Gently gather the dough into a ball and turn out onto a lightly floured work surface. Flatten into a disc, cover with plastic wrap, and refrigerate for 30 minutes.

2 Preheat the oven to moderately hot 200°C (400°F/Gas 6). Lightly grease a 27 cm shallow fluted flan tin with a removable base.

3 Roll the dough out between 2 sheets of baking paper until large enough to line the flan tin. Remove the paper and carefully lift the pastry into the flan tin, pressing it gently into the fluted sides. Trim any excess pastry. Line the pastry with crumpled baking paper and fill with baking beads or rice. Place the flan tin on a baking tray and bake for 15–20 minutes. Remove the paper and beads, reduce the oven to moderate 180°C (350°F/Gas 4) and bake for a further 20 minutes, or until the pastry case is dry and golden.

4 Meanwhile, to make the salsa verde, combine all the ingredients in a food processor and blend until almost smooth.

5 To make the filling, boil, steam or microwave the potato until just tender, but do not overcook. Drain and set aside.

6 Heat the oil in a large frying pan and add the garlic, capsicum and onion. Cook over medium–high heat for 3 minutes, stirring often. Add the zucchini, dill, thyme and capers and cook for 3 minutes more, stirring frequently. Add the potato and artichokes, reduce the heat to

low and cook for 3–4 minutes, or until the potato and artichokes are heated through. Season to taste with salt and freshly ground black pepper.

Rub the butter into the flour and salt with your fingers.

Use a flat-bladed knife to combine the mixture until it comes together in beads.

Press the pastry gently into the sides of the greased flan tin.

7 To assemble the tart, spread ¼ cup of the salsa verde over the base of the pastry case. Spoon the vegetable mixture into the case and drizzle with half the remaining salsa verde. Pile the spinach in the centre and drizzle with remaining salsa verde. Serve immediately.

NUTRITION PER SERVE
Protein 5.5 g; Fat 30 g; Carbohydrate 27 g; Dietary Fibre 3.5 g; Cholesterol 50 mg; 1590 kJ (380 cal)

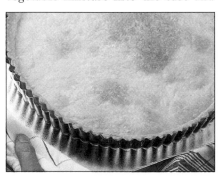

Bake the pastry case for 20 minutes, or until it is dry and golden.

Process the salsa verde ingredients until the mix is almost smooth.

Spoon the hot vegetable mixture into the pastry case.

VEGETABLES

There are numerous delicious vegetable accompaniments to any of our roasts. Choose two or three of your favourites at their fresh, seasonal best to enhance and supplement your roast.

Celeriac and tarragon purée

Bring 2 cups (500 ml) vegetable stock, 2 cups (500 ml) water and the juice of 1 lemon to the boil. Add 3 peeled and chopped medium celeriacs, and cook for 10–15 minutes, or until tender. Drain and place in a food processor with 40 g butter and 1 tablespoon cream. Season and process until smooth. Add 1 tablespoon finely chopped fresh tarragon and process for a further 10 seconds. If it is too thick, add a little more cream. *Serves 6*

Vichy carrots

Trim and peel 1 kg carrots and cut into batons. Bring a pan of water to the boil and cook the carrots for 3–5 minutes, or until tender. Drain well. Melt 40 g butter in the pan and add 2 teaspoons of sugar. Return the carrots to the pan and toss together until the carrots start to colour a little. Add 2 teaspoons lemon juice and 2 teaspoons chopped fresh parsley and toss together. *Serves 6*

Broccoli with almonds

Cut 500 g broccoli into small florets. Heat 2 teaspoons oil and 20 g butter in a large frying pan, add 1 crushed garlic clove and 20 g flaked almonds. Cook for 1–2 minutes, or until the almonds are golden. Remove and set aside. Add the broccoli to the pan and toss, cooking for 3–5 minutes, or until the broccoli is just tender. Return the almonds to the pan and stir to combine. Serve hot. *Serves 4–6*

Honey-roasted pumpkin

Preheat the oven to moderately hot 200°C (400°F/Gas 6). Bring a large pan of water to the boil. Add 1 kg peeled butternut pumpkin, cut into 3 cm chunks, and 2 tablespoons honey. Boil for 3–5 minutes, or until just tender. Drain well. Place into a baking dish and drizzle with 1 tablespoon oil and 1 tablespoon honey. Toss to coat. Bake for 30–40 minutes, or until cooked through. Serve sprinkled with 2 teaspoons toasted sesame seeds. *Serves 6–8*

Left to right: Celeriac and tarragon purée; Vichy carrots; Broccoli with almonds; Honey-roasted pumpkin; Duchess potatoes; Brussels sprouts and chestnuts.

Duchess potatoes

Preheat the oven to moderate 180°C (350°F/Gas 4). Quarter 1 kg floury potatoes and steam or boil until just tender. Drain well, return to the pan and mash. Beat together 2 eggs, 1/3 cup (80 ml) cream and 1/4 teaspoon grated nutmeg. Season to taste with salt and black pepper. Add to the potato and mash until smooth and thick, but not too stiff. Allow to cool slightly. Put the potato in a piping bag with a 1.5 cm star nozzle. Pipe in swirls, not too close together, onto two greased baking trays. Brush with an egg yolk. Bake for 15–20 minutes, or until golden. *Serves 6–8*

Brussels sprouts and chestnuts

Make slits in the skins of 500 g chestnuts and put them in a pan. Cover with cold water and place over high heat. Bring to the boil, then reduce the heat and simmer for 10 minutes, drain and leave until cool enough to handle. Peel off the skins. Trim 1 kg sprouts and cut a cross in the bottom of each sprout. Bring a pan of water to the boil, add the sprouts and cook at a fast simmer for 5–8 minutes, or until just tender. Melt 30 g butter in a large frying pan and add the chestnuts. Cook until they begin to brown and then add the sprouts, tossing together. Season well with salt, pepper and nutmeg. *Serves 6–8*

Risotto-stuffed onions

Preheat the oven to moderately hot 200°C (400°F/Gas 6). Peel 8 medium onions (about 200 g each) and trim the bases, leaving them intact. Cut the top off the onions, leaving a wide opening. Place in a baking dish, drizzle with 1 tablespoon oil and bake for 1–1½ hours, or until golden. Heat 20 g butter in a pan, add 70 g chopped mushrooms and 20 g chopped prosciutto, and cook until the mushrooms have softened. Add ½ cup (110 g) arborio rice and stir until well coated in the butter. Gradually stir in 2½ cups (600 ml) hot chicken stock, about ½ cup at a time, making sure the liquid has been absorbed before adding another portion. When all the stock has been added, stir through 2 tablespoons grated Parmesan and 2 tablespoons chopped fresh parsley. Scoop out the flesh from the middle of each onion, leaving at least 3 layers of skin. Chop the remaining flesh and stir through the risotto mixture. Spoon the filling into the onion shells, piling a little on top. Return to the oven for a further 10 minutes and serve. *Serves 8*

Roasted parsnips

Preheat the oven to moderately hot 200°C (400°F/Gas 6). Peel 1 kg parsnips and cut in half lengthways. Boil in salted water for 5 minutes, then drain well. Put 2 tablespoons oil in a baking dish and put the dish in the oven to heat up. When the oil is hot, add the parsnip and toss in the oil. Season with salt and pepper and roast for about 30 minutes, or until well browned and crisp. Garnish with thick curls of Parmesan and sea salt. *Serves 6*

Braised fennel

Slice 4 small fennel bulbs into quarters. Reserve fronds. Melt 20 g butter in a frying pan and add 1 tablespoon sugar, stirring, then add the fennel, and cook until browned all over. Pour on 100 ml white wine and 150 ml chicken stock and bring to the boil, then reduce the heat and simmer, covered, for 10 minutes, or until tender. Remove the lid and turn up the heat until most of the liquid has evaporated and the sauce has become sticky. Stir in 1 tablespoon sour cream. Garnish with the reserved fronds.
Serves 8

Roast potatoes

Preheat the oven to moderate 180°C (350°F/Gas 4). Cut 1.2 kg all-purpose potatoes in half. Place in a pan of water and bring to the boil, then reduce the heat and simmer for about 5 minutes. Drain well and cool on paper towels. Scrape the rounded side of each potato with a fork to form a rough surface and place in a single layer on a greased baking tray. Melt 20 g butter, mix with 1 tablespoon oil, and brush half over the potatoes. Roast the potatoes for about 50 minutes, or until crisp and golden brown, brushing halfway through with the remaining butter and oil mixture. *Serves 6–8*

Leeks in a white sauce

Trim and wash 2 leeks, cut in half lengthways and then into 5 cm pieces. Heat 30 g butter in a heavy-based pan, add the leeks and cook for 5 minutes, turning gently, or until tender. Place in an ovenproof serving dish. Melt 20 g butter in a pan, add 1 tablespoon plain flour and stir over medium heat for 1 minute. Remove from the heat and gradually add 1 cup (250 ml) milk. Return to the heat, stirring until the sauce boils and thickens. Pour over the top of the leeks. Sprinkle over 2 tablespoons grated cheese and 1 tablespoon dry breadcrumbs. Place under a hot grill for 2–3 minutes, or until crisp and golden on top. *Serves 4–6*

Left to right: Risotto-stuffed onions; Roasted parsnips; Braised fennel; Roast potatoes; Leeks in a white sauce.

ORANGE POPPY SEED VEGETABLES

Preparation time: 20 minutes
Total cooking time: 1 hour
<u>Serves 6–8</u>

500 g new potatoes, halved
6 parsnips, peeled and quartered
   lengthways
500 g orange sweet potato, diced
350 g baby carrots, peeled, with tops
   left on
6 pickling onions, halved
1/3 cup (80 ml) oil
2 tablespoons poppy seeds
200 g triple cream brie,
   thinly sliced

ORANGE DRESSING
1/2 cup (125 ml) orange juice
2 cloves garlic, crushed
1 tablespoon Dijon mustard
1 teaspoon white wine vinegar
1 teaspoon sesame oil

1 Preheat the oven to moderately hot 200°C (400°F/Gas 6). Place the potato, parsnip, sweet potato, carrots, onion and oil in a large, deep baking dish. Toss to coat all the vegetables with the oil. Bake the vegetables for 50–60 minutes, or until they are crisp and tender, tossing every 15 minutes. Sprinkle with the poppy seeds.

2 To make the orange dressing, whisk the orange juice, garlic, Dijon mustard, vinegar and sesame oil together in a bowl.

3 Pour the dressing over the warm vegetables and toss to coat well. Transfer the vegetables to a large bowl, top with the brie and serve immediately, while still warm.

NUTRITION PER SERVE (8)
Protein 10 g; Fat 17 g; Carbohydrate 32 g; Dietary Fibre 6.5 g; Cholesterol 25 mg; 1360 kJ (325 cal)

Bake the vegetables until they are crisp and tender, then sprinkle with poppy seeds.

Whisk the orange dressing ingredients together in a bowl.

CHARGRILLED VEGETABLE TERRINE

Preparation time: 30 minutes + overnight refrigeration
Total cooking time: Nil
Serves 8

350 g (11 oz) ricotta
2 cloves garlic, crushed
8 large slices chargrilled eggplant, drained
10 slices chargrilled red capsicum, drained
8 slices chargrilled zucchini, drained
45 g (1½ oz) rocket leaves
3 marinated artichokes, drained and sliced
85 g (3 oz) semi-dried tomatoes, drained and chopped
100 g (3½ oz) marinated mushrooms, drained and halved

1 Line a 23½ x 13 x 6½ cm (9 x 5 x 2½ inch) loaf tin with plastic wrap, leaving plenty hanging over the sides. Place the ricotta and garlic in a bowl and beat until smooth. Season well and set aside.

2 Line the base of the tin with half the eggplant, cutting and fitting to cover the base. Top with a layer of half the capsicum, then all the zucchini slices. Spread evenly with the ricotta mixture and press down firmly. Place the rocket leaves on top. Arrange the artichoke, tomato and mushrooms in three rows lengthways.

3 Top with another layer of capsicum and finish with the eggplant. Cover securely with the overlapping plastic wrap. Put a piece of cardboard on top and weigh it down with weights or small food cans. Refrigerate overnight.

4 To serve, peel back the plastic wrap and turn the terrine out onto a plate. Remove the plastic wrap and cut into thick slices.

NUTRITION PER SERVE
Protein 6 g; Fat 5 g; Carbohydrate 3 g; Dietary Fibre 2 g; Cholesterol 20 mg; 350 kJ (85 cal)

NOTE: You can buy chargrilled vegetables and marinated mushrooms and artichokes at local delis. Or you can make your own.

STORAGE TIME: Cover any leftovers with plastic wrap and store in the refrigerator for up to 2 days.

Put the ricotta and crushed garlic in a bowl and beat until smooth.

Arrange the mushrooms, tomato and artichoke in three rows over the rocket.

Cover the terrine with cardboard and weigh down with small food cans.

VEGETABLE CASSEROLE WITH HERB DUMPLINGS

Preparation time: 30 minutes
Total cooking time: 50 minutes
Serves 4

1 tablespoon olive oil
1 large onion, chopped
2 cloves garlic, crushed
2 teaspoons sweet paprika
1 large potato, chopped
1 large carrot, sliced
400 g can chopped tomatoes
1½ cups (375 ml) vegetable stock
400 g orange sweet potato, cut into
    1.5 cm cubes
150 g broccoli, cut into florets
2 zucchini, thickly sliced
1 cup (125 g) self-raising flour
20 g chilled butter, cut into small
    cubes
2 teaspoons chopped fresh
    flat-leaf parsley
1 teaspoon fresh thyme
1 teaspoon chopped fresh rosemary
⅓ cup (80 ml) milk
2 tablespoons sour cream

1 Heat the oil in a saucepan and add the onion. Cook over low heat, stirring occasionally, for 5 minutes, or until soft. Add the garlic and paprika and cook, stirring, for 1 minute.

2 Add the potato, carrot, tomato and stock. Bring to the boil, then reduce the heat and simmer, covered, for 10 minutes. Add the sweet potato, broccoli and zucchini and simmer for 10 minutes, or until tender. Preheat the oven to 200°C (400°F/Gas 6).

3 To make the dumplings, sift the flour and a pinch of salt into a bowl. Rub the butter into the flour with your fingertips until it resembles fine breadcrumbs. Stir in the herbs and make a well in the centre. Add the milk and mix with a flat-bladed knife, using a cutting action, until the mixture comes together in beads. Lift the dough onto a lightly floured surface, then divide into eight portions. Shape each portion into a ball.

4 Add the sour cream to the casserole. Transfer to a 2 litre ovenproof dish and top with the dumplings. Bake for 20 minutes, or until the dumplings are golden and a skewer comes out clean when inserted in the centre.

NUTRITION PER SERVE
Protein 8 g; Fat 10 g; Carbohydrate 27 g; Dietary Fibre 7.5 g; Cholesterol 16 mg; 967 kJ (230 cal)

Cook all the vegetables until they are tender.

Rub the butter into the flour until it resembles fine breadcrumbs.

Divide the dough into eight equal portions.

COUSCOUS PATTIES

Preparation time: 35 minutes +
   15 minutes refrigeration +
   10 minutes standing
Total cooking time: 30 minutes
Makes 4

1 cup (185 g/6 oz) couscous
4 tablespoons oil
1 eggplant, finely diced
1 onion, finely chopped
1 clove garlic, crushed
2 teaspoons ground cumin
2 teaspoons ground coriander
1 red capsicum, finely diced
2 tablespoons chopped fresh
   coriander
2 teaspoons grated lemon rind
2 teaspoons lemon juice
5 tablespoons natural yoghurt
1 egg, lightly beaten
oil, for shallow-frying

1 Place the couscous in a bowl. Add 1 cup (250 ml/8 fl oz) of boiling water and leave for 10 minutes, or until all the water has been absorbed. Fluff up the grains with a fork.

2 Heat 2 tablespoons of the oil in a frying pan and fry the eggplant until soft and golden, then place in a bowl. Heat 1 tablespoon of the oil in the pan. Add the onion, garlic, cumin and ground coriander. Cook for 3–4 minutes, or until soft, then add to the bowl. Heat the remaining oil and cook the capsicum for 5 minutes, or until soft. Place in the bowl and stir.

3 Add the vegetable mixture to the couscous with the fresh coriander, lemon rind, lemon juice, yoghurt and egg. Season to taste and mix well.

4 Divide the mixture into four portions and form large patties—they should be 2 cm (¾ inch) thick. Cover and refrigerate for 15 minutes. Shallow-fry the patties for 5 minutes on each side until golden. Drain well and serve with yoghurt.

NUTRITION PER PATTY
Protein 9 g; Fat 25 g; Carbohydrate 35 g; Dietary Fibre 4 g; Cholesterol 5 mg; 1760 kJ (420 cal)

When the couscous has absorbed the water, fluff up the grains with a fork.

Season the patty mixture with salt and cracked pepper and mix well.

With damp hands, form the mixture into four large patties.

MIXED LEAF SALAD

Preparation time: 20 minutes
Total cooking time: Nil
<u>Serves</u> 6–8

DRESSING
1 clove garlic, halved
½ cup (125 ml/4 fl oz) extra virgin
   olive oil
2 tablespoons white wine vinegar
2 teaspoons Dijon mustard
½ teaspoon sugar
50 g (1¾ oz) snow pea sprouts
150 g (5 oz) mixed lettuce leaves
80 g (2¾ oz) baby English spinach
   leaves
50 g (1¾ oz) edible flower petals

1 To make the dressing, skewer the garlic onto a toothpick and sit it in a jug with the oil, vinegar, mustard and sugar. Leave the garlic to infuse.

2 Trim the ends from the snow pea sprouts. Rinse the lettuce and spinach leaves under running water and drain well. Toss with the snow pea sprouts and flowers in a large bowl, cover with plastic wrap and refrigerate until ready to serve.

3 To serve, remove and discard the garlic clove from the dressing, whisk until well blended and then season. Place the salad in a serving bowl and drizzle with the dressing.

NUTRITION PER SERVE
Protein 1 g; Fat 15 g; Carbohydrate 1 g; Dietary Fibre 1 g; Cholesterol 0 mg; 585 kJ (140 cal)

Carefully separate the petals from the edible flowers.

Skewer the garlic onto a toothpick and allow it to infuse into the dressing.

Drizzle the dressing over the tossed salad in a serving bowl.

COLESLAW

Preparation time: 20 minutes
Total cooking time: Nil
Serves 8–10

½ green (savoy) cabbage
¼ red cabbage
3 carrots, coarsely grated
6 radishes, coarsely grated
1 red capsicum, chopped
4 spring onions, sliced

¼ cup (15 g/½ oz) chopped flat-leaf
  parsley
1 cup (250 g/8 oz) mayonnaise

1 Remove the hard cores from the cabbages and shred the leaves with a sharp knife. Place the leaves in a large bowl.

2 Add the carrot, radish, capsicum, spring onion and parsley to the bowl with the cabbage.

3 Add the mayonnaise, season with salt and freshly ground black pepper and toss until the ingredients are well combined.

NUTRITION PER SERVE (10)
Protein 5 g; Fat 10 g; Carbohydrate 10 g; Dietary Fibre 10 g; Cholesterol 8 mg; 610 kJ (145 cal)

NOTE: As an alternative to using mayonnaise, the coleslaw could be dressed with any kind of dressing, depending on your own preference.

STORAGE: You should cover and refrigerate the chopped vegetables for up to 3 hours before serving. Add the mayonnaise just before serving the coleslaw.

Coarsely grate the carrots and the radishes using a metal grater.

Remove the hard cores from the cabbages with a sharp knife.

Add the mayonnaise and season with salt and freshly ground black pepper.

SPINACH SALAD

Preparation time: 20 minutes
Total cooking time: 20 minutes
Serves 2–4

3 slices white bread, crusts removed
150 g (5 oz) English spinach leaves
2–3 tablespoons pine nuts
3 rashers bacon, chopped
8 button mushrooms, finely sliced
1/4 cup (7 g/1/4 oz) basil leaves,
   shredded
1–2 cloves garlic, crushed

2–3 tablespoons olive oil
balsamic vinegar or freshly squeezed
   lemon juice, to taste

1 Preheat the oven to moderately hot 190°C (375°F/Gas 5). Cut the bread into small cubes, spread on a baking tray and bake for 10 minutes, or until the bread cubes are golden.

2 Gently rinse the spinach leaves under cold water. Bundle them in a clean tea towel and shake gently to remove the water. Tear into pieces and place in a large serving bowl. Put the pine nuts in a non-stick frying pan and stir gently over low heat until golden brown. Remove and cool

slightly. Add the bacon to the pan and cook for 5–6 minutes, or until crispy. Remove and drain on absorbent paper towels.

3 Add the pine nuts, bacon, bread cubes, mushrooms and basil to the spinach leaves. Whisk the garlic and oil together and pour over the salad, mixing gently. Drizzle with the vinegar or lemon juice. Sprinkle with salt and freshly ground pepper, and serve immediately.

NUTRITION PER SERVE (4)
Protein 10 g; Fat 20 g; Carbohydrate 10 g; Dietary Fibre 3 g; Cholesterol 15 mg; 1105 kJ (265 cal)

Cut the bread into small cubes and spread on a baking tray.

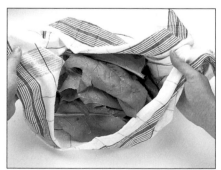

Bundle the spinach leaves in a tea towel and shake to remove the excess water.

Pour the combined garlic and oil over the salad, mixing gently.

WARM RADICCHIO SALAD WITH CRUSHED TOMATO VINAIGRETTE

Preparation time: 40 minutes
Total cooking time: 25 minutes
Serves 4

¼ cup (60 ml/2 fl oz) oil
6 cloves garlic, thinly sliced
1–2 tablespoons olive oil
7 egg tomatoes, cored and halved
¼ cup (60 ml/2 fl oz) olive oil
2 tablespoons red wine vinegar
1 teaspoon honey
920 g (1 lb 14 oz) chicory
1 onion, halved and sliced
1 radicchio lettuce

1 Heat the oil in a small pan, add the garlic and fry for a few minutes, or until lightly browned. Drain on paper towels.

2 Heat a little of the olive oil in a frying pan and cook the tomatoes, cut-side-down, until they are browned and very soft. Turn to brown the other side. Transfer to a bowl to cool, then peel and discard the skins. Coarsely mash the flesh with a fork.

3 To make the vinaigrette, whisk half of the crushed tomatoes, the extra virgin olive oil, vinegar and honey until combined. Season well.

4 Trim the coarse stems from the chicory, wash the leaves and drain. Cut into short lengths. Heat a little more olive oil in the frying pan, add the onion and cook until transparent. Add the chicory and stir until just wilted. Add the remaining tomatoes and stir until combined. Season.

5 Tear any large radicchio leaves into smaller pieces. Toss through the chicory mixture. Transfer to a large serving bowl, drizzle with the vinaigrette and sprinkle with garlic.

NUTRITION PER SERVE
Protein 7 g; Fat 35 g; Carbohydrate 9 g; Dietary Fibre 8 g; Cholesterol 0 mg; 1620 kJ (385 cal)

Fry the garlic in the oil over moderate heat until lightly browned.

Cook the tomatoes until they are browned and very soft.

Tear any large radicchio leaves into smaller pieces.

POTATO SALAD

Preparation time: 15 minutes
Total cooking time: 25 minutes
Serves 8

8 large waxy potatoes,
    chopped into 2 cm cubes
1/3 cup (90 g) whole-egg
    mayonnaise
1 1/2 cups (45 g) fresh
    coriander leaves
2 tablespoons olive oil
1 teaspoon lemon juice
1 teaspoon olive oil
6 small spring onions,
    very thinly sliced
1 tablespoon balsamic
    vinegar
4 tomatoes, seeded and
    finely chopped
300 g bacon, thinly sliced
1 hard-boiled egg
1 1/2 cups (45 g) snow pea
    sprouts or watercress

1 Boil or microwave the potato until just tender—do not overcook. Refresh under cold water, drain and place in a large bowl.

2 Put the whole-egg mayonnaise, coriander leaves, olive oil and lemon juice in a blender and process until smooth. Season to taste with salt and ground black pepper.

3 Heat the oil in a frying pan, add the spring onion and balsamic vinegar and stir. Cook over low heat for 3 minutes, cool, and then add to the mayonnaise mixture with the chopped tomato. Pour over the potato and toss to coat. Cover with plastic wrap and refrigerate until ready to serve.

4 Fry the bacon until very crispy and drain on paper towels. Grate or finely chop the hard-boiled egg. Add the bacon, egg and snow pea sprouts to the salad, toss and serve.

NUTRITION PER SERVE
Protein 11 g; Fat 11 g; Carbohydrate 20 g; Dietary Fibre 3.5 g; Cholesterol 40 mg; 935 kJ (225 cal)

Add the mayonnaise and tomato mixture to the potato and toss to coat.

Fry the bacon until crispy and drain well on paper towels.

WARM MUSSEL AND POTATO SALAD

Preparation time: 20 minutes
Total cooking time: 20 minutes
Serves 4

500 g (1 lb) baby new potatoes
1 kg (2 lb) fresh black mussels
45 g (1½ oz) baby spinach leaves

DRESSING
⅓ cup (80 ml/2¾ fl oz) olive oil
⅓ cup (80 ml/2¾ fl oz) cream
1 teaspoon grated lemon rind
2 tablespoons lemon juice
1 teaspoon caster sugar
1 tablespoon chopped lemon thyme

1 Cook the potatoes until tender. Drain and keep warm.

2 Scrub the mussels and remove the beards, discarding any that are open. Place in a pan with 2 cups (500 ml/16 fl oz) water, cover and cook gently until they have just opened. Do not overcook. Cover with cold water and remove from the shells. Discard any mussels that have not opened. Pat dry with paper towels.

3 To make the dressing, put the oil, cream, lemon rind and juice, sugar and lemon thyme in a small bowl and whisk to combine. Season to taste.

4 Combine everything in a large bowl. Add the dressing and toss.

NUTRITION PER SERVE
Protein 45 g; Fat 35 g; Carbohydrate 20 g; Dietary Fibre 2 g; Cholesterol 275 mg; 2310 kJ (550 cal)

Grate a lemon on the fine side of a grater to get 1 teaspoon of grated rind.

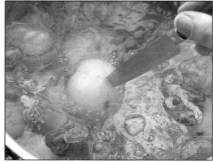

Cook the potatoes in boiling water until just tender.

Wash and scrub the mussels and remove the beards. Discard any that are open.

ORANGE AND FENNEL SALAD

Preparation time: 15 minutes
Total cooking time: Nil
Serves 4

3 oranges, peeled and sliced
2 baby fennel bulbs, thinly sliced
1 large avocado, sliced
100 g (3¼ oz) rocket leaves
2 tablespoons pine nuts

DRESSING
2 tablespoons orange juice
1 teaspoon Dijon mustard
¼ teaspoon ground cumin
⅓ cup (80 ml/2¾ fl oz) extra virgin
   olive oil

1 Layer the orange slices, fennel, avocado and rocket leaves on a serving platter.

2 To make the dressing, whisk the orange juice, mustard, cumin and olive oil. Season to taste.

3 Drizzle the dressing over the salad and top with the pine nuts.

NUTRITION PER SERVE
Protein 5 g; Fat 40 g; Carbohydrate 15 g; Dietary Fibre 9 g; Cholesterol 0 mg; 1745 kJ (415 cal)

NOTE: Blood oranges may be used instead of regular oranges in this recipe. They look lovely and will give the salad a sweet, tart flavour. Blood oranges are only in season for a very short period of time. The orange juice in the dressing works in the same way as lemon juice and will prevent the avocado from browning.

Thinly slice the fennel bulbs, discarding the green tops.

Peel the avocado and remove the seed, then cut into thin slices.

Put the orange juice, mustard and cumin in a small bowl, and add the olive oil.

CHICKPEA AND ROAST VEGETABLE SALAD

Preparation time: 25 minutes +
30 minutes standing
Total cooking time: 40 minutes
Serves 8

500 g (1 lb) butternut pumpkin,
cubed
2 red capsicums, halved
4 thin eggplants, halved lengthways
4 zucchini, sliced in half lengthways
4 onions, quartered
olive oil, for brushing
2 x 300 g (10 oz) cans chickpeas,
rinsed and drained
2 tablespoons chopped fresh flat-leaf
parsley

DRESSING
1/3 cup (80 ml/2³/4 fl oz) olive oil
2 tablespoons lemon juice
1 clove garlic, crushed
1 tablespoon chopped fresh thyme

1 Preheat the oven to 220°C
(425°F/Gas 7). Brush two baking
trays with oil and lay out the
vegetables. Brush with the olive oil.

2 Bake for 40 minutes, or until the
vegetables are tender and begin to
brown on the edges. Cool. Remove
the skins from the capsicum if you
want. Chop the capsicum, eggplant
and zucchini into pieces, then put the
vegetables in a bowl with the
chickpeas and half the parsley.

3 Whisk together all the dressing
ingredients in a bowl. Season,
then toss through the vegetables. Set
aside for 30 minutes and sprinkle
with the remaining parsley.

NUTRITION PER SERVE
Protein 8.5 g; Fat 12 g; Carbohydrate
20 g; Dietary Fibre 7.5 g; Cholesterol
0 mg; 935 kJ (225 cal)

Rinse the chickpeas under cold water then drain thoroughly.

Chop the roasted capsicum, eggplant and zucchini into small pieces.

Put the olive oil, lemon juice, garlic and thyme into a bowl and whisk to combine.

ROAST BEETROOT AND ONION WEDGE SALAD

Preparation time: 30 minutes
Total cooking time: 1 hour
   30 minutes
Serves 4–6

4 medium beetroots
3 red onions
1/3 cup (80 ml/2¾ fl oz) oil
20 g (¾ oz) butter
1 teaspoon ground cumin
1 teaspoon soft brown sugar
2 tablespoons orange juice
2 tablespoons orange zest
chopped chives, to garnish

SOUR CREAM DRESSING
150 g (5 oz) sour cream
2 tablespoons chopped chives
1 tablespoon chopped thyme
1 teaspoon lemon juice

1 Preheat the oven to 180°C (350°F/Gas 4). Trim the leafy tops from the beetroot, leaving a 4 cm (1½ inch) stalk, and wash. Keep the beetroot whole to avoid bleeding during baking. Cut each onion into 6 large wedges, leaving the bases intact so the wedges hold together. Put the oil in a baking dish and add the onion wedges and beetroot. Bake for 1¼ hours. Remove the beetroot and onion onto separate plates and set aside to cool. Peel and discard the beetroot skins. Trim the tops and tails to neaten, and cut into large wedges.

2 Heat the butter in a frying pan, add the cumin and brown sugar, and cook for 1 minute. Add the orange juice and simmer for 5 minutes, or until the juice has reduced slightly. Add the baked beetroot wedges and orange zest, and stir gently over low heat for 2 minutes.

3 To make the dressing, combine the sour cream, chopped chives, thyme and lemon juice. Arrange the cooked beetroot and onion wedges on a large serving plate and serve with the dressing. Sprinkle with the chopped chives to garnish.

NUTRITION PER SERVE (6)
Protein 3 g; Fat 25 g; Carbohydrate 10 g; Dietary Fibre 4 g; Cholesterol 40 mg; 1185 kJ (280 cal)

Trim the leafy tops from the beetroots, leaving a short stalk.

Cut the onions into wedges, leaving as much of the base intact as possible.

Add the beetroot wedges and orange zest to the pan.

ROASTED BALSAMIC ONIONS

Preparation time: 15 minutes +
   overnight refrigeration
Total cooking time: 1 hour 30 minutes
Serves 8 (as part of an antipasto platter)

1 kg (2 lb) pickling onions, unpeeled
3/4 cup (185 ml/6 fl oz) balsamic
   vinegar
2 tablespoons soft brown sugar
3/4 cup (185 ml/6 fl oz) olive oil

1 Preheat the oven to 160°C (315°F/
Gas 2–3). Place the unpeeled onions in a baking dish and roast for
1 1/2 hours. Leave until cool enough to handle. Trim the stems from the onions and peel away the skin (the outer part of the root should come away but the onions will remain intact). Rinse a 1-litre wide-necked jar with boiling water and dry in a warm oven (do not dry with a tea towel). Add the onions to the jar.

2 Combine the vinegar and sugar in a small screw-top jar and stir to dissolve the sugar. Add the oil, seal the jar and shake vigorously until combined—the mixture will be paler and may separate on standing.

3 Pour the vinegar mixture over the onions, seal, and turn upside down to coat. Marinate overnight in the refrigerator, turning occasionally.

Return to room temperature and shake to combine the dressing.

NUTRITION PER SERVE
Protein 0.5 g; Fat 7.5 g; Carbohydrate 20 g; Dietary Fibre 2 g; Cholesterol 0 mg; 677 kJ (162 cal)

NOTE: Pickling onions are very small, usually packed in 1 kg (2 lb) bags. The ideal size is 35 g (1 1/4 oz) each. The sizes in the bag will range from 20 g (3/4 oz) to 40 g (1 1/4 oz). The cooking time given is suitable for all sizes so do not cook the larger ones for longer. The marinating time is a minimum one and the onions can be marinated for up to 3 days. If the marinade separates after a few hours simply stir occasionally.

When cool, trim the stems from the onions and peel away the skin.

Add the oil to the vinegar and sugar and shake vigorously to combine.

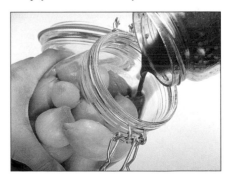

Pour the vinegar mixture over the onions, turning the jar to coat thoroughly.

SPICED PEARS

Preparation time: 10 minutes
Total cooking time: 1 hour
Serves 8

1/3 cup (80 ml/2 3/4 fl oz) kecap
    manis
3 tablespoons soy sauce
2 teaspoons sesame oil
1 teaspoon five-spice powder
6 ripe buerre bosc pears, unpeseled
    and quartered

1 Preheat oven to 150°C (300°F/ Gas 2). Line two shallow baking trays with foil and place a wire rack in each. Mix up the kecap manis, soy sauce, sesame oil and five-spice powder.
2 Brush the quartered pears with the soy mixture. Place apart, skin-side-down, in a single layer on the racks. Bake for 30 minutes. Brush the pears again with the marinade and continue baking for a further 30 minutes, or until the pears are tender and caramelised at the edge.
3 Serve the pears warm or at room temperature with cheese and biscuits or cold meat.

NUTRITION PER SERVE
Protein 1 g; Fat 1 g; Carbohydrate 15 g; Dietary Fibre 2.5 g; Cholesterol 0 mg; 280 kJ (65 cal)

HINT: The foil will catch any excess drops of the soy mixture. If the mixture scorches or burns during cooking, replace the foil lining halfway through the cooking time.

NOTE: Kecap manis (ketjap manis) is an Indonesian sauce similar to—but sweeter than—soy sauce. It is generally flavoured with garlic and star anise.

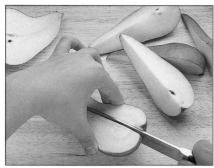

Wash but don't peel the pears, then cut them into quarters.

Mix together the kecap manis, soy sauce, sesame oil and five-spice powder.

Arrange the pears, skin-side-down, in a single layer on the wire racks.

SEAFOOD AND AVOCADO SALAD

Preparation time: 30 minutes
Total cooking time: 35 minutes
Serves 4

350 g (11¼ oz) orange sweet potato,
    cubed
1 tablespoon virgin olive oil
40 g (1¼ oz) butter
1 teaspoon oil
1 clove garlic
250 g (8 oz) scallops, trimmed
2 teaspoons lemon juice
24 raw prawns (about 600 g/
    1¼ lb), peeled and deveined,
    tails intact
½ mizuna lettuce
½ red oakleaf lettuce
1 Lebanese cucumber, peeled,
    seeded and cut into thin slices
2 avocados, thickly sliced
1 tablespoon chopped opal or
    green basil
opal or green basil leaves, to garnish

DRESSING
120 g (4 oz) butter
2 egg yolks
1 tablespoon white wine vinegar
2 tablespoons lime juice

1 Preheat the oven to moderately hot 190°C (375°F/Gas 5). Put the sweet potato cubes in a shallow ovenproof dish and toss to coat with the olive oil. Spread in a single layer, so that the cubes are not touching, then bake for 15 minutes. Sprinkle lightly with salt, turn over, then bake for a further 10 minutes, or until just cooked. Leave to cool.

2 Meanwhile, heat half the butter and the oil in a large pan. Add the garlic and stir for 10–15 seconds. Add the scallops and sauté over medium-high heat for 3–4 minutes, or until cooked through but not browned. Sprinkle with half the lemon juice and season lightly with salt and white pepper. Drain on paper towels.

3 Add the remaining butter to the same pan and, when it foams, add the prawns. Sauté over high heat for 2–3 minutes, or until crisp and opaque. Sprinkle with the remaining lemon juice and season lightly with salt. Discard the garlic clove and drain the prawns on paper towels.

4 Put the mizuna and oakleaf lettuce leaves in a large, shallow bowl. Add the cucumber, sweet potato, scallops and prawns, and toss lightly. Arrange the avocado slices over the top.

5 To make the dressing, melt the butter and keep it hot. Blend the egg yolks and vinegar in a food processor for 5 seconds. With the machine still running, slowly pour in the hot melted butter (the heat will thicken the mixture). Add the lime juice and season with salt and white pepper. Process briefly to combine. Drizzle over the salad and toss lightly. Sprinkle with the chopped basil and garnish with the basil leaves.

NUTRITION PER SERVE
Protein 45 g; Fat 70 g; Carbohydrate ~15 g; Dietary Fibre 5 g; Cholesterol 435 mg; 3605 kJ (860 cal)

Trim the dark vein from the scallops, leaving the roe attached.

Add the prawns to the foaming butter and sauté over high heat.

Blend the egg yolks and vinegar, and slowly pour in the hot melted butter.

PICKLED PRAWNS

Preparation time: 20 minutes +
    48 hours refrigeration
Total cooking time: nil
Serves 4–6

40 large cooked prawns
1 fennel bulb, or 2 baby fennel bulbs
    (600 g)
2 small red onions, thinly sliced
rind of 2 oranges, cut into
    thin strips
rind of 2 limes, cut into
    thin strips
6–8 tablespoons lime juice
    (juice of 4 limes)
1/3 cup (80 ml) orange juice
1 cup (250 ml) olive oil
1/2 cup (125 ml) tarragon
    vinegar
2 red birdseye chillies, finely
    sliced
1 teaspoon sugar

1 Peel and devein the prawns, leaving the tails intact. Slice the fennel thinly, removing any tough outer leaves first and reserving some of the green fronds for use as a garnish. Place the prawns, fennel, onion and orange and lime rind in a non-metallic container and mix well.

2 Mix the lime juice, orange juice, olive oil, tarragon vinegar, chilli, sugar and 1 teaspoon salt together and pour over the prawn mixture. Cover, either with a lid or plastic wrap, and refrigerate for 48 hours. Stir the mixture once or twice during this time to make sure every part of the prawn comes into contact with the marinade.

3 Garnish the prawns with the reserved fennel fronds and serve with crusty bread and a mixed salad.

NUTRITION PER SERVE
Protein 6.5 g; Fat 20 g; Carbohydrate 7 g; Dietary Fibre 3.5 g; Cholesterol 35 mg; 1731 kJ (414 cal)

Thinly slice the fennel, reserving some of the fronds for garnish.

Stir the mixture during the marinating time to ensure the prawns are evenly covered.

MELON AND CRAB SALAD WITH REDCURRANT MINT DRESSING

Preparation time: 1 hour
Total cooking time: 2 minutes
Serves 4

6 large cooked blue swimmer crabs,
    or 375 g (12 oz) frozen crab
    meat, thawed and squeezed dry
¼ small honeydew melon
¼ small watermelon
¼ small rockmelon
1 mizuna lettuce, washed, dried and
    chilled
2 ruby grapefruit, segmented
nasturtium flowers, to garnish

REDCURRANT MINT DRESSING
2 tablespoons redcurrant jelly
2 tablespoons red wine vinegar
½ cup (125 ml/4 fl oz) light olive oil
1 tablespoon finely shredded mint

1 To prepare the whole crabs, use your thumb to pull the apron back and lift off the shell. Pull away the white gills along the sides and discard. Wash the crab well. Remove the flesh from the body with your fingers. Crack the legs open using a nutcracker and remove the flesh.

2 Remove the seeds and skin from the melons and chop the flesh or use a melon baller to scoop out rounds.

3 To make the dressing, heat the jelly and vinegar over low heat until the jelly has dissolved. Allow to cool, then gradually whisk in the olive oil until smooth. Add the shredded mint and season to taste.

4 Tear the mizuna into pieces and arrange with the pieces of melon and grapefruit segments on individual serving plates. Top each with some of the crab meat and drizzle with the dressing. Serve garnished with the nasturtium flowers.

NUTRITION PER SERVE
Protein 15 g; Fat 30 g; Carbohydrate 15 g; Dietary Fibre 3 g; Cholesterol 80 mg; 1665 kJ (395 cal)

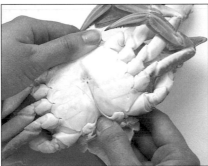

Using your thumb, pull back the apron and lift off the crab shell.

Pull away the white gills from the sides of the crab.

Chop the melons or use a melon baller to scoop out rounds.

Heat the redcurrant jelly and vinegar until the jelly has dissolved.

MIXED SEAFOOD SALAD

Preparation time: 1 hour +
1 hour refrigeration
Total cooking time: 12 minutes
Serves 8

24 cooked king prawns
16 cooked yabbies
1/2 cup (125 ml) white wine
pinch of dried thyme
pinch of dried tarragon or
    a bay leaf
24 scallops, with roe attached
400 g skinless salmon or trout
6 hard-boiled eggs
150 g mesclun
    (mixed lettuce leaves)
2 tablespoons coarsely chopped
    fresh flat-leaf parsley
2 avocados, sliced
2 tablespoons lemon juice

DILL VINAIGRETTE
1/2 cup (125 ml) extra virgin
    olive oil
2 tablespoons white wine
    vinegar
1 teaspoon sugar
2 teaspoons Dijon mustard
1 tablespoon chopped
    fresh dill

GREEN GODDESS DRESSING
2 egg yolks
2 teaspoons Dijon mustard
3 tablespoons lemon juice
1 cup (250 ml) olive oil
4 anchovy fillets, chopped
1 clove garlic, crushed
1/4 cup (60 g) sour cream
1/4 cup (15 g) chopped fresh
    mixed herbs

1 Peel and devein the prawns. Place the yabbies on their backs, exposing the underside. Cut through below the base of the head to remove and discard the head piece. Using scissors, cut down either side of the soft undershell, pull back and remove the flesh in one piece.

2 Put 1 cup (250 ml) water in a pan and add the wine, herbs and a pinch of salt and pepper. Bring to the boil, then reduce the heat and simmer for 5 minutes. Add the scallops and poach for 1–2 minutes, or until they have just turned white, then remove with a slotted spoon and drain on a wire rack. Add the fish fillets and poach until cooked and just tender, remove with a slotted spoon and drain on a wire rack. Break into large pieces.

3 To make the dill vinaigrette, combine all the ingredients and whisk until blended, then season.

4 Combine the prawns, yabbies, scallops and fish in a bowl. Pour the dill vinaigrette into the bowl, cover and refrigerate for 1 hour. Peel and slice the eggs, reserving 2 yolks.

5 To make the green goddess dressing, process the egg yolks, Dijon mustard and 2 tablespoons lemon juice in a food processor or blender for 30 seconds, or until light and creamy. With the motor running, add the oil in a thin, steady stream, increasing the flow as the mayonnaise thickens. Add 2–4 teaspoons lemon juice, the anchovy fillets, garlic, sour cream and fresh herbs. Season with salt and freshly ground white pepper and pulse for 30 seconds to combine the mixture well.

6 Place half the lettuce leaves in the base of a deep serving bowl. Arrange about half the seafood on the lettuce, reserving the dill

vinaigrette. Sprinkle with half the parsley, top with half the avocado, drizzle with half the lemon juice, then finish with half the sliced eggs,

Peel the prawns and then remove the intestinal tract running down the back.

Discard the head piece of the yabbies and try to remove the flesh in one piece.

Poach the scallops in a mixture of wine and herbs.

including the extra whites. Season with salt and freshly ground black pepper. Repeat the layers and season to taste with salt and freshly ground black pepper again. Drizzle with the reserved dill vinaigrette. Crumble the reserved egg yolks over the top and serve with green goddess dressing.

NUTRITION PER SERVE
Protein 30 g; Fat 63 g; Carbohydrate 1.6 g; Dietary Fibre 1 g; Cholesterol 337 mg; 2936 kJ (700 cal)

Drain the poached fish fillets on a wire rack and break into large pieces.

Whisk together all the ingredients for the vinaigrette and season well.

Process the green goddess dressing for 30 seconds to achieve the right consistency.

CHICKEN BALLOTTINE

Preparation time: 45 minutes
Total cooking time: 1 hour
    20 minutes + standing
Serves 8

1 x 1.8 kg chicken, boned
   (ask your butcher to do this)
190 g chicken breast fillet
1 tablespoon olive oil

FILLING
⅓ cup (60 g) chopped dried apricots
⅓ cup (60 g) chopped
   dried figs
1 cup (80 g) fresh white breadcrumbs
190 g chicken mince
60 g sliced prosciutto, chopped
1 tablespoon chopped glacé ginger
1 tablespoon chopped fresh chives
1 egg, lightly beaten
2 tablespoons chopped fresh
   parsley

1 Preheat the oven to moderate 180°C (350°F/Gas 4). Turn the wing and drumstick flesh inside the chicken and lay the chicken out flat, skin-side-down.

2 Place the fillet in a plastic bag and, using your hand, flatten out to an even thickness. Cover the chicken and fillet and refrigerate.

3 To make the filling, place the apricots and the figs in a small bowl, cover with boiling water and leave for 3 minutes to soften, then drain. Combine with the remaining filling ingredients and season.

4 Place the filling over the chicken and top with the fillet. Roll the chicken to enclose the filling, tucking the ends in as you go. Use a sewing needle and double cotton to sew up the chicken and secure the filling. Tie the chicken with string to help retain its shape. Brush with oil and place in a baking dish. Bake for 1 hour 20 minutes, or until golden brown and cooked through. Cover with foil and leave to stand for 10–15 minutes before removing the string and thread. Cut into slices to serve.

NUTRITION PER SERVE
Protein 60 g; Fat 15 g; Carbohydrate 14 g; Dietary Fibre 2 g; Cholesterol 210 mg; 1785 kJ (427 cal)

Place the filling over the boned chicken, cover with the fillet and roll up.

Tie the chicken securely with string to ensure it keeps its shape while cooking.

PORK AND VEAL TERRINE

Preparation time: 20 minutes + overnight refrigeration
Total cooking time: 1 hour 20 minutes
Serves 6

8–10 thin slices rindless bacon
1 tablespoon olive oil
1 onion, chopped
2 cloves garlic, crushed
1 kg (2 lb) pork and veal mince
1 cup (80 g/2¾ oz) fresh bread-crumbs
1 egg, beaten
¼ cup (60 ml/2 fl oz) brandy
3 teaspoons chopped fresh thyme
¼ cup (15 g/½ oz) chopped fresh parsley

1 Preheat the oven to moderate 180°C (350°F/Gas 4). Lightly grease a 25 x 11 cm (10 x 4¼ inch) terrine. Line the terrine with the bacon so that it hangs over the sides.

2 Heat the oil in a frying pan, add the onion and garlic and cook for 2–3 minutes, or until the onion is soft. Mix the onion with the mince, breadcrumbs, egg, brandy, thyme and parsley in a large bowl. Season with salt and pepper. Fry a small piece of the mixture to check the seasoning, and adjust if necessary.

3 Spoon the mixture into the bacon-lined terrine, pressing down firmly. Fold the bacon over the top of the terrine, cover with foil and place in a baking dish.

4 Place enough cold water in the baking dish to come half way up the side of the terrine. Bake for 1–1¼ hours, or until the juices run clear when the terrine is pierced with a skewer. Remove the terrine from the water-filled baking dish and pour off the excess juices. Cover with foil, then put a piece of heavy cardboard, cut to fit, on top of the terrine. Put weights or food cans on top of the cardboard to compress the terrine. Refrigerate overnight, then cut into slices to serve.

NUTRITION PER SERVE
Protein 15 g; Fat 7.5 g; Carbohydrate 10 g; Dietary Fibre 1 g; Cholesterol 60 mg; 800 kJ (190 cal)

NOTE: The terrine can be stored in a refrigerator for up to 5 days.

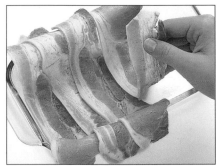

Line the terrine dish with the bacon strips so that they drape over the sides.

Mix together the onion mixture, mince, breadcrumbs, egg, brandy and herbs.

Press the mixture firmly into the terrine dish and fold the bacon over the top.

Strain the liquid through a fine sieve and leave to cool.

When cool enough to handle, pull the chicken flesh off the bones.

Process the chicken flesh with the butter and spices until smooth.

Pour the yellow clarified butter over the potted chicken.

POTTED CHICKEN

Preparation time: 15 minutes
　+ 2 hours refrigeration
Total cooking time: 1 hour
Serves 6

6 chicken thighs, skin removed
1 onion, sliced
1 carrot, sliced
6 peppercorns
1 bay leaf
pinch of ground mace
pinch of cayenne pepper
1/4 teaspoon freshly grated nutmeg
200 g (6¹/2 oz) unsalted butter,
　softened

1 Place the chicken thighs, onion, carrot, peppercorns and bay leaf in a pan and add 2 cups (500 ml/16 fl oz) of water. Bring to the boil, skimming off any foam. Reduce the heat, then cover and simmer for 30 minutes, or until tender and cooked through.

2 Remove the chicken, then rapidly boil the remaining liquid until it has reduced to about ¹/4 cup (60 ml/1fl oz). Strain through a fine sieve and allow to cool.

3 Remove the chicken flesh from the bones. Place the flesh in a food processor with the liquid and process until smooth. Add the mace, cayenne pepper, nutmeg and 150 g (5 oz) of the butter. Season to taste with salt and pepper and process until combined and smooth.

4 Put the chicken mixture in a 3-cup (750 ml/24 fl oz) ceramic dish. Melt the remaining butter in a small pan and pour the yellow clarified butter onto the surface of the chicken, leaving the white milk solids in the pan. Refrigerate for 2 hours, or until the butter sets.

NUTRITION PER SERVE
Protein 25 g; Fat 30 g; Carbohydrate 1.5 g; Dietary Fibre 0.5 g; Cholesterol 140 mg; 1590 kJ (380 cal)

Use a sharp knife to chop the tarragon leaves into small pieces.

Cover the base of the tin with chives and top with the cream cheese mixture.

Use a palette knife to spread the cream cheese mixture evenly into the tin.

Starting from the longest edge, roll the cream cheese and herbs into a log.

HERB CHEESE LOG

Preparation time: 25 minutes +
  3 hours refrigeration
Total cooking time: Nil
Serves 6

500 g (1 lb) cream cheese,
    at room temperature
1 tablespoon lemon juice
1 clove garlic, crushed
2 teaspoons chopped fresh thyme
2 teaspoons chopped fresh tarragon
1 tablespoon chopped fresh
    flat-leaf parsley
1 cup (50 g/1²⁄₃ oz) chopped fresh
    chives

1 Put the cream cheese in a large bowl and beat with electric beaters until soft and creamy. Mix in the lemon juice and garlic. Mix together the thyme, tarragon and the parsley.

2 Line a 20 x 30 cm (8 x 12 inch) tin with foil. Spread the chives over the base, then spoon the cream cheese mixture over the chives. Using a palette knife, gently spread the mixture into the tin, pushing it into any gaps. Sprinkle the combined herbs evenly over the cheese.

3 Lift the foil from the tin and place on a work surface. Roll into a log, starting from the longest edge, peeling back the foil as you go. Cover and place on a baking tray. Refrigerate for at least 3 hours, or preferably overnight. Serve with water crackers or fresh crusty bread.

NUTRITION PER SERVE
Protein 7 g; Fat 28 g; Carbohydrate 2.5 g; Dietary Fibre 0.5 g; Cholesterol 80 mg; 1188 kJ (285 cal)

NOTE: You can also choose to make a roulade by simply rolling it into a log from the shortest edge rather than the longest one.

RAISED PORK PIE

Preparation time: 20 minutes +
  refrigeration + overnight setting
Total cooking time: 65 minutes
Serves 6

1.2 kg minced pork
²/₃ cup (90 g) pistachio nuts,
  shelled and chopped
2 green apples, peeled and finely
  chopped
6 fresh sage leaves, finely chopped
4 cups (500 g) plain flour
150 g butter
2 eggs, lightly beaten
1 egg yolk
200 ml vegetable stock
200 ml unsweetened apple juice
2 teaspoons gelatine

1 Preheat the oven to moderately hot
200°C (400°F/Gas 6). Put the pork,
pistachio nuts, apple and sage leaves in
a bowl, mix well and season. Fry a
piece of the mixture to taste and adjust
the seasoning. Cover and refrigerate.
Wrap a piece of plastic wrap around a
6 cm high, 20 cm straight-sided tin,
then turn the tin over, and grease the
outside base and side of the tin.

2 Put the flour and 1 teaspoon salt in
a bowl and make a well in the
centre. Put the butter in a pan with
210 ml water, bring to the boil and add
to the flour, with the eggs. Mix with a
wooden spoon until combined, then
turn out onto a work surface and bring
the mixture together to form a smooth
dough. Wrap in plastic wrap and
refrigerate for 10 minutes.

3 Cut off a third of the pastry and
wrap in plastic wrap—do not
refrigerate. Roll the remainder into a
circle large enough to just cover the

*Combine the ingredients for the filling
and season to taste.*

*The dough must be combined to a
smooth consistency.*

*Cover the outside of the tin with the
pastry, working fast so that it does not set.*

outside of the tin. Lift onto a rolling pin and place over the tin, working fast before the pastry sets. Refrigerate until the pastry hardens. Carefully pull out the tin and remove the plastic wrap. Attach a paper collar made of 2 layers of greased baking paper around the outside of the pastry so it fits snugly and secure with a paper clip at the top and bottom. Fill the pie, then roll out the remaining pastry to form a lid. Attach it to the base with some water, pressing or crimping it to make it look neat. Cut a small hole in the top of the pie.

4 Put the pie on a baking tray, bake for 40 minutes and check the pastry top. If it is still pale, bake for another 10 minutes, then remove the paper. Brush with egg yolk mixed with 1 tablespoon water and bake for another 15 minutes, or until the sides are brown. Cool completely.

5 Bring the stock and half the apple juice to the boil. Sprinkle the gelatine over the surface of the remaining apple juice in a jug and leave to go spongy, then pour into the stock and mix until the gelatine dissolves. Place a small funnel (piping nozzles work well) in the hole of the pie and pour in a little of the gelatine mixture, leave to settle and then pour in some more until the pie is full. Fill the pie completely so there are no gaps when the gelatine mixture sets. Leave to set overnight.

NUTRITION PER SERVE
Protein 60 g; Fat 35 g; Carbohydrate 72 g; Dietary Fibre 5.5 g; Cholesterol 257 mg; 3545 kJ (845 cal)

NOTE: If wrapped tightly with plastic wrap, pork pies will last in the refrigerator for up to 4–5 days.

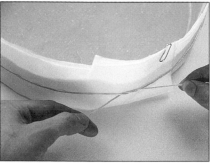

The greased paper collar should fit snugly around the outside of the pastry.

Cut a small hole in the top of the pie to allow the gelatine to be poured in.

Gradually pour the gelatine into the cooked and cooled pie until it is full.

TURKEY LEFTOVERS

Roast turkey is a seasonal dish for most people—Christmas and, for some, Thanksgiving. If the thought of days of turkey sandwiches is all a bit overwhelming, here are some tasty alternatives.

Turkey empanadas

Heat 1 tablespoon oil in a frying pan, add 1 small finely chopped onion and 1 crushed garlic clove. Cook over medium heat for 2 minutes, then add 2 teaspoons paprika, 1 teaspoon ground cumin and ½ teaspoon ground cinnamon, and stir until fragrant. Add 2 tablespoons sherry, 400 g can puréed tomatoes and 400 g finely chopped cooked turkey. Simmer for about 10 minutes, or until thick. Remove from the heat, stir in ½ cup (110 g) chopped pitted green olives, 3 chopped hard-boiled eggs and 1 tablespoon chopped fresh parsley, and season. Transfer to a bowl and allow to cool. Using 4½ sheets of ready-rolled shortcrust pastry, cut 12 cm rounds from each sheet (you will need 18 rounds). Place 1½ tablespoons of the mixture on one half of each round, brush the edge lightly with water and fold the pastry over to enclose the filling. Press the edges with a fork to seal. Deep-fry the empanadas, in batches, for about 3–5 minutes, or until golden brown. Drain on paper towels.
Makes 18

Leek, turkey and sweet corn soup

Heat 20 g butter in a large pan and add 1 thinly sliced leek. Cook over medium heat until soft. Add 3½ cups (875 ml) chicken stock and 420 g can creamed corn. Season with salt and pepper. Bring to the boil and then reduce the heat and simmer for 5 minutes. Add 250 g shredded cooked turkey. *Serves 4*

Left to right: Turkey empanadas; Leek, turkey and sweet corn soup; Potato and apple salad; Turkey filo parcels; Turkey san choy bau.

Potato and apple salad

Cut 4 spring onions into thin strips and fry until crisp. Boil 750 g new potatoes until just tender; drain and allow to cool, then cut in half. Cut an unpeeled red apple into thin wedges and toss with 1 tablespoon lemon juice. Boil 2 thickly sliced zucchini until tender, then drain and refresh in cold water. For the dressing, combine ½ cup (125 g) whole-egg mayonnaise, 3 teaspoons Dijon mustard, 1 tablespoon wholegrain mustard and 2 tablespoons lemon juice. Season to taste. Cut 400 g cooked turkey into thin strips and toss with the potato, apple, zucchini, 2 tablespoons chopped fresh parsley and the dressing until combined. Top with the crispy spring onion. *Serves 6*

Turkey filo parcels

Preheat the oven to moderate 180°C (350°F/Gas 4). Heat 20 g butter in a large pan, add 200 g sliced mushrooms and 4 diced bacon rashers. Cook over high heat until the mushrooms are soft and there is no liquid left. Stir through 350 g chopped, cooked turkey, 150 g ricotta, 2 sliced spring onions and ¼ cup (15 g) shredded fresh basil. Season with black pepper. Cover 24 sheets of filo pastry with a damp tea towel. Working with 3 sheets at a time, brush each layer with melted butter. Cut the pastry into 3 strips. Place 1 tablespoon of filling at the end of each strip and fold the pastry over to form a triangle. Continue folding until you reach the end of the pastry. Repeat with the remaining pastry and filling. Place on a baking tray, brush with butter and sprinkle with sesame seeds. Bake in the oven for 35 minutes, or until crisp. *Makes 24*

Turkey san choy bau

Soak 8 small iceberg lettuce leaves in cold water while preparing the filling. Soak 5 dried Chinese mushrooms in a bowl of boiling water for 15 minutes, or until soft. Drain, discard the stems and finely chop. Heat 1 teaspoon sesame oil and 2 teaspoons oil in a pan, add 2 crushed garlic cloves, 1 tablespoon grated fresh ginger and 100 g thinly sliced canned baby corn, and toss over heat until fragrant. Add 300 g finely chopped cooked turkey, the Chinese mushrooms, ½ cup (90 g) finely chopped water chestnuts, 100 g bean sprouts, 2 chopped spring onions, 1 tablespoon chopped fresh coriander, 1 teaspoon sugar, 1 tablespoon oyster sauce and 1 tablespoon soy sauce. Toss the mixture well to heat. Drain the lettuce and carefully pat dry. Spoon the turkey filling into each lettuce cup and serve. *Serves 4*

HAM LEFTOVERS

A 7 kg ham serves around 20 people. But don't worry, leftover ham can be kept wrapped in a damp tea towel in the refrigerator for up to 10 days. Try some of these delicious ways of finishing it off.

Ham and cider casserole

Preheat the oven to moderately hot 200°C (400°F/Gas 6). Heat 1 tablespoon butter in a heavy-based pan and add 1 chopped onion. Fry for 2–3 minutes, or until tender, then add 2 sliced leeks and continue frying until the leeks are cooked through. Stir in 2 crushed garlic cloves. Place the onion and leek mixture in the base of an ovenproof dish. Scatter with 400 g (8 slices) chopped ham, season with pepper and pour on 100 ml apple cider. Spoon 1 can (300 g) rinsed, drained butter beans over and around the ham and sprinkle with 1/3 cup (25 g) fresh breadcrumbs and 1 tablespoon freshly grated Parmesan. Dot with 20 g butter and bake for 20 minutes. *Serves 4*

Layered cob

Place 2 red capsicums under a hot grill, turning occasionally, until the skin blackens and blisters. Cool under a tea towel or in a plastic bag, then peel away the skin and cut the flesh into slices. Slice 500 g eggplant and grill until golden on both sides. Briefly steam 400 g washed and trimmed English spinach until wilted, allow to cool, and squeeze out any excess liquid. Cut a large round from the top of a 22 cm cob loaf and reserve. Scoop out the white bread, leaving a 1 cm border. Brush the inside of the loaf and the inside of the lid with 2 tablespoons oil, combined with 2 crushed garlic cloves. Place half the eggplant slices in the bottom, layer the red capsicum on top, then 150 g sliced ham. Top with 2 cups (500 g) ricotta mixed with 2 tablespoons chopped fresh parsley, 1/4 cup (25 g) grated Parmesan and season with salt and pepper. Spread the spinach leaves over the top, then add the remaining eggplant. Put the lid on and wrap tightly with plastic wrap. Place a plate on top and weigh down with some cans and leave overnight. *Serves 6–8*

Left to right: Ham and cider casserole; Layered cob; Split pea and ham soup; Ham and leek pie; Ham, bean and tomato salad.

Split pea and ham soup

Rinse 500 g yellow split peas in cold water, then drain. Place the peas, your leftover ham bone, 2 chopped carrots, 2 chopped celery sticks, 1 large chopped onion, 2 bay leaves and 3 litres water in a pan, cover and bring to the boil. Reduce the heat and simmer, partly covered, for 2 hours, or until the peas are tender. Skim off any scum that rises to the surface. Remove the ham bone and remove the meat from the bone, discarding any fat or skin. Finely chop the ham and set aside. Remove the bay leaves. Purée the soup until smooth, adding a little more water if needed, then stir in the ham. Season with pepper and salt if needed. Note: This soup thickens on standing and it's great to freeze too. *Serves 8*

Ham and leek pie

Preheat the oven to moderately hot 200°C (400°F/Gas 6). Boil 2 medium potatoes until just tender and then slice. Melt 20 g butter in a frying pan, add 2 sliced leeks and cook until golden. Add 300 g ham cut into large cubes and toss to combine. Place the potato slices in the bottom of a greased 23 cm pie plate, top with the ham and leek mixture. Pour in 1/3 cup (80 ml) cream, combined with 2 lightly beaten eggs and 2 tablespoons chopped fresh parsley. Sprinkle with 1/2 cup (60 g) grated cheese. Wet the edge of the pie plate with a little water, place 1 sheet thawed ready-rolled puff pastry on top, trim the edges and press down to seal. Cut two slits in the top of the pastry and decorate with any leftover pastry. Bake for 40 minutes, or until golden. *Serves 6–8*

Ham, bean and tomato salad

Top and tail 200 g green beans and 200 g sugar snap peas. Cut the beans on the diagonal into 4 cm lengths. Place the beans, peas and 200 g frozen broad beans in a pan of boiling water and cook for 1 minute. Drain and refresh in cold water. Discard the outer skin from the broad beans. Cut 200 g sliced ham into thin strips and combine with the beans and peas, 250 g halved cherry tomatoes, 3/4 cup (115 g) cashews, 2 tablespoons chopped fresh parsley and 2 tablespoons chopped fresh chives in a large bowl. For the dressing, combine 1/4 cup (60 ml) olive oil, 2 tablespoons cider vinegar, 1/2 teaspoon sugar and 2 tablespoons chopped fresh mint in a screw-top jar and shake well. Pour the dressing over the salad and toss well. Season. *Serves 6*

PUDDINGS AND DESSERTS

FEW THINGS sum up the Christmas season quite so well as a steaming, hot Christmas pudding. Add some brandy butter or vanilla custard and you have a dessert to look forward to all year. But given the festive spirit, there's no need to stop at just one. Why not try some trifle or berries in Champagne jelly as well? And what would Christmas be without mince pies and Christmas cake?

BOILED CHRISTMAS PUDDING

Preparation time: 40 minutes
+ 2 nights standing
Total cooking time: 7 hours
Serves 10–12

1²/₃ cups (310 g) mixed
    dried fruit
¼ cup (45 g) mixed peel
4 cups (500 g) mixed sultanas,
    currants and raisins
½ cup (125 ml) brown ale
2 tablespoons rum or brandy
rind and juice of 1 orange
rind and juice of 1 lemon
225 g suet, grated
1¹/₃ cups (245 g) soft brown
    sugar
3 eggs, lightly beaten
2½ cups (200 g) fresh white
    breadcrumbs
¾ cup (90 g) self-raising flour
1 teaspoon mixed spice
¼ teaspoon freshly grated nutmeg
²/₃ cup (100 g) blanched almonds,
    chopped

1 Finely chop the mixed dried fruit. Place in a large bowl with the mixed peel, sultanas, currants, raisins, ale, rum, orange and lemon rind and juice. Cover and leave overnight.

2 Mix the fruit mixture with the remaining ingredients and a pinch of salt in a large bowl. Leave to stand for 10 minutes to thicken.

3 Cut an 80 cm square from a clean piece of calico or an old tea towel and boil it for 20 minutes. Wring out (wearing rubber gloves to prevent scalding) and spread on a clean work surface. Dust the calico with a thick layer of plain flour, leaving a border around the edge. Spread the flour out with your hands—it is important that you get an even covering because the flour forms a seal to prevent the pudding absorbing any water. Place the pudding mixture onto the centre of the calico and bring the points of the material together. Gather in all the excess material, trying to make the folds neat and even (they will leave an imprint on the finished pudding). Tie the top tightly with a piece of unwaxed string—no water should get in. Tie a loop into the end of one of the pieces of string to act as a handle. Hook a wooden spoon handle through the loop and lower the pudding into a pan of boiling water. The pudding should not rest on the base of the pan. Make sure the pan is large enough for the pudding to move around.

4 Cover the pan and boil for 5 hours. If the water level drops, add more boiling water around the edge of the pudding. Remove from the water and hang in a well-ventilated, dry place where it will not touch anything. Make sure the calico ends all hang to one side so they do not drip all over the pudding. Leave overnight.

5 Untie the cloth and, if there are damp patches at the top, spread it out to make sure it dries. When it is dry, re-wrap and tie with a new piece of string. The pudding will store hanging in a cool, dry place for up to 4 months. To serve, boil for 2 hours, hang for 15 minutes, then remove from the cloth and cut into wedges.

NUTRITION PER SERVE (12)
Protein 7.5 g; Fat 20 g; Carbohydrate 76 g; Dietary Fibre 5.5 g; Cholesterol 60 mg; 2211 kJ (528 cal)

Mix all the ingredients together in a large bowl and leave for 10 minutes.

Dust a calico square with a thick layer of plain flour, spreading it with your hands.

Put the pudding mixture in the centre of the calico square and draw the material up.

When gathering all the material together, try to keep the folds as neat as possible.

Tie a loop in the string sealing the pudding and use this as a handle.

Using the string handle, lower the pudding into a large pan of boiling water.

STEAMED CHRISTMAS PUDDING

Preparation time: 40 minutes + overnight standing
Total cooking time: 8 hours
Serves 10–12

4 cups (500 g) mixed sultanas, currants and raisins
1²/3 cups (310 g) mixed dried fruit, chopped
¼ cup (45 g) mixed peel
½ cup (125 ml) brown ale
2 tablespoons rum or brandy
juice and rind of 1 orange
juice and rind of 1 lemon
225 g suet, grated (see Note)
1¹/3 cups (245 g) soft brown sugar
3 eggs, lightly beaten
2½ cups (200 g) fresh white breadcrumbs
¾ cup (90 g) self-raising flour
1 teaspoon mixed spice
¼ teaspoon freshly grated nutmeg
²/3 cup (100 g) blanched almonds, roughly chopped

1 Place the sultanas, currants, raisins, dried fruit, mixed peel, ale, rum, orange and lemon juice and rind into a large bowl. Cover and leave overnight.

2 The next day, mix together the fruit mixture, suet, brown sugar, eggs, breadcrumbs, flour, spices, almonds and a pinch of salt in a large bowl. The mixture should fall from the spoon—if it is too stiff, add a little more ale. Place a 2 litre pudding basin on a trivet in a large pan with a lid, which will comfortably hold it, and pour in enough water to reach halfway up the side of the basin. Remove the basin and put the water on to boil.

3 Grease the pudding basin and line the base with a circle of baking paper. Fill with the pudding mixture. Cut a sheet of baking paper and a sheet of foil big enough to fit comfortably over the top of the basin and come halfway down the sides. Lay the baking paper on top of the foil, grease the paper, then make a pleat in the centre. Put the cover, paper-side-down on top of the pudding and fold everything down over the edge. Cover with a lid if your basin has one, or tie a double piece of string securely around the rim of the basin, just under the lip, and make a handle which runs across the top with another piece of string.

4 Place the basin carefully on the trivet in the pan and turn the water down to a fast simmer. Cover the pan and steam for 8 hours, replenishing with boiling water when necessary. If you want to keep your pudding and reheat it later, then steam it for 6 hours and steam it for another 2 hours on the day you would like to eat it. Store in a cool, dry place for up to 3 months.

NUTRITION PER SERVE (12)
Protein 7 g; Fat 20 g; Carbohydrate 75 g; Dietary Fibre 5 g; Cholesterol 60 mg; 2167 kJ (518 cal)

NOTE: Buy suet from your butcher.
Metal pudding basins are better heat conductors than ceramic basins so puddings will cook more quickly in them. Check the pudding about 30 minutes before the cooking time is up. To test, insert a skewer into the centre of the pudding. If it comes out clean, the pudding is cooked.

Grate the suet with the rough side of a cheese grater.

Mix all the ingredients together, adding more ale if the mixture is too dry.

Cut a round of baking paper to fit the base of the pudding basin.

Make a pleat in the foil and paper cover so the pudding can expand when cooking.

Cover the pudding with the greased paper facing down.

Tie the cover securely to the basin with string and make a handle across the top.

SWEET SAUCES

Sinfully thick and creamy, these sauces make perfect accompaniments for Christmas cakes or puddings. For something a little lighter, try serving them with fresh fruit.

Left to right: Brandy butter; Brandy cream sauce; Zabaglione; Whisky sauce; Crème Anglaise; Vanilla custard.

Brandy butter

Using electric beaters, beat 250 g softened unsalted butter and 1½ cups (185 g) sifted icing sugar until smooth and creamy. Gradually add ¼ cup (60 ml) brandy, beating thoroughly. Refrigerate until required. *Makes about 1 cup (250 ml)*

Brandy cream sauce

Beat 2 egg yolks and ⅓ cup (90 g) caster sugar until thick and pale and all the sugar has dissolved. Stir in ⅓ cup (80 ml) brandy and fold in 1 cup (250 ml) cream. Beat 2 egg whites in a clean, dry bowl until soft peaks form. Fold into the sauce and serve immediately. *Makes 1½ cups (375 ml)*

Zabaglione

In a heatproof bowl, beat together 8 egg yolks and ⅓ cup (90 g) caster sugar with electric beaters until thick and pale. Put the bowl over a simmering pan of water and beat continuously, gradually adding 1¼ cups (315 ml) Marsala. Beat for 5 minutes, or until thick and frothy. If you can draw a line through the zabaglione with a spoon and it leaves a trail, it is ready. *Makes 2 cups (500 ml)*

Whisky sauce

Melt 2 tablespoons butter in a pan over low heat. Remove from the heat, add 1/3 cup (40 g) plain flour and stir until combined. Gradually whisk in 2 cups (500 ml) milk and 2 tablespoons caster sugar. Return to medium heat and whisk until it boils and thickens. Reduce the heat and simmer for 10 minutes, stirring occasionally. Remove from the heat, and stir in 1/3 cup (80 ml) whisky, 2 teaspoons butter and 1 tablespoon thick cream. Cover with plastic wrap until ready to serve. *Makes 2 cups (500 ml)*

Crème Anglaise

Whisk 3 egg yolks and 2 tablespoons caster sugar together in a heatproof bowl for 2 minutes, or until light and creamy. Heat 1 1/2 cups (375 ml) milk until almost boiling, then pour onto the mixture, whisking constantly. Return to the clean pan and stir for 5 minutes, or until thickened enough to coat the back of a spoon. Don't allow the mixture to boil or it will curdle. Remove from the heat, stir in 1/2 teaspoon vanilla essence and transfer to a jug. Serve immediately. *Makes 2 cups (500 ml)*

Vanilla custard

Combine 1 cup (250 ml) milk and 1/4 cup (60 ml) cream in a pan. Bring to the boil, then remove from the heat immediately. In a bowl, whisk 3 egg yolks, 1/2 cup (125 g) caster sugar and 2 teaspoons cornflour. Slowly pour the hot milk and cream into the egg mixture, whisking continuously. Return to the pan and stir over low heat for 5 minutes, or until thickened—do not boil. Remove from the heat and stir in 1/2 teaspoon vanilla essence. Serve immediately. *Makes 2 cups (500 ml)*

SUGAR-FREE PUDDING

Preparation time: 30 minutes
Total cooking time:
    1 hour 30 minutes
Serves 6–8

6 ripe bananas, mashed
1 egg, lightly beaten
2 cups (370 g) mixed dried fruit
1 cup (80 g) fresh breadcrumbs

ORANGE CREAM
300 ml cream
2 tablespoons orange juice
1 tablespoon grated orange rind
1 teaspoon vanilla essence

1 Grease a 1.25 litre pudding basin with melted butter and place a round of baking paper in the bottom.

2 Place the basin in a large pan, on a trivet or upturned saucer, and pour in enough cold water to come halfway up the side of the basin. Remove the basin and put the water on to boil.

3 Combine the banana, egg, dried fruit and breadcrumbs in a bowl. Spoon into the prepared basin.

4 Lay a sheet of foil on the work surface and cover with a sheet of baking paper. Make a large pleat in the middle. Grease the paper with melted butter and place, paper-side-down, across the top of the basin. Tie string securely around the rim of the basin and over the top to make a handle. The handle is used to lift the pudding in and out of the pan.

5 Gently lower the basin into the boiling water, reduce the heat to a fast simmer and cover with a tight-

fitting lid. Cook for 1½ hours, checking the water after an hour and topping up to the original level with boiling water as needed.

6 To make the orange cream, combine the cream, orange juice, rind and vanilla in a bowl and mix well. Serve over the pudding.

NUTRITION PER SERVE (8)
Protein 5.5 g; Fat 18 g; Carbohydrate 60 g; Dietary Fibre 5.5 g; Cholesterol 75 mg; 1720 kJ (410 cal)

NOTE: This pudding is low-fat. If you're keeping an eye on the calories, skip the orange cream.

Cover the pudding mix with a pleated layer of foil and greased baking paper.

Using the string handle, lower the pudding into boiling water.

To make the orange cream, simply combine all the ingredients in a bowl.

ICE CREAM CHRISTMAS PUDDING

Preparation time: 1 hour +
overnight standing +
2 nights freezing
Total cooking time: nil
Serves 10

⅓ cup (50 g) toasted almonds,
chopped
¼ cup (45 g) mixed peel
½ cup (60 g) raisins, chopped
½ cup (60 g) sultanas
⅓ cup (50 g) currants
⅓ cup (80 ml) rum
1 litre good-quality vanilla
ice cream
½ cup (105 g) red and green
glacé cherries, quartered
1 teaspoon mixed spice
1 teaspoon ground cinnamon
½ teaspoon ground nutmeg
1 litre good-quality chocolate
ice cream

1 Mix the almonds, peel, raisins, sultanas, currants and rum in a bowl, cover with plastic wrap and leave overnight. Chill a 2 litre pudding basin in the freezer.

2 Soften the vanilla ice cream slightly and mix in the glacé cherries. Working quickly, press the ice cream around the inside of the chilled basin, spreading it evenly to cover the base and side of the basin. Return the basin to the freezer and leave overnight. Check the ice cream a couple of times and spread it evenly to the top.

3 The next day, mix the spices and chocolate ice cream with the fruit mixture. Spoon it into the centre of the pudding bowl and smooth the top. Freeze overnight, or until very firm. Turn the pudding out onto a chilled plate, decorate and leave to stand for 5 minutes. Cut into wedges to serve.

NUTRITION PER SERVE
Protein 7 g; Fat 25 g; Carbohydrate 45 g; Dietary Fibre 1.5 g; Cholesterol 46 mg; 1798 kJ (430 cal)

NOTE: If you want to put coins and charms into the pudding, wrap each one in baking paper and poke into the base of the pudding.

Cover the inside and base of the basin with the ice cream and cherry mixture.

Spoon the chocolate ice cream mixture into the bowl and smooth the surface.

FRESH FRUIT MINCE PIES

Preparation time: 1 hour +
30 minutes refrigeration
Total cooking time: 50 minutes
Makes 24

PASTRY
1¾ cups (220 g) plain flour
150 g butter, chilled and chopped
¾ cup (80 g) ground hazelnuts
2 tablespoons caster sugar
1–2 tablespoons iced water

FILLING
¾ cup (115 g) blueberries
1 cup (200 g) peeled and
    finely chopped apple
½ cup (60 g) raisins
½ cup (75 g) currants
½ cup (60 g) sultanas
¼ cup (30 g) slivered almonds,
    toasted
¼ cup (60 g) caster sugar
2 tablespoons mixed peel
½ cup (125 ml) brandy
1 teaspoon grated lemon rind
½ teaspoon mixed spice
½ teaspoon ground ginger
sifted icing sugar, for dusting

1 To make the pastry, sift the flour into a large bowl and add the chopped butter. Rub the butter into the flour with your fingertips until it resembles fine breadcrumbs. Stir in the nuts and sugar. Make a well in the centre and add the water. Mix using a flat-bladed knife until the mixture comes together in beads. Gather the mixture into a ball and turn out onto a lightly floured surface. Press together into a ball and

Rub the butter into the flour with your fingertips until it resembles breadcrumbs.

Mix with a flat-bladed knife until the mixture comes together in beads.

Gather the mixture into a ball and turn out onto a lightly floured surface.

flatten slightly into a disc. Cover with plastic wrap and refrigerate for 30 minutes.

2 Preheat the oven to moderate 180°C (350°F/Gas 4). Between sheets of baking paper, roll the dough out to a 3 mm thickness. Using a 7 cm round pastry cutter, cut 24 pastry rounds and line two 12 hole deep patty pans with the rounds. Line each pastry case with baking paper and fill with baking beads. Bake for 10 minutes, remove the paper and beads and bake for a further 10 minutes.

3 Meanwhile, press together the pastry scraps and re-roll them to 3 mm thickness. Using 4.5 cm star, bell or holly-shaped cutters, cut 24 shapes from the pastry to make the tart lids.

4 To make the filling, place the blueberries, apple, raisins, currants, sultanas, slivered almonds, sugar, mixed peel, brandy, lemon rind, mixed spice and ground ginger in a pan and simmer, stirring well, for 5–10 minutes, or until the mixture is thick and pulpy. Spoon the filling evenly among the cases and top each case with a pastry lid.

5 Bake the pies for 20 minutes, or until the pastry lids are golden. Leave in the tins for 5 minutes before transferring to a wire rack to cool. Dust with the icing sugar before serving.

NUTRITION PER MINCE PIE
Protein 2 g; Fat 8 g; Carbohydrate 17 g; Dietary Fibre 1.5 g; Cholesterol 16 mg; 623 kJ (150 cal)

NOTE: Fruit mince pies will keep well for up to 7 days in an airtight container. If you prefer, they can be frozen for up to 3 months.

Line the pastry cases with baking paper and fill with baking beads.

Spoon the fruit mince filling evenly among the pastry cases.

Top the pies with a star-shaped pastry lid and bake until golden.

TRADITIONAL FRUIT MINCE

Preparation time: 20 minutes
Total cooking time: nil
Makes 2 litres (64 fl oz)

2 large green apples (about
    440 g/14 oz), peeled, cored
    and chopped
250 g (8 oz) packet suet mix
375 g (12 oz) raisins

1½ cups (345 g/11 oz), firmly
    packed soft brown sugar
250 g (8 oz) sultanas
250 g (8 oz) currants
150 g (5 oz) mixed peel
100 g (3¼ oz) slivered almonds,
    chopped
1 tablespoon mixed spice
½ teaspoon nutmeg
½ teaspoon cinnamon
2 teaspoons grated orange rind
1 teaspoon grated lemon rind
1 cup (250 ml/8 fl oz) orange juice
½ cup (125 ml/4 fl oz) lemon juice
150 ml (5 fl oz) brandy

1 Combine all the ingredients and ½ cup (125 ml/4 fl oz) brandy in a large bowl. Mix together thoroughly.

2 Spoon the fruit mince into clean, warm jars. Use a skewer to remove air bubbles and to pack the mixture in firmly. Leave a 1.5 cm (⅝ inch) space at the top of the jar and wipe the jar clean with a cloth. Spoon a little brandy over the surface of the fruit mince and seal. Label and date.

3 Set aside for at least 3 weeks, or up to 6 months, before using in pies and tarts. (Keep the fruit mince refrigerated in hot weather.)

Peel and core the apples. Cut them into quarters and then finely chop.

Take care when grating the rind not to include any pith as it will taste bitter.

Remove any air bubbles with a clean metal skewer before sealing the jar.

QUICK FRUIT MINCE

Preparation time: 20 minutes
Total cooking time: nil
<u>Makes</u> 2 cups (500 ml/16 fl oz)

1/4 cup (35 g/1 1/4 oz) currants
1/3 cup (40 g/1 1/4 oz) sultanas
2 tablespoons mixed peel
1/4 cup (30 g/1 oz) slivered almonds
1 apple, grated
1/4 cup (45 g/1 1/2 oz) soft brown
 sugar
1/4 teaspoon ground nutmeg
1/4 teaspoon ground cinnamon
1 teaspoon grated orange rind
1 teaspoon grated lemon rind
100 g (3 1/2 oz) can stoneless cherries,
 drained and quartered, or 150 g
 (5 oz) fresh cherries, pitted
100 g (3 1/2 oz) white seedless grapes,
 halved
1 tablespoon whisky

1 To make the fruit mince mixture, combine all the ingredients in a large bowl and stir well to ensure they are evenly mixed.

2 Spoon into clean, warm jars and seal. Label and date.

NOTE: Use this quick fruit mince as a filling for mini tarts or as a topping for pancakes. The mince will only keep for a short period (up to 5 days in the refrigerator) because it is made with fresh fruit and has very little alcohol within it.

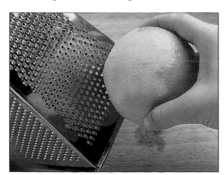

Finely grate the rind—do not grate any white pith as it will taste bitter.

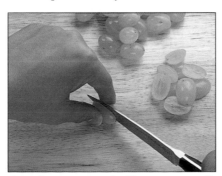

Cut the grapes in half using a small, sharp knife.

Combine all the ingredients in a large bowl and mix well.

FRESH FRUIT PAVLOVA

Preparation time: 30 minutes
Total cooking time: 55 minutes
Serves 6–8

6 egg whites
2 cups (500 g) caster sugar
1½ tablespoons cornflour
1½ teaspoons vinegar
2 cups (500 ml) cream,
   whipped
2 bananas, sliced
2 punnets (500 g) strawberries,
   sliced
4 kiwi fruit, sliced
pulp from 4 passionfruit

1 Preheat the oven to slow 150°C (300°F/Gas 2). Line a large oven tray with baking paper and draw a 26 cm circle on the paper, then turn the paper over. Beat the egg whites with electric beaters in a large dry bowl until soft peaks form. Gradually add all but 2 tablespoons of the sugar, beating well after each addition. Combine the cornflour and vinegar with the last of the sugar and beat for 1 minute before adding it to the bowl. Beat for 5–10 minutes, or until all the sugar has dissolved.

2 Spread the meringue mixture onto the tray inside the circle. Shape the meringue evenly, running the flat side of a palette knife along the edge and over the top.

3 Run the palette knife up the edge of the meringue mixture all the way round, making furrows. This strengthens the pavlova and stops the edge from crumbling, as well as giving it a decorative finish.

4 Bake the meringue for 40 minutes, or until pale and crisp. Reduce the heat to very slow 120°C (250°F/ Gas ½) and bake for another 15 minutes Turn off the oven and leave the pavlova inside to cool, using a wooden spoon to keep the door slightly ajar. When completely cooled, top with whipped cream and fruit. Drizzle with passionfruit pulp and serve.

NUTRITION PER SERVE (8)
Protein 6.5 g; Fat 27 g; Carbohydrate 80 g; Dietary Fibre 5 g; Cholesterol 85 mg; 2360 kJ (565 cal)

Beat the egg whites with electric beaters until soft peaks form.

Spread the meringue mixture over the circle on the baking paper.

Use a palette knife to make furrows all around the edge of the meringue mixture.

BERRY TRIFLE

Preparation time: 35 minutes +
  overnight refrigeration
Total cooking time: 5 minutes
Serves 8–10

1½ cups (2 x 225 g jars) redcurrant
  jelly
⅔ cup (170 ml) fresh orange juice
600 ml cream
250 g mascarpone
¼ cup (30 g) icing sugar
1 teaspoon vanilla essence
¼ teaspoon ground cinnamon
250 g thin sponge finger (savoiardi)
  biscuits
1½ cups (375 ml) Marsala

400 g fresh raspberries
250 g large fresh strawberries, hulled
  and quartered
400 g fresh blueberries

1 Melt the redcurrant jelly over medium heat. Remove from the heat, stir in the orange juice and set aside until the mixture reaches room temperature.

2 Place the cream, mascarpone, icing sugar, vanilla essence and cinnamon in a bowl. Using an electric mixer, whisk until soft peaks form.

3 Cut the biscuits in half and dip in the Marsala. Arrange half over the base of a 3.25 litre serving bowl.

4 Sprinkle a third of the berries over the biscuits and drizzle with half of the Marsala and a third of the redcurrant sauce. Spoon half the

cream mixture over the sauce. Repeat the layering with the remaining half of the dipped biscuits and Marsala, a third of the berries and sauce, and the remaining cream.

5 Arrange the remaining berries over the cream in a mound in the centre of the bowl. Reserve the final third of the redcurrant sauce, cover and refrigerate. Cover the trifle with plastic film and refrigerate for at least 6 hours, or preferably overnight. Before serving, pour the reserved redcurrant sauce over the berries to glaze. (Gently reheat the sauce if the consistency is too thick.)

NUTRITION PER SERVE (10)
Protein 10 g; Fat 35 g; Carbohydrate 40 g; Dietary Fibre 3.5 g; Cholesterol 144 mg; 2398 kJ (575 cal)

Whisk the cream mixture with an electric beater until soft peaks form.

Pour one third of the redcurrant sauce over the layers of berries and biscuits.

Repeat the layering process with half the Marsala-dipped biscuits.

BERRIES IN CHAMPAGNE JELLY

Preparation time: 10 minutes
  + refrigeration
Total cooking time: 5 minutes
<u>Serves 8</u>

1 litre Champagne or sparkling
  white wine
1 1/2 tablespoons gelatine
1 cup (250 g) sugar
4 strips lemon rind
4 strips orange rind
1 2/3 cups (250 g) small fresh
  strawberries, hulled
1 2/3 cups (255 g) fresh blueberries

1 Pour 2 cups (500 ml) Champagne or sparkling white wine into a bowl and let the bubbles subside.

Sprinkle the gelatine over the Champagne in an even layer. Leave until the gelatine is spongy—do not stir. Place the remaining Champagne in a large pan with the sugar, lemon and orange rind, and heat gently, stirring constantly, until all the sugar has dissolved.

2 Remove the pan from the heat, add the gelatine mixture and stir until thoroughly dissolved. Leave the jelly to cool completely, then remove the lemon and orange rind.

3 Divide the strawberries and blueberries among eight 1/2 cup (125 ml) stemmed wine glasses (or eight small glass bowls) and gently pour the jelly over them. Refrigerate until the jelly has fully set. Take the jellies out of the refrigerator at least 15 minutes before serving.

NUTRITION PER SERVE
Protein 3 g; Fat 0 g; Carbohydrate 37 g;
Dietary Fibre 1.5 g; Cholesterol 0 mg;
965 kJ (230 cal)

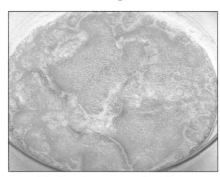

Sprinkle the gelatine over the Champagne in an even layer and leave until spongy.

Pour the jelly into the wine glasses, covering the berries.

MACERATED FRUITS WITH MASCARPONE

Preparation time: 20 minutes
Total cooking time: 10 minutes
Serves 4–6

2 oranges
1 cup raspberries
1 cup blueberries
2 tablespoons caster sugar
1/3 cup water
2 tablespoons sugar
225g marscapone, to serve

Place each orange on a board and cut a 2 cm-wide slice from each end—cut down to where pulp starts.

1 Remove rind in wide strips. Remove pith; cut the rind into thin strips.

2 Separate the orange segments then combine these with the berries, sprinkle with caster sugar and toss lightly. Cover and refrigerate.

3 Dissolve sugar in water in a small pan over low heat. Bring to the boil, reduce heat and add the orange rind. Simmer for 2 minutes until rind is tender; cool. Reserve 1 tablespoon of rind, combine syrup and remaining rind with berry mixture. Spoon into goblets and garnish with reserved rind; serve with mascarpone.

Use a small, sharp knife to cut the pith away from the rind.

Separate the orange segments by cutting between the membrane and flesh.

Once you have dissolved the sugar in water, add the orange rind to the pan.

PASHKA

Preparation time: 2½ hours plus
overnight refrigeration
Total cooking time: 15 minutes
Serves 8–10

½ cup (100 g) glacé pineapple
½ cup (100 g) glacé ginger
⅓ cup (60 g) mixed peel
¼ cup (60 g) sultanas
2 tablespoons white or dark rum
100 g butter, softened
½ cup caster sugar
2 egg yolks
½ cup (60 g) slivered almonds,
    toasted

2 teaspoons finely grated lemon rind
2 teaspoons finely grated orange rind
2 tablespoons lemon juice
750 g fresh ricotta cheese, sieved
½ cup sour cream
whole blanched almonds and glacé
    apricots, for decoration

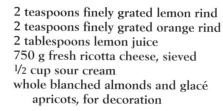

Chop the pineapple and ginger.

1 In a medium bowl, combine the
pineapple and ginger with the
mixed peel, sultanas and rum. Soak
for 2 hours. Thoroughly wet a piece
of muslin and wring out excess water.
Use to line an 8-cup capacity
pudding bowl.

2 Beat butter and sugar in medium
bowl until light and creamy. Beat
in egg yolks one at a time. Add
almonds, rinds and lemon juice; mix

well. Transfer to large bowl. Fold in
cheese, sour cream and fruit mixture.

3 Press mixture into prepared basin;
fold edges of cloth over top.
Cover top with plastic wrap, place a
saucer on top and weigh down with a
can placed on top of saucer. Place
bowl on a plate and refrigerate
overnight. Turn out of basin and peel
away muslin. Place on serving plate
with smaller end facing up. Decorate
with glacé apricots. Serve small
wedges to serve.

NOTE: Pashka is a traditional Russian
Easter dish. Storage time: This dish
will keep for up to 2 days if placed in
the refrigerator.
Hint: If muslin is unavailable, use a
new 'Chux' type cloth.

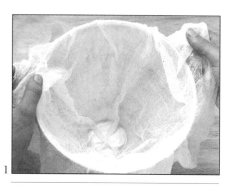

PLUM COBBLER

Preparation time: 15 minutes
Total cooking time: 45 minutes
Serves 6–8

750 g fresh blood plums
1 tablespoon water
¼ cup caster sugar

COBBLER TOPPING
1 cup self-raising flour
½ cup plain flour

¼ cup caster sugar
125 g butter, chopped
1 egg
½ cup milk
icing sugar, for dusting

Preheat your oven to a moderate
180°C (350°F/Gas 4). Lightly grease
an 8-cup capacity baking dish. Cut
the plums into quarters and then
remove their seeds.

1 Place the plums into a medium
pan, then add water and sugar.
Stir, uncovered, over a low heat for
5 minutes or until the sugar dissolves
and the fruit softens slightly. You

should then spread the plum mixture
over the bottom of the lightly greased
baking dish.

2 To create the cobbler topping, sift
the two flours into a bowl; add
the sugar and then stir. Rub in the
butter using your fingertips until the
mixture is fine and crumbly.
Combine the egg and milk, and then
whisk until smooth. Stir this into the
flour mixture.

3 Place large spoonfuls of the
mixture on top of the plums. Bake
for 30–40 minutes or until golden
and cooked through. Dust with icing
sugar before serving.

RUM BABA WITH FIGS

Preparation time: 40 minutes +
    2 hours standing
Total cooking time: 35 minutes
Makes 10
Serves 4–6

1½ cups plain flour
2 teaspoons dried yeast
¼ teaspoon salt
2 teaspoons sugar
⅓ cup lukewarm milk
80 g butter
3 eggs, lightly beaten
2 cups water
1½ cups caster sugar
⅓ cup dark rum
¾ cup apricot jam
2 tablespoons dark rum, extra
4–6 figs

Brush 10 ½-cup dariole moulds lightly with oil.

1 Place 1 tablespoon of the flour, and the yeast, salt, sugar and milk in a small bowl. Leave, covered with plastic wrap, in a warm place for about 10 minutes or until the mixture is foamy. Using your fingertips, rub butter into the remaining flour in a large mixing bowl, until the mixture is a fine crumbly texture.

2 Add the yeast mixture and the eggs to the flour mixture. Beat with a wooden spoon for 2 minutes, until smooth and glossy; scrape the mixture down the side of the bowl. Leave, covered with plastic wrap, in a warm place for 1½ hours, until risen.

3 Preheat the oven to 210°C (400°F/Gas 6). Using a wooden spoon, beat the mixture again for 2 minutes. Divide mixture evenly between the tins. Set aside, covered with plastic wrap, for another 30 minutes, until dough is well risen.

4 Bake for 20 minutes, until golden brown. Meanwhile, combine the water and sugar in a medium pan. Stir over medium heat without boiling until sugar has completely dissolved. Bring to the boil; reduce heat slightly and simmer, without stirring, for 15 minutes. Remove from heat, cool slightly and add rum.

5 Turn babas out onto a wire rack placed over a shallow oven tray. Brush warm babas liberally with warm rum syrup until they are well soaked; allow to drain. Strain excess syrup to remove any crumbs if necessary; reserve syrup.

6 Heat apricot jam in a small pan or in the microwave; strain through a fine sieve. Add extra rum, stir to combine and brush warm jam all over babas to glaze. To serve, place one or two babas on each plate, drizzle a pool of reserved syrup around them. Cut the figs in half and place on plate beside babas.

STORAGE TIME: Rum babas are best served on the day they are made.
NOTE: If you do not have dariole or baba moulds, use empty baked bean tins. The 130 g size is best.
It is important when working with a yeast dough that the temperature of the liquid used, as well as the surrounding temperature during rising, is neither too cold nor too hot. Measure ingredients accurately as they must be in the correct proportions. The yeast must not be stale. Oven temperature is also particularly important. If you have any reason to doubt the accuracy of your oven temperature readings, test with an oven thermometer so that you can make adjustments if needed.

4

5

6

ICE CREAM BOMBE

Preparation time: 20 minutes +
overnight freezing +
25 minutes refrigeration
Total cooking time: 3 minutes
Serves 8

BOMBE
1 large mango, finely
chopped
1 cup (160 g) canned pineapple
pieces
¼ cup (60 ml) Grand Marnier
1²/₃ cups (250 g) fresh strawberries,
puréed
400 g condensed milk
600 ml cream
80 g dessert nougat, chopped
(see Note)
¼ cup (35 g) roughly chopped
unsalted pistachio kernels
strawberries, extra, halved and
stems intact, to garnish

TOFFEE BARK
¹/₃ cup (90 g) caster sugar

1 Line a 2 litre ceramic pudding
bowl with plastic wrap, allowing it
to hang over the side of the bowl.
Put in the freezer until ready to
use. Drain the mango and pineapple
in a sieve.

2 Mix together the Grand Marnier,
strawberry purée and condensed
milk. Whisk the cream to soft peaks,
then add to the condensed milk
mixture and continue whisking until
thick. Fold in the drained fruits,
nougat and pistachio kernels. Pour
the mixture into the pudding bowl,
cover with plastic wrap and freeze
overnight, or until firm.

3 To serve, remove the plastic wrap
from the base and invert the
pudding onto a chilled serving plate.
Remove the pudding bowl, but leave
the plastic wrap and refrigerate for
15–25 minutes to soften.

4 To make the toffee bark, line an
oven tray with baking paper. Heat
the sugar over gentle heat in a
heavy-based pan for 4–5 minutes, or
until melted and golden. Carefully
pour onto the prepared tray. Tilt the
tray to get a thin, even layer of toffee

over the paper and cool slightly.
While still pliable, drape the paper
over a rolling pin and cool for 30–60
seconds before peeling away strips of
toffee in large irregular shapes. Cool.
To serve, remove the plastic wrap and
decorate the bombe with toffee bark
and some extra strawberries.

NUTRITION PER SERVE
Protein 8 g; Fat 40 g; Carbohydrate
56 g; Dietary Fibre 2 g; Cholesterol
120 mg; 2595 kJ (620 cal)

NOTE: Dessert nougat is a soft nougat
that is available from confectionery shops
and delicatessens.

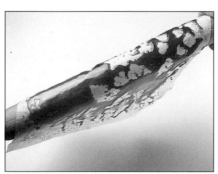

*Drape the toffee-coated baking paper over
a rolling pin and allow to set.*

*Peel the toffee bark away from the paper
in large, irregular shapes.*

PRALINE ICE CREAM WITH TOFFEE GLASS

Preparation time: 25 minutes + 6
  hours refrigeration
Total cooking time: 7 minutes
Serves 4

70 g almonds (with skins)
1/4 cup caster sugar
3/4 cup cream
250 g mascarpone
125 g melted white chocolate, cooled
2 tablespoons sugar

Line a flat baking tray with foil;
brush foil lightly with oil.

1 Combine almonds and sugar in a
small pan over low heat. Tilt pan
slightly (do not stir) and watch until
sugar melts and turns golden—this
should take about 3–5 minutes.

2 Pour mixture onto prepared tray,
leave until set and completely
cold. Break into chunks, place into a
plastic bag and crush with a rolling
pin, or process briefly in a food
processor until crumbly in texture.

3 Whip cream until stiff peaks form.
Place mascarpone and chocolate
in a mixing bowl; stir to combine.
Using a metal spoon, fold in whipped
cream and crushed praline. Transfer
to a 4-cup capacity ceramic or glass
bowl, freeze for 6 hours or overnight.
Remove from freezer 15 minutes
before serving to soften slightly. Serve
scoops of ice cream decorated with
Toffee Glass. Serve with fresh figs
and dessert wafers, if desired

4 To make Toffee Glass: Line a flat
baking tray with aluminium foil,
brush lightly with oil. Sprinkle sugar
evenly onto prepared tray. Place
under hot grill for 2 minutes until
sugar is melted and golden. Check
often towards the end of cooking
time as sugar may burn quickly.
Remove from heat, leave until set
and cold, then break into shards.

STORAGE TIME: Praline Ice Cream
may be made up to 2 days in
advance; cover tightly in the freezer.
Toffee glass is best made within
30 minutes of serving, particularly if
the weather is humid.

ICE CREAM FRUIT BOX

Preparation time: 45 minutes
Total cooking time: 1 hour and
fifteen minutes
Serves: 8–10

COCONUT CAKE
2 x 20cm (8 inch) square tins
500 g (16 oz) self-raising flour
90 g (3 oz) desiccated coconut
440 g (14 oz) caster sugar
120 g (4 oz) ground almonds
500 ml (16 fl oz) buttermilk
4 eggs
2 teaspoons vanilla essence
300 g (10 oz) butter, melted

FRUIT BOX
2 litres vanilla ice cream
160 g (5¼ oz) apricot jam
3 kiwi fruit
1 star fruit
500 g (1 lb) strawberries

GLAZE
110 g (3¾ oz) apple or fruit salad
    baby gel
3 tablespoons sugar
3 tablespoons apricot jam
1 tablespoon Cointreau or
    Grand Marnier

This is a great treat for a Christmas
party. The layer of fruit hides a layer
of cake, which in turn hides a secret
ice cream centre. You can vary the
fresh fruit, depending on your
individual preference.

1 Preheat the oven to moderate
180°C (350°F/Gas 4). Brush the
two 20 cm (8 inch) square cake tins
with melted butter or oil. Line the
bases with baking paper.

2 Mix the sifted flour, coconut,
sugar and almonds in a large bowl
and make a well in the centre.

3 Pour the combined buttermilk,
eggs, vanilla and butter into the
well and stir in with a metal spoon
until smooth.

4 Pour the mixture into the two tins
and smooth the surfaces. Bake for
1 hour, or until a skewer comes out
clean when inserted into the centre of
the cakes. Leave them in the tins for
10 minutes before turning out onto
wire racks to cool.

5 Remove the ice cream from the
freezer and leave it to soften a
little. Cut the domed tops from the
cakes, leaving a flat surface. Keep one
of the cake tops (use the other for
trifle or cake crumbs). Cut around
the inside of each cake but not all the
way through, leaving a 1.5 cm
(¼ inch) thick shell around the sides
and base. Scoop out the cake from
the centre of each.

6 Fill the hollow centres of the cakes
with the ice cream and pack down
firmly. Carefully replace one of the
cake tops. Wrap the cakes in plastic
wrap and place them in the freezer
overnight, or until the ice cream is
completely firm.

7 Warm the jam in a small pan over
a low heat. Unwrap the cakes and
brush a little jam around the edge of
the cake that doesn't have a top. Put
the other cake on top and press
down. Return to the freezer.

8 To make the fruit glaze, put all the
ingredients into a small pan and
stir them over a low heat until the
sugar has dissolved completely.
Simmer gently for 3–5 minutes, then
keep it warm.

9 Thinly slice the kiwi and star fruit
and half the strawberries (you can
peel the fruit, or leave the skin on if
you prefer). Place the cake on a board
or serving plate and brush all over
with the warm jam. Arrange the kiwi
fruit and strawberry slices in rows
over the top and sides of the cake,
pressing them gently so that they
stick to the jam. Gently brush the
glaze over the fruit. Pile the
remaining strawberries on top of the
cake and arrange some star fruit slices
on top. Serve immediately.

NOTE: You can fill the cake with ice
cream up to 3 days in advance and
keep it in the freezer. However, once
the fruit has been put on the cake it
can't be returned to the freezer and
so needs to be served immediately.

STORAGE: The cake can actually be
kept in an airtight container in the
fridge for up to a week, or stored for
3 days in an airtight container in a
cool dry place before you make the
ice cream centre. It can also be frozen
for up to 2 months.

*Use the jam to stick the strawberry and kiwi
fruit on the cake, in rows.*

*Brush a little jam around the edge of the cake
and put the other one on top.*

*Remove the centre of the cakes, leaving a shell
to be filled with ice cream.*

1

1

2

3

MINI TOFFEE PUFFS WITH LIQUEUR CREAM

Preparation time: 30 minutes
Total cooking time: 25 minutes
Serves 4–6

35 g butter
1/4 cup water
1/4 cup plain flour
1 egg, lightly beaten

LIQUEUR CREAM
1/2 cup cream
1 tablespoon Grand Marnier

TOFFEE
1 cup caster sugar
1/3 cup water

Preheat oven to 220°C (425°F/Gas 7). Line an oven tray with baking paper.

1 Combine the butter and water in a pan. Stir over low heat until the butter is melted and the mixture just boils. Remove from heat and add the flour all at once. Using a wooden spoon, beat mixture smooth. Return to heat then beat until mixture thickens and comes away from side of pan. Remove from heat, cool slightly. Transfer to a bowl. Using electric beaters, add egg gradually, beating until mixture is thick and glossy.

2 Drop teaspoonfuls of mixture about 4 cm apart on prepared tray. Bake for 10 minutes, reduce heat to 180°C and bake another 5–10 minutes, or until golden and well puffed. Pierce side of each puff to release steam. Turn off oven, return puffs to oven to dry; cool.

3 To make Liqueur Cream: Using electric beaters, beat cream until soft peaks form. Add Grand Marnier,

4

beat until just combined. Place cream in piping bag fitted with a small plain nozzle. Pipe into puffs.

4 To make Toffee: Combine sugar and water in a pan. Stir over low heat until sugar dissolves, brushing down the sides of the pan. Bring to boil, simmer until golden. Quickly spoon over puffs and allow to set.

NOTE: Make Toffee Puffs up to 6 hours in advance; store in airtight container.

CRUNCHY MERINGUES WITH COFFEE CREAM

Preparation time: 30 minutes
Total cooking time: 2 hours
Serves 8

2 egg whites
1/4 cup caster sugar
1/4 cup demerara sugar

COFFEE CREAM
1/2 cup strong black coffee
2 tablespoons caster sugar
2 teaspoons cornflour
1 tablespoon brandy
3/4 cup cream, lightly whipped

Line a flat baking tray with non-stick baking paper. Preheat oven to moderate 180°C (350°F/Gas 4).

1 Using electric beaters, beat egg whites in small, dry bowl until soft peaks form. Gradually add caster sugar, beating well until mixture is thick and glossy. Gradually beat in demerara sugar until it is evenly distributed (it will not dissolve).

2 Using a fluted nozzle, pipe 24 meringues onto prepared tray. Bake in preheated oven for 1 minute, then reduce oven temperature to 150°C (300°F/Gas 2) and bake for 1 1/2 hours or until meringues are crisp. Remove from oven, set aside for 1 minute, then lift meringues from paper and place on wire rack to cool.

3 To make Coffee Cream: Place coffee and sugar in small pan, bring to boil. In small bowl, combine cornflour and brandy to a smooth paste, add to pan, stirring until mixture thickens slightly; cool. Gradually fold in cream. To serve, arrange 3 meringues on each serving plate, with fresh fruit if desired. Dust meringues with icing sugar. Serve Coffee Cream separately.

NOTE: Make meringues a day ahead, sauce near serving time.

CHOCOLATE MOUSSE TORTE WITH RASPBERRY FILLING

Preparation time: 1 hour +
   3 hours refrigeration
Total cooking time: 50 minutes
Serves 10–12

BOTTOM LAYER
2 cups (250 g) chopped walnuts
200 g butter, chopped
3/4 cup (185 g) caster sugar
4 eggs, separated
200 g dark chocolate, melted
   and cooled
300 g fresh raspberries, or
   frozen raspberries, thawed
   and drained

TOP LAYER
2 eggs
1/4 cup (60 g) sugar
200 g white chocolate, melted
   and cooled
250 g mascarpone cheese
2 tablespoons Grand Marnier
2 tablespoons orange juice
2 teaspoons gelatine
1 cup (250 ml) cream, whipped

cocoa powder, to decorate
150 g dark chocolate melts

1 Preheat the oven to moderate 180°C (350°F/Gas 4). Spread the walnuts onto a tray and bake for about 8–10 minutes, or until fragrant and lightly toasted (make sure they don't burn). Cool, then place in a food processor and process until finely ground. Brush a round 22 cm springform tin with melted butter and line the base and side with baking paper.

2 Using electric beaters, beat the butter and sugar until light and creamy. Add the egg yolks one at a time, beating well after each addition. Add the chocolate and beat until combined. Stir the ground walnuts into the mixture.

3 Using clean beaters, beat the egg whites in a clean, dry bowl until soft peaks form. Fold a quarter of the beaten egg white into the chocolate mixture, then gently fold in the remainder. Work carefully, so there are no white streaks in the mixture, but without losing too much volume. Spoon into the prepared tin, and bake for 35–40 minutes, or until the side of the cake has risen and the top has a crust (the centre will still be soft). Leave to cool, then refrigerate for about 1 hour, or until firm. The centre of the cake will sink on cooling, which is fine.

4 Remove the cake from the tin and peel the paper from the side. Invert onto a flat serving plate and remove the paper from the base. Put the cleaned ring part of the tin back around the cake (not the base). Sprinkle the raspberries over the top of the cake, leaving a gap of about 1 cm around the edge.

5 To make the top layer, beat the eggs and sugar until thick and pale and increased in volume. On low speed, beat in the chocolate, mascarpone and Grand Marnier until combined (don't overbeat). Place the orange juice in a bowl and sprinkle on the gelatine in an even layer. Leave until the gelatine is spongy— do not stir. Bring a small pan of water to the boil, remove from the heat and place the bowl in the pan. The water should come halfway up the sides of the bowl. Stir the gelatine until clear and dissolved. Allow to cool slightly. Stir into the chocolate mixture, then gently fold in the whipped cream.

6 Spoon the mousse onto the cooled cake base, covering the raspberries and making sure it reaches right to

Fold the beaten egg white through the chocolate, making sure there are no streaks.

Sprinkle the raspberries over the top of the cake, leaving a gap around the edge.

Cover the raspberries with the white chocolate mousse mixture.

the side of the tin. Smooth the surface as much as is possible. Refrigerate for 2 hours, or until set.

7 Run a flat-bladed knife around the inside of the tin. Cut a large star shape from a piece of cardboard and use as a stencil over the cake, resting the cardboard over the tin and dusting generously with cocoa, to make a big chocolate star on the top. Carefully remove the tin.

8 Cut a piece of glossy contact or baking paper as wide as the tin is high, and long enough to fit around the cake. Melt the chocolate melts, cool slightly, and spread over the paper, right up to the edges. Wrap the paper carefully around the cake, chocolate side against the cake, before the chocolate sets. Leave for the chocolate to set. When set, gently peel away the paper. Serve.

NUTRITION PER SERVE (12)
Protein 13 g; Fat 55 g; Carbohydrate 45 g; Dietary Fibre 3 g; Cholesterol 170 mg; 717 kJ (170 cal)

Make a star on the top of the cake using cocoa and a cardboard stencil.

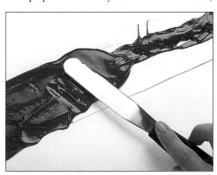

Spread the slightly cooled melted chocolate evenly over the contact.

Wrap the chocolate around the side of the cake and remove the contact when set.

YULE LOG

Preparation time: 40 minutes
Total cooking time: 15 minutes
Serves 8

½ cup (60 g) plain flour
2 tablespoons cocoa powder
3 eggs
⅓ cup (90 g) caster sugar
50 g butter, melted and cooled
1 tablespoon caster sugar, extra

FILLING
125 g white chocolate, chopped
½ cup (125 ml) cream
50 g hazelnuts, toasted and
    finely chopped

TOPPING
125 g dark chocolate, chopped
½ cup (125 ml) cream
icing sugar, to dust

1 Brush a 30 x 35 cm Swiss roll tin with oil or melted butter and line the base and sides with baking paper. Preheat the oven to moderate 180°C (350°F/Gas 4). Sift the flour and cocoa powder together twice. Using electric beaters, beat the eggs and sugar for 5 minutes, or until light and fluffy and increased in volume.

2 Sift the flour mixture over the eggs and pour the butter around the edge of the bowl. Using a large metal spoon, gently fold the mixture together to incorporate the flour and butter. Take care not to overmix and lose too much volume.

3 Spread the mixture into the prepared tin and bake for about 12 minutes, or until the sponge springs back to the light touch. Sprinkle the extra caster sugar over a clean tea towel. Turn the sponge out onto the tea towel, close to one end. Roll up the sponge and tea towel together lengthways, and leave to cool completely.

4 To make the filling, put the white chocolate in a small heatproof bowl. Bring a small pan of water to the boil, then remove from the heat. Add the cream to the chocolate and stand the bowl over the pan of water, making sure the base of the bowl does not touch the water, until the chocolate is soft. Stir until smooth. Repeat with the dark chocolate and cream for the topping. Leave the white chocolate mixture until it has cooled to room temperature and is the consistency of cream. Leave the dark chocolate mixture until it cools to a spreadable consistency.

5 Using electric beaters, beat the white chocolate mixture until soft peaks form—do not overbeat. Unroll the sponge, remove the tea towel and paper and spread with the filling, finishing 2 cm from the end. Sprinkle with the hazelnuts. Re-roll the sponge, and trim the ends. Cut one end off on the diagonal and place it alongside the log to create a branch.

6 Place the roll onto a serving plate, and spread the dark chocolate topping all over it. Run the tines of a fork along the length of the roll, to give a 'bark' effect. Just before serving, dust generously with icing sugar. Decorate with some fresh green leaves.

NUTRITION PER SERVE
Protein 8 g; Fat 35 g; Carbohydrate 45 g; Dietary Fibre 1.5 g; Cholesterol 130 mg; 2072 kJ (495 cal)

NOTE: Keep, covered in plastic wrap, in the refrigerator for 4–5 days.

Using electric beaters, beat the eggs and sugar until light and fluffy.

Pour the sponge mixture into the prepared tin and spread evenly.

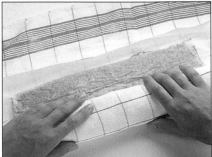

Roll the sponge up lengthways in a tea towel and leave to cool.

Melt the white chocolate and add the cream, stirring until smooth.

Unroll the sponge and spread with the filling, leaving a 2 cm border.

Use a fork to make a 'bark' effect on the log topping.

CHRISTMAS CAKE

Preparation time: 40 minutes
+ overnight soaking
Total cooking time:
3 hours 40 minutes
Serves 20

250 g sultanas
250 g raisins
300 g currants
200 g mixed peel
100 g whole red glacé cherries
100 g glacé (cooking) ginger,
    roughly chopped
150 g chopped glacé apricots
½ cup (125 ml) brandy
½ cup (125 ml) orange juice
1½ cups (185 g) walnuts
250 g butter, chopped and at
    room temperature
1 cup (230 g) firmly packed soft
    brown sugar
½ cup (160 g) orange marmalade
5 eggs
2 cups (250 g) plain flour
1 teaspoon bicarbonate of soda
1 teaspoon ground cinnamon
1 teaspoon ground nutmeg

1 Combine all the fruit in a large bowl, working with your fingers to separate any lumps. Add the brandy and orange juice, and stir well. Cover with plastic wrap and leave overnight (or for at least 4 hours) for the fruit to absorb most of the liquid, stirring occasionally.

2 Preheat the oven to warm 160°C (315°F/Gas 2–3). Brush a 23 cm round or square cake tin with oil or melted butter. Cut 2 strips of baking paper, long enough to fit around the sides of the tin in one piece and tall enough to come 5 cm above the top edge. Fold down a cuff about 2 cm deep along the length of each strip. Make diagonal cuts up to the fold line on each strip, approximately 1 cm apart. Fit the strips around the inside of the tin, pressing the cuts so they fit flat around the bottom edge of the tin. Cut 2 pieces of paper to fit the base of the tin and place in the base of the tin.

3 Put the walnuts on a baking tray and place into the preheated oven for about 8–10 minutes (watch to make sure they don't burn), or until fragrant and lightly toasted. Cool and roughly chop.

4 Using electric beaters, beat the butter, sugar and marmalade in a large bowl until light and creamy. Scrape down the sides of the bowl with a rubber spatula. Add the eggs one at a time, beating well after each addition. The mixture will appear curdled but don't worry.

5 Add the butter mixture and the walnuts to the soaked fruit. Sift the flour, bicarbonate of soda and spices on top, then mix together gently but thoroughly. Make sure there are no pockets of flour in the mixture, but do not beat too vigorously.

6 Spoon the mixture into the prepared tin, then wrap the outside of the tin with a double thickness of newspaper, and secure with string. Bake for 3–3½ hours, or until a skewer inserted into the centre of the cake comes out clean and the cake has shrunk slightly from the edge of the tin. Cool in the tin before turning it out.

NUTRITION PER SERVE
Protein 6 g; Fat 18 g; Carbohydrate 65 g; Dietary Fibre 3.5 g; Cholesterol 75 mg; 1910 kJ (457 cal)

Add the brandy and orange juice to the fruit mixture and stir well.

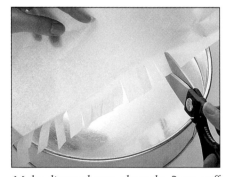

Make diagonal cuts along the 2 cm cuff folded in the baking paper strips.

Fit the baking paper strips inside the tin so that they fit around the bottom.

The mixture appears curdled after the eggs are added but don't worry.

Wrap a double thickness of newspaper around the tin and tie securely with string.

The cake is cooked when a metal skewer inserted into the centre comes out clean.

ICING YOUR CAKE

A beautifully decorated Christmas cake doesn't have to be beyond you. Decorating your cake will be a lot easier if you follow these instructions, and the best part is you can do it up to a month before Christmas.

ONCE YOU have cooked your Christmas cake, it is time to decorate it. Firstly you must cover the cake with marzipan. Then you have a choice between ready-made soft icing or, if you want to be a little more adventurous, royal icing. You can also add handmade decorations such as Christmas trees, presents, holly leaves or Christmas messages. The icing amounts given here will cover a 23 cm cake, such as the Christmas cake on page 98.

MARZIPAN ICING

To make marzipan icing, you will need 2 tablespoons apricot jam and 800 g marzipan or almond icing.

1 Trim the dome from the cake to give it a flat surface and turn it upside-down on a board which is

Fill any holes in the surface of the cake with rolled-up balls of marzipan.

Brush the melted jam all over the surface of the cake with a pastry brush.

Drape the marzipan over a rolling pin and move it carefully onto the cake.

Use a sharp knife to trim the marzipan around the base of the cake.

4 cm larger than the cake. Fill any holes in the surface of the cake with small pieces of marzipan. Heat the jam in a small pan with 1 teaspoon water, then push it through a fine sieve and brush it all over the cake with a pastry brush.

2 Briefly knead the marzipan on a clean work surface dusted lightly with icing sugar until it is smooth. Roll it out to a circle large enough to just cover the base and side of the cake—don't roll it out too big or you may get folds in it.

3 Drape the marzipan over a rolling pin lightly dusted with icing sugar, then carefully lift it over the cake and unroll it onto the cake, smoothing it over the base and side and pressing out any folds and wrinkles with icing sugar-dusted hands. Carefully pierce

any air bubbles with a pin. Trim the marzipan around the base of the cake with a sharp knife and leave the cake in a cool, dry place overnight.

SOFT ICING

To make soft icing, you will need 1 egg white and 1 kg ready-made soft icing.

1 Lightly beat the egg white in a clean, dry bowl and then brush it all over the surface of the marzipan in a thin layer. (This will help the icing stick to the marzipan.)

2 Briefly knead the icing on a clean work surface, lightly dusted with icing sugar, until it is smooth and pliable. Roll it out just large enough to cover the cake, dusting your rolling pin and bench with more icing sugar if needed.

3 Roll the icing over the rolling pin and drape it carefully over the cake, gently pressing the icing over the cake. Dust your hands with icing sugar and smooth out any wrinkles and folds. You can also use a 'smoother' available from cake decorating shops. Or, make your own smoother with a smooth-edged piece of laminex and a wooden block glued to the back as a handle. Trim the icing around the base of the cake with a sharp knife and leave the cake in a cool, dry place overnight.

Press the soft icing over the cake and smooth out any wrinkles or folds.

ROYAL ICING

To make royal icing, you will need 500 g pure icing sugar and 3 lightly beaten egg whites.

1 Sift the icing sugar into a large bowl and make a well in the centre, add the egg whites and gradually incorporate them into the icing sugar, stirring from the centre outwards until everything is completely mixed in. The mixture will be fairly stiff. Beat it with an electric hand mixer until it is fluffy—the mixture should be spreadable but not runny.

2 Icing your cake is much easier if you have a turntable. If not, place your cake on an upturned cake tin to give you a little bit more height and

Spoon a third of the royal icing onto the cake and smooth out with a palette knife.

Pull the palette knife over the surface of the cake to smooth the icing out.

Use the palette knife to create a snow scene on the surface of the cake.

make turning the cake easier. Spoon about a third of the icing onto the surface of the marzipan-covered cake and spread it out to the edge of the cake with a palette knife. If you have one, use a steel ruler to smooth the surface; if not use the palette knife. Hold each end of the palette knife and pull it towards you over the icing (you may need to do this a few times, adding more icing as necessary). Ice the side of the cake and when you have a surface that is as smooth as possible, leave the cake to dry. (If you want to create a snow scene, press down with a palette knife and lift at intervals all over the icing to make peaks, and then leave to dry.)

ICING DECORATIONS

To make your icing decorations you will need ready-made soft icing, icing sugar, assorted food colourings and thin ribbons, if desired.

Christmas trees: Colour various sized pieces of icing green and roll them into cone shapes. Use a pair of scissors to make snips into the side of the cone all over. Leave to dry. Cut small stars out of yellow tinted icing and leave to dry. Stick the stars to the top of the tree with some royal icing. Dust with sifted icing sugar.

Presents: Make little shapes of icing in varying sizes and leave them to dry. Paint each one in a different colour and leave to dry. Then paint bows and ribbons, stripes and spots on the presents in different colours. Arrange a selection of decorations on your cake, attaching them with a little royal icing. You can also tie a ribbon or frill around the cake and, if you wish, write a Christmas greeting.

Runout letters: Trace a Christmas greeting from a lettering book or Christmas card onto a piece of paper in simple, easy-to-read letters. Place the paper on a board and cover with a piece of baking paper. Make up some icing using an egg white and enough pure icing sugar to make a smooth icing which will hold its shape. Tint with colour and spoon it into a paper piping bag. Pipe around the outline of the letters and then fill in the centre. If the icing is too stiff and doesn't sit flat, brush it with a paint brush dipped in egg white. Leave to dry overnight and then very carefully peel the letters off the

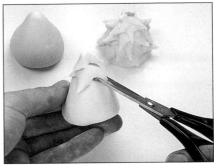

Make Christmas tree decorations out of green coloured icing.

Paint small pieces of icing different colours to make presents.

Write your greeting on baking paper and attach to the cake when dry.

paper and stick them to the cake with a little royal icing.

Leaves: Use a holly-shaped cutter to cut leaves out of the icing. Shape the leaves and leave to dry. When dry, paint the leaves green. Roll small amounts of icing into balls to represent holly berries. Paint the balls red and leave to dry. Holly leaves can also be used alone as a border around the edge of the cake to represent a wreath.

NOTE: Never use real holly berries to decorate your cake—they are toxic!

STORAGE: Keep your iced and decorated Christmas cake in an airtight container in a cool, dry place for 4–5 months. Do not refrigerate or the icing will go sticky.

BOILED FRUIT CAKE

Preparation time: 20 minutes
Total cooking time:
  2 hours 10 minutes
Serves 16–18

2 cups (250 g) raisins
2 cups (250 g) sultanas
1 cup (150 g) currants
²/₃ cup (100 g) blanched
  almonds, chopped
100 g red glacé cherries
1 cup (230 g) firmly packed
  soft brown sugar
125 g butter, chopped
¼ cup (80 ml) brandy
2 eggs, lightly beaten
³/₄ cup (90 g) plain flour
³/₄ cup (90 g) self-raising
  flour
1 tablespoon mixed spice

1 Combine all the dried fruits, almonds, glacé cherries, sugar, butter, brandy and 1 cup (250 ml) water in a large pan. Bring to the boil (stir occasionally to ensure the sugar dissolves and butter melts evenly through the mixture), then remove from the heat and cool.

2 Preheat the oven to warm 160°C (315°F/Gas 2–3). Brush the base and side of a 20 cm round tin with oil or melted butter. Cut 2 strips of baking paper long enough to fit around the outside of the tin and tall enough to come 5 cm above the top edge. Fold down a cuff about 2 cm deep along the length of each strip. Make diagonal cuts up to the fold line on each strip approximately 1 cm apart. Fit the strips around the inside of the tin, pressing the cuts so they sit flat around the bottom edge of the tin. Cut 2 circles of baking paper, using the tin as your guide. Place the two circles of baking paper into the base of the tin.

3 Add the eggs to the mixture, then sift in the flours and mixed spice. Mix together thoroughly, working quickly and lightly—don't beat vigorously. Pour the mixture into the prepared tin, smooth the top of the cake with wetted hands and bake for 1 ½–2 hours, or until a skewer inserted into the centre of the cake comes out clean. Cool completely in the tin, then turn out.

NUTRITION PER SERVE (18)
Protein 4 g; Fat 9.5 g; Carbohydrate 45 g; Dietary Fibre 2.5 g; Cholesterol 40 mg; 1186 kJ (285 cal)

Stir to ensure the sugar dissolves and butter melts evenly through the mixture.

Add the eggs, flours and mixed spice and mix thoroughly.

Smooth over the top of the cake with wetted hands before baking.

LIGHT FRUIT CAKE

Preparation time: 20 minutes
Total cooking time:
    1 hour 40 minutes
Serves 16–18

**250 g butter, chopped and
    at room temperature**
1 cup (250 g) caster sugar
4 eggs
1 teaspoon vanilla essence
**2 cups (250 g) self-raising
    flour**
1/2 cup (60 g) plain flour
1 teaspoon mixed spice
500 g mixed dried fruit
1/2 cup (125 ml) milk

1 Preheat the oven to moderate 180°C (350°F/Gas 4). Brush a 20 cm round tin with oil or melted butter. Cut 2 strips of baking paper long enough to fit around the outside of the tin and tall enough to come 5 cm above the top edge. Fold down a cuff about 2 cm deep along the length of each strip. Make diagonal cuts up to the fold line on each strip approximately 1 cm apart. Fit the strips around the inside of the tin, pressing the cuts so they sit flat around the bottom edge of the tin. Cut two circles of baking paper, using the tin as a guide, and place the circles in the base of the tin.

2 Using electric beaters, beat the butter and sugar together until light and creamy. Add the eggs one at a time, beating well after each addition. Add the vanilla essence and beat the mixture until combined. The mixture will appear curdled at this stage but this is fine.

3 Sift the flours and mixed spice together in a bowl, add the dried fruit and toss to coat with the flour, separating any clumps of fruit with your fingers. Add to the butter mixture, with the milk, and mix gently until combined. Transfer to the prepared tin. Tap the base gently to release any air bubbles.

4 Bake for 1 hour 40 minutes, or until a skewer inserted into the centre of the cake comes out clean and the cake has shrunk slightly from the edge of the tin. Leave in the tin for 15 minutes, then turn out onto a wire rack to cool.

NUTRITION PER SERVE (18)
Protein 4.5 g; Fat 13 g; Carbohydrate 47 g; Dietary Fibre 2.5 g; Cholesterol 75 mg; 1335 kJ (320 cal)

Using electric beaters, beat the butter and sugar together until light and creamy.

Coat the fruit in the flour and spice, separating any clumps with your fingers.

CHRISTMAS FROSTED FRUITS

Preparation time: 1 hour + overnight soaking of fruit and drying time
Total cooking time: To make 18 x 25 cm oval cake, bake for 3½ hours.
Serves: 10–12

one 18 x 25 cm (7 x 10 inch) oval
    fruit cake

FRUIT CAKE
500 g (1 lb) sultanas
375 g (12 oz) raisins, chopped
250 g (8 oz) currants
250 g (8 oz) glacé cherries, quartered
250 ml (8 fl oz) brandy or rum, plus
    1 tablespoon to glaze
250 g (8 oz) butter
230 g (7½ oz) soft dark brown sugar
2 tablespoons apricot jam
2 tablespoons treacle or syrup
1 tablespoon grated lemon or orange
    rind
4 eggs
350 g (11 oz) plain flour
1 teaspoon each of ginger, mixed
    spice and cinnamon

FROSTED FRUITS
selection of seasonal fruits such as
    white and dark cherries, red or
    white currants, blackcurrants,
    apricots or tiny plums or pears
1 egg white
caster sugar

ICING
1 egg white
1–3 teaspoons lemon juice
125 g (4 oz) pure icing sugar, sifted

1 Put the fruit in a bowl with the brandy and soak overnight.

2 Preheat the oven to slow 150°C (300°F/Gas 2). Brush a deep 18 x 25 cm (7 x 10 inch) oval cake tin with melted butter or oil. Cut 2 strips of baking paper long enough to fit around the outside of the tin and wide enough to come 5 cm (2 inches) above the top of tin. Fold down a cuff about 2 cm (1 inch) deep along the length of each strip. Make diagonal cuts up to the fold line approximately 1 cm (½ inch) apart. Fit the strips around the inside of the tin, pressing the cuts so that they sit flat around the bottom edge of the tin. Cut 2 circles of baking paper, using the tin as a guide, and use to line the base. Wrap a folded piece of newspaper around the outside of the tin and tie securely with string.

3 Beat the butter and sugar to just combine. Beat in the jam, treacle and rind. Add the eggs one at a time, beating after each addition.

4 Stir the fruit and the combined sifted flour and spices alternately into the mixture.

5 Spoon into the tin and smooth the surface. Tap the tin on the bench to remove any air bubbles. Dip your hand in water and level the surface. Sit the cake tin on several layers of newspaper in the oven and bake for 3½ hours, or until a skewer comes out clean when inserted into the centre. Brush with the extra tablespoon of brandy. Cover the top of the cake with paper and wrap in a tea towel. Cool completely in the tin.

6 To make the frosted fruits: Wash the fruit and make sure it is completely dry before starting (if possible, wash beforehand and leave for several hours). Line a tray with a paper towel. Place the egg white in a shallow bowl and whisk until just foamy. Put some caster sugar on a large plate. Work with one piece of fruit at a time, except for the berries (which can be sugared in small bunches). Brush the egg white lightly over the fruit, making sure the entire piece of fruit is covered with it, but not too heavily.

7 Sprinkle the sugar over the fruit and shake off any excess, then leave on the tray to dry. The drying time will depend on the humidity. Always frost more fruit than you need, so you have a good selection to choose from when arranging.

8 To make the icing, whisk the egg white until just foamy. Beat in 1 teaspoon of the lemon juice. Add the icing sugar gradually, beating well after each addition. The icing should be thick and white—add a little more lemon juice if necessary, but don't make it too runny.

9 Place the cake on a serving plate or stand. Working quickly, pouring the icing over the top. Using a palette knife, carefully smooth the icing to the edge of the cake, allowing it to run slowly down the side. Leave the cake for 10 minutes to let the icing set a little. Arrange the frosted fruits on top of the cake.

NOTE: The fruits can be frosted several hours in advance.

Paint the fruit with a little egg white, then sprinkle with the caster sugar.

To make the icing, whisk the egg white, then add lemon juice and icing sugar.

Smooth the icing over the cake, allowing it to run slowly down the side.

CANDIED CITRUS CAKE

Preparation time: 45 minutes
Total cooking time: 1½ hours
Serves: 6–8

BUTTER CAKE
one x 2 litre (5 pint) charlotte tin

280 g (9 oz) butter
225 g (7 oz) caster sugar
1½ teaspoons vanilla essence
4 eggs
225 g (7 oz) self-raising flour
150 g (5 oz) plain flour
185 ml (6 fl oz) milk

CANDIED RIND
2 oranges
2 tangelos
2 lemons
2 limes
310 g (10 oz) caster sugar

LEMON ICING
125 g (4 oz) icing sugar
20 g (³/4 oz) butter, melted
1–2 tablespoons lemon juice

The tanginess of candied citrus rind appeals to many cake lovers who might find chocolate decorations and whipped cream a little overpowering. We used butter cake for this recipe, but you could also use coconut cake if you prefer.

1 Preheat the oven to moderate 180°C (350°F/Gas 4). Brush a 2 litre (5 pint) charlotte tin with melted butter or oil and then line the base with baking paper.

2 Beat the butter and sugar with electric beaters until the mixture becomes light and creamy. Then beat in the vanilla essence. Add the eggs one at a time, again beating well after each addition.

3 Using a large metal spoon, fold in the combined sifted flours alternately with the milk, until smooth. Spoon the mixture into the tin and smooth the surface. Bake for 1¼ hours, or until a skewer comes out clean when inserted into the centre of the cake.

4 Leave the cake in the tin for at least 5 minutes before turning out onto a wire rack to cool completely.

5 To make the candied rind: Use a vegetable peeler to peel the rind from the fruit. Then use a sharp knife to remove any pith (the bitter white layer of flesh just inside the rind). Cut the rind into long thin strips.

6 Put the sugar in a pan with 125 ml (4 fl oz) water and stir over a low heat until completely dissolved. Bring to the boil, reduce the heat slightly, then add the rind in batches. Simmer each batch for 3–5 minutes, or until the rind is bright and transparent. Remove the rind with tongs and drain on a wire rack until cold.

7 To make the icing: Put the icing sugar and butter in a small bowl. Mix in the lemon juice gradually, until the icing is pourable but not runny.

8 Use a serrated knife to cut the dome from the top of the cake to level the surface out. Turn the cake upside down on a wire rack and smooth the icing over the top of the cake, allowing it to run down the side but do not let it completely cover the side. Leave the icing to set. Transfer the cake to a serving plate or stand and then pile the candied rind on top of the cake.

NOTE: Butter cake can be kept in an airtight container in the fridge for up to a week, or for 3–4 days in an airtight container in a cool dry place. It can be frozen for up to 2 months. The candied rind can be stored for up to 3 days in an airtight container. Place the rind in a single layer between sheets of baking paper. Refrigerate in hot weather.

Cut away the pith from the rind or it will leave a bitter taste.

Simmer the rind in the syrup until it is bright and transparent.

Turn the cake upside down on a wire rack and smooth the icing over the top.

GLACE FRUIT AND NUT LOAF

Preparation time: 30 minutes
Total cooking time:
    1 hour 45 minutes
Serves 12

50 g butter, softened
¼ cup (55 g) firmly packed
    soft brown sugar
2 tablespoons breakfast marmalade
2 eggs
1 cup (125 g) plain flour
1 teaspoon baking powder
1 teaspoon ground nutmeg
1¼ cups (225 g) pitted dates
1½ cups (185 g) raisins
1 cup (155 g) brazil nuts
⅔ cup (140 g) red, yellow and green
    glacé cherries
½ cup (110 g) chopped glacé
    pear or pineapple
½ cup (120 g) chopped glacé
    apricots
½ cup (120 g) chopped glacé
    peaches
⅓ cup (120 g) chopped glacé figs
1 cup (100 g) walnut halves
⅔ cup (100 g) blanched almonds

TOPPING
2 teaspoons gelatine
2 tablespoons breakfast marmalade
150 g glacé pineapple or pear rings
100 g red, yellow and green
    glacé cherries
¼ cup (40 g) blanched almonds,
    toasted

1 Grease a 20.5 x 8 x 7 cm bar tin and line the base and sides with baking paper. Preheat the oven to slow 150°C (300°F/Gas 2).

2 Place the butter, sugar and marmalade in a bowl and mix together until pale and creamy. Add the eggs and beat until combined.

3 Sift the flour, baking powder and nutmeg into a large bowl. Add the fruit and nuts and mix together until each piece is coated in the flour mixture. Add to the egg mixture and combine well.

4 Put the mixture in the prepared tin, pushing well into each corner. Bake for 1½–1¾ hours, or until a skewer inserted into the centre comes out clean. Cool in the tin for 10 minutes before turning out. Remove the baking paper and transfer to a wire rack to cool.

5 For the topping, sprinkle the gelatine over the marmalade and 2 tablespoons water in a small bowl. Bring a pan of water to the boil, then remove from the heat. Stand the bowl in the pan and stir until the gelatine has dissolved. Brush the top of the cake with some of the gelatine mixture, and arrange the pineapple, cherries and almonds over the top. Brush or drizzle with more gelatine mixture and allow to set.

NUTRITION PER SERVE
Protein 9 g; Fat 25 g; Carbohydrate 87 g; Dietary Fibre 6 g; Cholesterol 40 mg; 2496 kJ (596 cal)

Coat the fruit and nuts in the flour mixture before adding to the egg mixture.

Drizzle extra gelatine over the glacé fruit and nut topping and allow to set.

STOLLEN

Preparation time: 30 minutes +
1 hour 45 minutes proving
Total cooking time: 40 minutes
Serves 6–8

1/3 cup (80 ml) lukewarm water
1/3 cup (80 ml) lukewarm milk
2 teaspoons sugar
7 g sachet dried yeast
120 g butter, softened
1/3 cup (90 g) caster sugar
1 egg
2 teaspoons vanilla essence
1/2 teaspoon ground cinnamon
3 cups (375 g) plain flour
1/2 cup (60 g) raisins
1/2 cup (75 g) currants
1/2 cup (95 g) mixed peel
1/2 cup (60 g) slivered almonds
30 g butter, melted
icing sugar, to dust

1 Combine the water, milk, sugar and yeast in a small bowl. Stand in a warm place for 10 minutes, or until the mixture is foamy. Meanwhile, beat the butter and sugar with electric beaters until light and creamy, then beat in the egg and vanilla essence.

2 Add the foamy yeast mixture, cinnamon and almost all the flour and mix to a soft dough, adding more flour if necessary. Turn out onto a lightly floured surface and knead for 10 minutes, or until the dough is smooth and elastic. Place in a lightly oiled bowl, cover with plastic wrap and leave for 1 hour 45 minutes in a warm place, or until doubled in volume. Preheat the oven to moderate 180°C (350°F/Gas 4). Brush an oven tray lightly with oil or melted butter.

3 When the dough has risen, tip it out of the bowl onto a floured work surface and punch it to expel the air and then press it out to a thickness of about 1.5 cm. Sprinkle the fruit and nuts over the dough, then gather up and knead for a few minutes to mix the fruit and nuts evenly through the dough.

4 Shape the dough into an oval about 18 cm wide and 30 cm long. Fold in half lengthways, and press down to flatten slightly, with the fold slightly off centre on top of the loaf. Place on the prepared tray, and bake for 40 minutes, or until golden brown. As soon as it comes out of the oven, brush the loaf with the melted butter, allowing each brushing to be absorbed until you have used all the butter up. Cool on a wire rack. Dust with icing sugar before cutting to serve.

NUTRITION PER SERVE (8)
Protein 9.5 g; Fat 20 g; Carbohydrate 57 g; Dietary Fibre 4.5 g; Cholesterol 72 mg; 1905 kJ (455 cal)

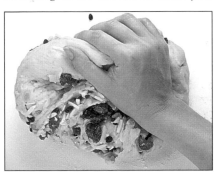

Sprinkle the fruit and nuts over the dough and knead to mix through evenly.

Fold the dough in half lengthways, with the fold on top, and flatten slightly.

FRUIT PASTES

Fruit pastes are a perfectly delicious method for preserving an overabundance of fruit. They may take a while to cook, but fruit pastes keep for up to a year because of their high concentration of sugar. They are delicious with coffee, as part of a cheese board or with cold meats.

Quince paste

Line a 28 x 18 cm (11 x 7 inch) tin with baking paper. Peel and core 2 kg (4 lb) quinces, reserving the cores. Cut into chunks and place in a pan. Chop the cores, put on a muslin square, tie with string and add to the pan with 2 cups (500 ml/16 fl oz) water and 2 tablespoons lemon juice. Cook, covered, over low heat for 30–40 minutes, or until soft and tender. Cool slightly, then squeeze any juices from the bag and discard. Purée the fruit in a blender or food processor until smooth, then press through a sieve. Weigh the purée and return it to the pan. Gradually add an equivalent measure of sugar (1 kg/2 lb fruit purée = 1 kg/2 lb sugar). Stir over low heat, without boiling, until all the sugar has dissolved. Cook, stirring with a wooden spoon to prevent sticking and burning, for 45–60 minutes, or until the mixture leaves the side of the pan and it is difficult to push the wooden spoon through. (If the mixture starts to stick to the bottom, transfer to a heatproof bowl, clean the pan and return to the pan to continue cooking.)

To package and store the pastes: Spread into the prepared tin and smooth with a palette knife. Cut into small squares, diamonds or triangles with a hot knife. Place a blanched or slivered almond in the centre of each or roll in caster sugar to coat. Wrap in foil and store in an airtight container in a cool, dry place. Disposable foil tins are ideal. Spread the hot fruit mixture into them and press a piece of greaseproof paper onto the mixture before wrapping.

NOTE: As the mixture thickens, it will start to splatter so make sure you use a deep-sided pan and wrap your hand in a tea towel.

Apricot paste

Line a 28 x 18 cm (11 x 7 inch) tin with baking paper. Select 2 kg (4 lb) apricots (some need to be a little green to help gel the paste). Remove the stalks, stones and any blemishes. Cut the greenish apricots into quarters and the remainder in half. Place in a pan with 1 cup (250 ml/8 fl oz) water and 2 tablespoons lemon juice. Bring to the boil, then reduce the heat and simmer, covered, for 15–20 minutes, or until the fruit is soft and tender. Cool. Purée the fruit until smooth, then press through a sieve. Weigh the purée and return it to the pan. Add an equivalent measure of sugar gradually. Stir over low heat, without boiling, until the sugar dissolves. Cook, stirring with a wooden spoon to prevent sticking and burning, for 45–60 minutes, or until the mixture leaves the side of the pan and it is difficult to push the wooden spoon through. (If the mixture sticks to the bottom, clean the pan then continue.)

Plum paste

Line a 28 x 18 cm (11 x 7 inch) tin with baking paper. Select 1.5 kg (3 lb) plums (some need to be a little green to help gel the paste). Remove the stalks, stones and any blemishes, then cut into quarters. Place in a pan with 1 cup (250 ml/8 fl oz) water and 2 tablespoons lemon juice. Bring to the boil, reduce the heat and simmer, covered, for 20–30 minutes, or until the fruit is soft

and tender. Cool. Purée the fruit, then press through a sieve. Weigh the purée and return it to the pan. Gradually add an equivalent measure of sugar. Stir constantly over low heat, without boiling, until the sugar dissolves. Cook, stirring with a wooden spoon to prevent sticking and burning, for 45–60 minutes, or until the mixture leaves the side of the pan and is difficult to push the wooden spoon through. (If the mixture sticks to the bottom, transfer it and clean the pan.)

Peach paste

Line a 28 x 18 cm (11 x 7 inch) tin with baking paper. Remove the stalks, blemishes and stones from 2 kg (4 lb) peaches (some need to be a little green to help gel the paste). Cut each peach into 8 pieces and place in a large pan with 1 cup (250 ml/8 fl oz) water and 3 tablespoons lemon juice. Bring to the boil, reduce the heat and simmer, covered, for 20–30 minutes, or until the fruit is soft and tender. Cool. Purée the fruit, then press through a sieve. Weigh the purée and return it to the pan. Gradually add an equivalent measure of sugar. Stir constantly over low heat, without boiling, until all the sugar has dissolved. Cook, stirring with a wooden spoon to prevent sticking and burning, for 45–60 minutes, or until the mixture leaves the side of the pan and it is difficult to push the wooden spoon through. (If the mixture sticks to the bottom, transfer it and clean the pan.)

Clockwise from top left: Quince paste; peach paste; apricot paste; plum paste.

LIQUEURS AND AFTER-DINNER COFFEES

Cumquat liqueur
Wash and dry 500 g cumquats, then pierce each with a fine skewer. Place cumquats in a large jar, layering with 2 cups of caster sugar. Pour in 1 litre of brandy, gin or vodka; seal and leave in a cool, dark place for at least a month, turning jar regularly. To serve, place one cumquat in each glass and pour liqueur over it. Makes 1 litre of liqueur.

Spicy coffee
Make a pot of strong black coffee (enough to make 4 cups) and add 1 teaspoon of cinnamon. Pour coffee into cups and add some Kahlua to taste. Top coffee with whipped cream and decorate with shreds of orange rind. Serves 4.

Clockwise from below: Coffee liqueur; Whisky cream; Spicy coffee; Cumquat liqueur; Vienna coffee; Irish coffee

Irish coffee

Make a pot of strong black coffee and pour into tall—preferably glass—mugs. Add sugar and Irish whiskey to taste, then pour thick cream slowly over the back of a spoon onto the coffee to create a 5 mm-thick layer. Serve immediately. Substitute dark rum for the whiskey to make Jamaican coffee.

Coffee liqueur

In a large jug, whisk together 1 cup sugar, 3 tablespoons instant coffee powder, 1 cup each of rum and boiling water, and 3 teaspoons of vanilla essence. Pour into a sterilised bottle, seal and store in a cool, dark place for two weeks to allow flavours to develop. Makes about 2½ cups.

Whisky cream

Combine 1 cup cream, 1½ cups evaporated milk, ½ cup condensed milk and 2 tablespoons drinking chocolate in large jug. Slowly stir in 1 cup Scotch whisky; transfer to a sterilised bottle. Store in the refrigerator for up to two weeks. Return to room temperature to serve. Makes 1 litre.

Vienna coffee

Make cups of milky coffee, stir in some grated milk chocolate. Top with a generous dollop of whipped cream and sprinkle with extra grated chocolate. Serve immediately.

PARTIES

EVERYONE LOVES a party—and Christmas is definitely party time. Office parties, family reunions, drinks with old friends, any excuse to spread a little festive spirit! Planning your Christmas celebration doesn't have to be a drama-ridden nightmare. A little organisation, and a delicious selection of finger food, fresh seafood and warm or chilled cocktails will have everyone revelling in festive cheer. You never know, you may even get to relax and enjoy yourself too!

NIBBLES

There's nothing fussy about these tasty snacks—leave them on side tables with some napkins and your guests will need no invitation to help themselves.

Seasoned popcorn
Ready in about 15 minutes.

¼ cup (60 ml) oil
⅔ cup (150 g) popping corn
40 g butter
⅔ cup (125 g) finely chopped Kalamata olives
1 fresh bird's eye chilli, finely chopped
1 clove garlic, crushed
1 tablespoon chopped fresh parsley
1 tablespoon chopped fresh oregano
1 teaspoon grated lemon rind

Heat the oil in a large saucepan, add the popping corn and cover. Cook over medium heat, shaking occasionally, until the popping stops. Transfer to a large bowl and discard any unpopped corn. Melt the butter in a large frying pan and add the remaining ingredients. Mix, then toss through the popcorn. Serve warm. Makes a large bowl.

Honey-roasted peanuts
Ready in about 30 minutes.

350 g raw shelled peanuts
½ cup (175 g) honey
1½ teaspoons Chinese five-spice powder

Preheat the oven to slow 150°C (300°F/Gas 2). Combine all the ingredients in a small saucepan and warm over low heat. Spread the nuts onto a large baking tray lined with baking paper and bake for 15–20 minutes, or until golden brown. Cool before serving. Makes 2½ cups.

NOTE: You can store the honey-roasted peanuts in an airtight container for up to 1 week.

Vegetable chips
Ready in under 30 minutes.

500 g orange sweet potato
500 g beetroot
500 g parsnip
oil, for deep-frying

Preheat the oven to moderate 180°C (350°F/Gas 4). Run a vegetable peeler along the length of the sweet potato and beetroot to make thin ribbons. Cut the parsnip into thin slices. Fill a deep heavy-based saucepan one third full of oil and heat to 190°C (375°F), or until a cube of bread dropped into the oil browns in 10 seconds. Cook the vegetables in batches for about 30 seconds, or until golden and crisp, turning with tongs, if necessary. Drain on crumpled paper towels and season with salt. Keep warm on a baking tray in the oven and cook the remaining chips. Makes a large bowl.

Parmesan wafers
Ready in about 30 minutes.

1¼ cups (125 g) good-quality
    grated Parmesan
1 tablespoon flour
2 tablespoons fresh thyme

Preheat the oven to hot 220°C (425°F/ Gas 7). Line two baking trays with baking paper and, using a 7 cm cutter as a guide, draw circles on the paper. Turn the paper upside down on the trays. Toss the cheese and flour together in a bowl, then sprinkle 2 teaspoons of the mixture over 3–4 circles on the paper, spreading the mixture to the edge of each round. Scatter a few thyme leaves over each round.
Bake in batches for about 3 minutes, or until melted but not firm. Using an egg-flip, turn the rounds over and cook for a minute more, or until they are firm and light golden. Remove each round from the tray and drape over a rolling pin or bottle until cool. Repeat with the rest of the ingredients. Makes 30.

Curried nuts
Ready in about 30 minutes.

500 g mixed nuts (almonds, brazil
    nuts, pecans, macadamias,
    cashew nuts)
1 egg white
2 tablespoons curry powder
1 teaspoon ground cumin

Preheat the oven to slow 150°C (300°F/Gas 2). Spread the nuts in a single layer on a baking tray and roast for 10 minutes. Whisk the egg white until frothy, then add the nuts, curry powder, cumin and 1 teaspoon salt. Toss together and return to the oven for a further 10–15 minutes, then allow to cool. Makes 4½ cups.

Marinated olives
Prepare a day ahead.

150 g Kalamata olives
150 g good-quality green olives
¾ cup (185 ml) extra virgin olive oil
2 sprigs fresh rosemary
2 sprigs fresh thyme
2 small fresh red chillies, seeded
1 large piece lemon peel
½ teaspoon fennel seeds
2 fresh thyme sprigs, extra

Place the olives, oil, rosemary, thyme, chilli, lemon peel and fennel in a large saucepan and warm over low heat. Transfer to a bowl and marinate overnight at room temperature. Remove the olives from the oil with a slotted spoon and discard the herbs, reserving the oil. Add the extra thyme to the bowl with the olives before serving. Makes 2 cups.

NOTES: Serve the oil with bread.

BLUE CHEESE AND PORT PATE

Preparation time: 10 minutes +
    refrigeration
Total cooking time: nil
Serves 8

350 g cream cheese,
    at room temperature
60 g unsalted butter,
    softened
1/3 cup (80 ml) port
300 g blue cheese,
    at room temperature,
    mashed
1 tablespoon snipped
    fresh chives
45 g walnut halves

1 Using electric beaters, beat the cream cheese and butter until smooth, then stir in the port. Add the blue cheese and chives and stir until just combined. Season to taste.

2 Spoon the mixture into a serving bowl and smooth the surface. Cover the pâté with plastic wrap and refrigerate until firm.

3 Arrange the walnuts over the top, pressing down lightly. Serve at room temperature with crusty bread, crackers and celery sticks.

NUTRITION PER SERVE
Protein 12 g; Fat 37 g; Carbohydrate 2.5 g; Dietary Fibre 0.5 g; Cholesterol 100 mg; 1650 kJ (395 cal)

Stir the blue cheese and chives into the cream cheese and butter mixture.

Arrange the walnut halves over the surface, pressing down lightly.

CHICKEN LIVER AND GRAND MARNIER PATE

Preparation time: 20 minutes +
  soaking and refrigeration
Total cooking time: 10 minutes
Serves 8

750 g chicken livers, trimmed
1 cup (250 ml) milk
200 g butter, softened
½ cup (60 g) finely chopped
  spring onions
1 tablespoon Grand Marnier
1 tablespoon frozen orange juice
  concentrate, thawed
½ orange, very thinly sliced

JELLIED LAYER
1 tablespoon frozen orange juice
  concentrate, thawed
1 tablespoon Grand Marnier
1¼ cups (315 ml) canned chicken
  consommé, undiluted
2½ teaspoons gelatine

1 Place the chicken livers in a large bowl, add the milk and stir to combine. Cover and refrigerate for 1 hour. Drain the livers and discard the milk. Rinse well in cold water, drain and pat dry with paper towels.

2 Melt a third of the butter in a frying pan, add the spring onion and cook for 2–3 minutes, or until tender, but not brown. Add the chicken livers and cook, stirring, over medium heat for 4–5 minutes, or until just cooked. Remove from the heat and cool a little.

3 Place the contents of the pan in a food processor and process until very smooth. Chop the remaining butter, and add to the food processor with the Grand Marnier and orange concentrate. Process until creamy and season. Place the pâté in a 1.25 litre serving dish, cover the surface of the pâté with plastic wrap and refrigerate for 1½ hours, or until firm.

4 To make the jellied layer, whisk the orange juice concentrate, Grand Marnier and ½ cup (125 ml) of the consommé together in a bowl, and sprinkle on the gelatine in an even layer. Set aside and leave until the gelatine is spongy—do not stir. Heat the remaining consommé, then remove from the heat and add the gelatine mixture to the pan. Stir gently to dissolve the gelatine and leave to cool and thicken until the mixture is the consistency of an uncooked egg white.

5 Press the orange slices lightly into the surface of the pâté and spoon the thickened jelly over the top. Refrigerate until set. Serve at room temperature with toast or crackers.

NUTRITION PER SERVE
Protein 20 g; Fat 25 g; Carbohydrate 8 g; Dietary Fibre 0 g; Cholesterol 260 mg; 1480 kJ (355 cal)

Cook the spring onion and chicken livers over medium heat until just cooked.

Blend the chicken liver mixture in a food processor until creamy.

Add the gelatine mixture to the heated consommé, then leave to cool and thicken.

DIPS

Dips are one of the easiest options for feeding the hordes at a party. They can be made well in advance and simply need to be placed on a side table for your guests to help themselves.

Guacamole
Ready in under 15 minutes.

2 large ripe avocados
2 tablespoons lime juice
1 tomato, seeded and finely diced
1 fresh red chilli, finely chopped
2 tablespoons finely diced red onion
1 1/2 tablespoons chopped fresh
    coriander leaves
1 1/2 tablespoons sour cream
1 tablespoon olive oil
1/2 teaspoon ground cumin
pinch of cayenne pepper

Put the avocado and lime juice in a large bowl, then mash. Stir in the diced tomato, chilli, onion, coriander, sour cream, olive oil and cumin. Season with cayenne pepper and some salt and pepper. Spoon into a serving bowl and sprinkle with cayenne pepper. Makes 2 cups. Ideal with crudités (see page 125), tortilla shards (see page 126) or corn chips.

Taramasalata
Ready in under 15 minutes.

4 slices white bread, crusts removed
1/3 cup (80 ml) milk
200 g smoked cod or grey mullet roe
1 egg yolk
1 clove garlic, crushed
150–170 ml olive oil
2 tablespoons lemon juice
1 tablespoon finely chopped fresh
    parsley

Soak the bread in milk for 5 minutes. Squeeze out the excess liquid and transfer to a food processor. Add the roe, egg yolk and garlic and process until smooth. With the motor running, slowly pour in the oil, stopping when the dip is thick and holds its form. Add the lemon juice and parsley. Season and add more lemon juice, if needed. Makes 1 2/3 cups. Ideal with crudités (see page 125) or plain bruschetta.

NOTE: You can add a few drops of red food colouring to deepen the colour.

Warm cheese dip
Ready in about 15 minutes.

40 g butter
3 spring onions, finely chopped
2 jalapeño chillies, finely chopped
1/2 teaspoon ground cumin
3/4 cup (185 g) sour cream
2 cups (250 g) grated Cheddar
green Tabasco, to drizzle

Melt the butter in a saucepan and add the spring onion, chilli and cumin. Cook without browning over low heat, stirring often, for 6–8 minutes. Stir in the sour cream and, when it is warm, add the Cheddar. Stir constantly until the cheese melts and the mixture is glossy and smooth. Transfer to a bowl, drizzle with a little Tabasco and serve warm. Makes 2 cups. Ideal with Parmesan puff straws (see page 125) or tortilla shards (see page 126).

Red capsicum skordalia
Ready in about 30 minutes

1 large floury potato (e.g. russet,
    King Edward), cut into large
    cubes
2 large red capsicums, seeded
    and cut into large flattish pieces
100 g slivered almonds, toasted
4 cloves garlic, crushed
200 ml olive oil
2 tablespoons red wine vinegar

Boil the potato until tender, then drain and return to the pan. Mash with a potato masher, then cool. Meanwhile, put the capsicum, skin-side-up, under a hot grill and cook until the skin blackens and blisters. Transfer to a plastic bag and leave to cool. Peel the skin and roughly chop the flesh. Finely grind the nuts in a food processor, then add the garlic and capsicum. Blend until smooth. With the motor running, slowly add the oil, then mix in the vinegar. Transfer to a bowl and fold in the mashed potato. Mix well. Makes 2 1/2 cups. Ideal with crudités (see page 125), orange sweet potato wedges (see page 126) or deep-fried cheese ravioli (see page 124).

Baba ganouj
Ready in about 1 hour 30 minutes.

2 eggplants (1 kg)
1/3 cup (80 ml) lemon juice
2 tablespoons tahini
1 1/2 tablespoons olive oil
3 cloves garlic, crushed
1/2 teaspoon ground cumin
pinch of cayenne pepper
1 tablespoon finely chopped fresh
    flat-leaf parsley
black olives, to garnish

Preheat the oven to moderately hot 200°C (400°F/Gas 6). Pierce the eggplants a few times with a fork, then cook them over an open flame for about 5 minutes, or until the skin is black and blistered all over. Then transfer the eggplants to a roasting tin and bake for 35–40 minutes, or until soft and wrinkled. Place in a colander over a bowl to drain off any bitter juices and stand for 30 minutes, or until they are cool. Peel the skin from the eggplants, and place the flesh in a food processor along with the lemon juice, tahini, oil, garlic, cumin and cayenne. Process this mixture until it becomes smooth and creamy. Season to taste with salt and stir in the chopped parsley. Spread onto a serving plate and garnish with the olives. Makes 1 2/3 cups. Ideal served with tortilla shards (see page 126).

Hummus
Prepare a day ahead.

200 g dried chickpeas
1/3 cup (80 ml) olive oil
3–4 tablespoons lemon juice
2 cloves garlic, crushed
2 tablespoons tahini
1 tablespoon ground cumin

Soak the chickpeas in water for 8 hours or overnight. Drain. Place in a saucepan, cover with cold water, bring to the boil and boil for 50–60 minutes. Drain, reserving 3/4–1 cup (185–250 ml) of the cooking liquid.

Place the chickpeas in a food processor with the oil, lemon juice, garlic, tahini, cumin and 1/2 teaspoon salt. Blend well until the mixture begins to look thick and creamy. With the motor running, gradually add the reserved cooking liquid until the mixture reaches the desired consistency. Makes 2 1/2 cups.

Ideal accompanied with herbed lavash (see page 124), herb grissini (see page 127), crudités (see page 125) or pitta bread.

Green mexican salsa
Ready in under 15 minutes.

300 g can tomatillos, drained
  (see Note)
1 small onion, chopped
1 jalapeño chilli, finely chopped
3 cloves garlic, crushed
2 tablespoons chopped fresh
  coriander leaves
1–2 teaspoons lime juice

Place the tomatillos in a food processor with the onion, chilli, garlic and 1 tablespoon of the coriander. Process until smooth, then blend in the lime juice to taste. Add the rest of the coriander and process just long enough to mix it through the dip. Makes 2 cups.

Ideal served with tortilla shards (see page 126) or corn chips.

NOTE: Tomatillos resemble green tomatoes with a papery husk. They are used a lot in Mexican cooking.

White bean dip
Ready in under 15 minutes.

2 x 400 g cans lima or cannellini
  beans, drained and rinsed
1/2 cup (125 ml) olive oil
1/3 cup (80 ml) lemon juice
3 cloves garlic, finely chopped
1 tablespoon finely chopped fresh
  rosemary

Place the beans in a food processor with the oil, lemon juice, garlic and rosemary and 1 teaspoon salt. Process until smooth, then season with cracked black pepper. Makes 3 cups.

Ideal with herb grissini (see page 127), orange sweet potato wedges (see page 126), tortilla shards (see page 126), plain bruschetta or Turkish bread.

NOTE: This dip improves with age, so you can make it up to 2 days ahead of time.

Dhal
Ready in about 30 minutes.

1 cup (250 g) red lentils, rinsed
1/4 teaspoon ground turmeric
1 tablespoon oil
1 tablespoon cumin seeds
1/2 teaspoon brown mustard seeds
1 onion, finely chopped
1 tablespoon grated fresh ginger
2 long fresh green chillies, seeded
    and finely chopped
1/3 cup (80 ml) lemon juice
2 tablespoons finely chopped fresh
    coriander leaves

Place the lentils in a saucepan with 3 cups (750 ml) cold water. Bring to the boil, then reduce the heat and stir in the turmeric. Simmer, covered, for 20 minutes, or until tender.

Meanwhile, heat the oil in a saucepan over medium heat, and cook the cumin and mustard seeds for 5–6 minutes, or until the seeds begin to pop. Add the onion, ginger and chilli and cook for 5 minutes, or until the onion is golden. Add the lentils and 1/2 cup (125 ml) water. Season with salt, reduce the heat and simmer for 10 minutes. Spoon into a bowl, stir in the lemon juice and garnish with coriander. Makes 3 cups.

Ideal with herbed lavash (see page 124), spicy poppadoms (see page 126) or chips.

Warm crab and lemon dip
Ready in about 30 minutes.

80 g butter
2 cloves garlic, crushed
3 French shallots, thinly sliced
1 teaspoon mustard powder
1/2 teaspoon cayenne pepper
1/2 cup (125 ml) cream
150 g cream cheese
1/2 cup (60 g) grated Cheddar
350 g can crab meat, drained
2 tablespoons lemon juice
2 teaspoons Worcestershire sauce
3 teaspoons chopped fresh tarragon
1/2 cup (40 g) fresh breadcrumbs
1 tablespoon chopped fresh parsley

Preheat the oven to warm 170°C (325°F/Gas 3). Melt half the butter in a saucepan, then cook the garlic and shallots for 2–3 minutes, or until just softened. Add the mustard powder, cayenne pepper and cream. Bring to a simmer and slowly whisk in the cream cheese, a little at a time. When the cream cheese is completely incorporated, whisk in the Cheddar and allow to cook, stirring constantly, over very low heat for 1–2 minutes, or until smooth. Remove from the heat and add the crab meat, lemon juice, Worcestershire sauce and 2 teaspoons of the tarragon. Season to taste with salt and cracked black pepper. Mix, then transfer to a small baking dish. Melt the remaining butter in a small saucepan, add the breadcrumbs, parsley and remaining tarragon and stir until just combined. Sprinkle over the crab mixture and bake for 15 minutes, or until golden. Serve warm. Makes 2 1/2 cups.

Ideal with Parmesan puff straws (see page 125), Turkish bread or Melba toasts.

DIPPERS

You can either serve these dippers with one of the home-made dips on the previous pages, or jazz up ready-made dips. Serve in large bowls or on platters.

Deep-fried cheese ravioli
Ready in under 15 minutes.

oil, for deep-frying
300 g fresh cheese ravioli

Fill a deep heavy-based saucepan or deep-fryer one third full of oil and heat to 180°C (350°F), or until a cube of bread dropped into the oil browns in 15 seconds. Cook the ravioli in batches until golden brown. Remove from the oil and drain on crumpled paper towels. Sprinkle with salt and cracked black pepper and serve hot. Makes about 30.

Ideal with red capsicum skordalia (see page 121) or green Mexican salsa (see page 122). Also good on their own.

Mixed asian crisps
Ready in under 15 minutes.

oil, for deep-frying
16 cassava crackers, broken into small pieces
16 round won ton wrappers
16 small uncooked plain prawn crackers (see Note)
1 sheet toasted nori, shredded

Fill a deep heavy-based saucepan or deep-fryer one third full of oil and heat to 180°C (350°F), or until a cube of bread dropped into the oil browns in 15 seconds. Deep-fry the cassava pieces until crisp. Remove with a slotted spoon and drain on paper towels. Repeat with the won ton wrappers and prawn chips. When they are all cool, combine and toss with the nori. Makes a big bowl.

Best on their own or with a Thai dipping sauce.

NOTE: Cassava crackers are made from the flour of the dried cassava root. Available from Asian food stores.

Herbed lavash
Ready in about 15 minutes.

½ cup (125 ml) olive oil
3 cloves garlic, crushed
6 slices lavash bread
2 teaspoons sea salt flakes
2 teaspoons dried mixed Italian herbs

Preheat the oven to moderate 180°C (350°F/Gas 4). Heat the oil and garlic in a small saucepan over low heat until the oil is warm and the garlic is fragrant but not browned. Brush the lavash bread on both sides with the garlic oil. Cut each piece of bread into eight triangular wedges and position side-by-side on baking trays. Sprinkle the upper side with the sea salt and herbs. Bake the lavash for 8–10 minutes, or until crisp. Makes about 48 pieces.

Ideal with hummus or dhal (see pages 122–3).

Crudités
Ready in about 15 minutes

100 g baby green beans, trimmed
170 g asparagus, trimmed and
    halved
100 g baby corn
24 sugar snap peas
2 heads of endive, trimmed
1 head of radicchio, trimmed
12 baby carrots, trimmed, leaving
    the leafy tops intact
2 red capsicums, sliced into 1 cm
    wide slices
fresh herbs (e.g. dill, chervil,
    coriander), to serve
lime quarters, to serve

Fill a large bowl with iced water and
set it aside. Bring a large saucepan of
salted water to the boil and blanch
the beans, asparagus, corn and peas
separately until tender, but still firm
to the bite. Remove with a slotted
spoon and refresh in the iced water,
then pat dry. Separate the endive
and radicchio leaves. Arrange all the
vegetables, including the carrots and
capsicum, in their groups on a
serving plate with your favourite dip.
Garnish with sprigs of fresh herbs
and lime quarters. Makes enough for
a platter.

Parmesan puff straws
Ready in under 30 minutes.

4 sheets ready-rolled puff pastry
50 g butter, melted
1²/₃ cups (165 g) finely grated
    Parmesan
1 egg, lightly beaten

Preheat the oven to moderately hot
200°C (400°F/Gas 6). Lightly brush
the pastry with the butter, then
sprinkle each sheet with ¹/₄ cup
(25 g) of the cheese and season with
salt and pepper. Fold each sheet in
half, bringing the top edge down
towards you. Brush the tops of each
sheet with the egg. Sprinkle each
with 2 tablespoons of extra grated
Parmesan and season with salt. Using
a very sharp knife, cut the dough
vertically into 1 cm wide strips.
Transfer each of the strips to a baking
tray lined with baking paper, spacing
them evenly apart. Grab each end of
the pastry and stretch and twist in
the opposite direction. Bake in the
oven for 8–10 minutes or until lightly
browned. Makes 80.

Ideal with warm cheese dip (see
page 120) or warm crab and lemon
dip (see page 123). Also good on
their own.

*From left: Deep-fried cheese ravioli,
Mixed Asian crisps, Herbed lavash,
Crudités, Parmesan puff straws.*

Tortilla shards
Ready in under 15 minutes.

2 tablespoons sweet paprika
1/4 teaspoon cayenne pepper
oil, for deep-frying
8 large flour tortillas, cut into long
    triangles

Combine the paprika and cayenne pepper in a small bowl. Fill a deep heavy-based saucepan one third full of oil and heat to 180°C (350°F/ Gas 4)), or until a cube of bread dropped into the oil browns in 15 seconds. Drop the tortilla shards in the oil in batches and deep-fry until crisp. Drain on crumpled paper towels and sprinkle lightly with the paprika mix while still hot. Serves 8–10.

Ideal with guacamole (see page 120), baba ganouj (see page 121), green Mexican salsa (see page 122) or white bean dip (see page 122).

Spicy poppadoms
Ready in about 15 minutes.

3 green cardamom seeds
1 1/2 tablespoons coriander seeds
1 tablespoon cumin seeds
2 cloves
1 teaspoon black peppercorns
1 bay leaf, crushed
1 teaspoon ground mace
1/4 teaspoon ground cinnamon
pinch of ground chilli
oil, for deep-frying
24 large poppadoms, broken into
    quarters

Toast the cardamom, coriander and cumin seeds, cloves, peppercorns and bay leaf in a dry frying pan over low heat for 2–3 minutes, or until richly fragrant. Cool for 5 minutes, then grind to a fine powder. Stir in the mace, cinnamon and chilli.

Fill a wide, large saucepan one third full with oil and heat to 180°C (350°F/Gas 4), or until a cube of bread dropped into the oil browns in 15 seconds. Deep-fry the pieces of poppadom, a few at a time, until crisp and golden. Drain on crumpled paper towels and sprinkle with the spice mix while still hot. Makes a large bowl.

Ideal with dhal (see page 123).

Orange sweet potato wedges
Ready in about 30 minutes.

1.3 kg orange sweet potato, peeled
    and sliced into 6 cm x 2 cm
    wedges
2 tablespoons olive oil
1 tablespoon fennel seeds
1 tablespoon coriander seeds
1/2 teaspoon cayenne pepper
1 teaspoon sea salt flakes

Preheat the oven to moderately hot 200°C (400°F/Gas 6). Place the sweet potato in a large baking dish and toss with the oil. In a mortar and pestle pound together the fennel and coriander seeds until they are roughly crushed. Add to the orange sweet potato along with the cayenne and sea salt flakes. Toss well and bake for about 30 minutes, or until browned and crisp. Serve warm. Serves 6–8.

Ideal with red capsicum skordalia (see page 121) or white bean dip (see page 122). Also great on their own.

Spring onion flatbreads
Ready in under 1 hour.

2 teaspoons oil
185 g spring onions, thinly sliced
1 clove garlic, crushed
1/2 teaspoon grated fresh ginger
1 3/4 cups (215 g) plain flour
1 1/2 tablespoons chopped fresh
  coriander
oil, for shallow-frying

Heat the oil in a frying pan, and cook the spring onion, garlic and ginger for 2–3 minutes, or until soft.

Combine the flour and 1 teaspoon salt in a bowl. Stir in the onion mixture and the chopped coriander. Gradually stir in 1 cup (250 ml) boiling water, stopping when a loose dough forms. Knead the dough with floured hands for 1 1/2–2 minutes, or until smooth. Cover with plastic wrap and rest for 30 minutes. Break off walnut-sized pieces of dough and roll out into thin ovals.

Fill a large frying pan with 2 cm oil and heat over medium heat. When shimmering, cook the breads 2–3 at a time for 25–30 seconds each side, or until crisp and golden. Drain on paper towels and serve warm. Makes 40.

Ideal with dhal (see page 123).

Herb grissini
Ready in under 2 hours.

7 g sachet dried yeast
1 teaspoon sugar
4 cups (500 g) plain flour
1/4 cup (60 ml) olive oil
1/2 cup (15 g) chopped fresh
  flat-leaf parsley
1/4 cup (15 g) chopped fresh basil
2 teaspoons sea salt flakes

Combine the yeast, sugar and 1 1/4 cups (315 ml) warm water in a small bowl and leave in a warm place for 5–10 minutes, or until foamy.

Sift the flour and 1 teaspoon salt into a bowl. Stir in the yeast and oil to form a dough, adding more water if necessary. Gather into a ball and turn out onto a lightly floured surface. Knead for 10 minutes, or until soft and elastic. Add the herbs, and knead for 1–2 minutes to incorporate evenly. Place the dough in a lightly oiled bowl and cover with plastic wrap. Leave in a warm place for 1 hour, or until doubled in volume. Preheat the oven to very hot 230°C (450°F/Gas 8) and lightly grease two large baking trays.

Punch down the dough and knead for 1 minute. Divide into 24 portions, and roll each portion into a 30 cm long stick. Place on the trays and lightly brush with water. Sprinkle with the salt flakes. Bake for 15 minutes, or until crisp and golden. Makes 24.

Ideal with white bean dip or hummus (see page 122).

From left: Tortilla shards, Spicy poppadoms, Orange sweet potato wedges, Spring onion flatbreads, Herb grissini.

SPICED CARROT SOUP SIP

Preparation time: 30 minutes
Cooking time: 1 hour 10 minutes
Serves 36 (Makes 1.25 litres)

1/3 cup (80 ml) olive oil
2 teaspoons honey
3 teaspoons ground cumin
3 teaspoons coriander seeds, lightly
    crushed
2 cinnamon sticks, broken in half
1.5 kg carrots, cut into even chunks
    (about 3 cm)
3 cups (750 ml) chicken stock
100 ml cream
3/4 cup (185 g) sour cream
3 tablespoons fresh coriander leaves

1 Preheat the oven to moderately hot 200°C (400°F/Gas 6). Combine the oil, honey, cumin, coriander seeds, cinnamon sticks, 1 teaspoon salt and plenty of cracked black pepper in a roasting tin. Add the chunks of carrot and mix well to ensure that all the carrot is coated in the spice mixture.

2 Roast for 1 hour, or until the carrot is tender, shaking the pan occasionally during cooking. Remove from the oven, discard the cinnamon sticks with tongs and allow the carrot to cool slightly.

3 Transfer half the carrot chunks, 1 1/2 cups (375 ml) of the stock and 1 cup (250 ml) water to a food processor or blender and blend until smooth. Strain through a fine sieve into a clean saucepan. Repeat with the remaining carrots, stock and another 1 cup (250 ml) water. Bring the soup to a simmer and cook for 10 minutes. Add the cream and season to taste. Ladle into a jug, then pour into shot glasses or espresso cups. Garnish each cup with 1/4 teaspoon sour cream and a coriander leaf.

NOTE: The soup can be refrigerated for 2 days or frozen for up to 8 weeks if placed in the freezer before the cream is added. Then reheat in a saucepan – bring to the boil, then simmer for 1 minute.

Stir the carrots into the spice mixture so that they are well coated.

Blend the carrots, stock and water until the mixture is smooth.

BLOODY MARY OYSTER SHOTS

Preparation time: 10 minutes +
30 minutes refrigeration
Cooking time: Nil
Serves 12

⅓ cup (80 ml) vodka
½ cup (125 ml) tomato juice
1 tablespoon lemon juice
dash of Worcestershire sauce
2 drops of Tabasco
pinch of celery salt
12 oysters
1 cucumber, peeled, seeded and
finely julienned

1 Combine the vodka, tomato juice, lemon juice, Worcestershire sauce, Tabasco and celery salt in a jug. Mix well, then refrigerate for 30 minutes, or until chilled. Just before serving, fill each shot glass about two thirds full. Drop an oyster in each glass, then top with a teaspoon of julienned cucumber. For the final touch, crack some black pepper over the top of each shot glass, then serve.

NOTE: It is better to use oysters fresh from the shell rather than from a jar because they have a much better, fresher taste. The tomato mixture can be made a day ahead of time and kept in the fridge. Stir before serving.
Variation: If you think your guests are game enough for some fire in their evening, make chilled sake shots—fill each glass two thirds full of sake, add an oyster, then garnish with cucumber.

Finely shred the peeled and seeded cucumber with a sharp knife.

Fill each glass about two thirds full, then drop in an oyster.

OYSTERS

Oysters whisper elegance and will set the tone for any celebration.
Buy two dozen oysters, then serve with one of these delicious toppings.

Basic oyster recipe

Buy 24 fresh oysters, remove from the shells and pat dry. Wash the shells, replace the oysters and cover with a damp cloth in the fridge. They are fabulous with a simple squeeze of lemon, or try one of these toppings.

NOTE: Oysters are sold freshly shucked on the half shell, or alive and unshucked. When buying fresh shucked oysters, look for a plump, moist oyster. The flesh should be creamy with a clear liquid (oyster liquor) surrounding it. Oysters should smell like the fresh sea and have no traces of shell particles. If you prefer to shuck them yourself, you should purchase tightly closed, unbroken shells.

Oysters are often served on a bed of rock salt or crushed ice to help them remain stable and upright and to keep them cool in summer.

Ginger shallot
Ready in about 15 minutes.

2 tablespoons Japanese soy sauce
1 tablespoon mirin
2 teaspoons sake
1/2 teaspoon sugar
1 1/2 tablespoons thinly sliced fresh ginger
2 tablespoons thinly sliced spring onion
2 teaspoons sesame oil
24 prepared oysters
toasted sesame seeds, to garnish

Place the soy sauce, mirin, sake and sugar in a small saucepan and mix together well. Simmer over low heat, stirring, until the sugar dissolves, then stir in the ginger and spring onion. Simmer for a minute, then add the sesame oil. Spoon about 1/2 teaspoon of the sauce over each oyster. Garnish with sesame seeds and serve.

Lemon herb dressing
Ready in about 15 minutes.

1 tablespoon chopped fresh dill
1 clove garlic, crushed
1 tablespoon finely chopped fresh flat-leaf parsley
2 teaspoons finely chopped fresh chives
2 tablespoons lemon juice
1/4 cup (60 ml) extra virgin olive oil
24 prepared oysters
chive bows, to garnish
brown bread, cubed, to garnish

Place the dill, garlic, parsley, chives, lemon juice and oil in a bowl and season to taste with salt and cracked black pepper. Mix together well, then drizzle a little of the dressing over each oyster. Garnish with chive bows and serve with tiny cubes of brown bread.

Tomato, chilli and coriander salsa
Ready in under 15 minutes.

2 vine-ripened tomatoes, seeded and finely diced
2 French shallots, finely chopped
2 small fresh red chillies, seeded and sliced
3 tablespoons chopped fresh coriander
1 tablespoon lime juice
24 prepared oysters

Place the tomato, shallots, chilli and coriander in a bowl and mix together well. Stir in the lime juice, then season with salt and pepper. Place a teaspoon of the salsa on each oyster.

Prosciutto and balsamic vinegar
Ready in under 15 minutes.

2 teaspoons olive oil
6 slices prosciutto, finely chopped
2 French shallots, finely chopped
1 tablespoon balsamic vinegar
24 prepared oysters

Heat the oil in a small frying pan over medium heat, add the prosciutto and shallots and fry until the prosciutto is crisp. Add the vinegar and cook for 1 minute to warm through. Spoon a little of the topping over each oyster.

Wasabi crème fraîche
Ready in under 15 minutes.

1/3 cup (80 ml) crème fraîche
2 tablespoons whole-egg mayonnaise
1 1/2 teaspoons wasabi paste
24 prepared oysters
flying fish roe, to garnish
small lime wedges, to garnish

Combine the crème fraîche, mayonnaise and wasabi paste in a bowl and whisk well. Place a teaspoon of the mixture on top of each oyster, then garnish with the roe and lime wedges.

From left: Ginger shallot, Lemon herb dressing, Tomato, chilli and coriander salsa, Prosciutto and balsamic vinegar, Wasabi crème fraîche.

SEAFOOD TERRINE

Preparation time: 1 hour + cooling
    and refrigeration
Total cooking time: 50 minutes
Serves 8

FIRST LAYER
500 g raw prawns, chilled
2 egg whites, chilled
freshly grated nutmeg, to taste
220 ml cream, chilled
150 g baby green beans

SECOND LAYER
**250 g salmon fillet without skin
    and bones, chopped**
2 egg whites, chilled
**2 tablespoons chopped
    fresh chives**
220 ml cream, chilled

TOMATO COULIS
2 tablespoons extra virgin olive oil
1 onion, very finely chopped
**750 g ripe Roma tomatoes, peeled,
    seeded and diced**
**2 tablespoons Grand Marnier,
    optional**

1 Preheat the oven to moderate 180°C (350°F/Gas 4). Brush a 1.5 litre (22 x 12 cm) loaf tin with oil and line the base with baking paper. To make the first layer, peel and devein the prawns and finely chop in a food processor. Add the egg whites one at a time, processing until smooth. Season with salt, pepper and nutmeg. Add the cream slowly and then stop the machine. Spoon into the tin, cover and refrigerate.

2 Cook the beans in boiling water until tender, then drain and plunge into cold water. Drain again and dry with paper towels. Arrange lengthways over the prawn mixture.

3 To make the second layer, process the salmon until finely chopped. Add the egg whites one at a time and process until smooth, then add the chives. Add the cream slowly and then stop the machine. Spread evenly over the beans.

4 Cover the loaf tin tightly with foil brushed with oil and place in a baking dish. Pour cold water into the

dish to come halfway up the sides of the tin. Bake for 35 minutes, or until lightly set in the centre. Leave to cool before removing the foil. Cover with plastic wrap and refrigerate until firm. Serve at room temperature.

5 To make the coulis, heat the oil in a pan, add the onion and cook over medium heat for 5 minutes, or until soft. Add the tomato and Grand

Marnier and bring to the boil. Boil for 8 minutes, or until thickened slightly. Cool, then process until smooth. Season to taste and serve with slices of the terrine.

NUTRITION PER SERVE
Protein 22.5 g; Fat 33 g; Carbohydrate 7 g; Dietary Fibre 2 g; Cholesterol 190 mg; 1749 kJ (415 cal)

Spread the second layer evenly over the beans, smoothing with the back of a spoon.

Boil the tomato coulis until it has thickened slightly.

GRAVADLAX

Preparation time: 20 minutes +
overnight refrigeration
Total cooking time: nil
Serves 20

3 tablespoons sugar
2 tablespoons coarse sea salt
1 teaspoon crushed black
   peppercorns
1 x 2.5 kg salmon, filleted and
   deboned but with the skin left on
   (ask your fishmonger to do this)
1 tablespoon vodka or brandy
4 tablespoons very finely
   chopped fresh dill

MUSTARD SAUCE
1½ tablespoons cider vinegar
1 teaspoon caster sugar
½ cup (125 ml) olive oil
2 teaspoons chopped fresh dill
2 tablespoons Dijon mustard

1 Combine the sugar, salt and peppercorns in a small dish. Remove any bones from the salmon fillets. Pat dry with paper towels and lay one fillet skin-side-down in a shallow tray or baking dish. Sprinkle with half the vodka or brandy and rub half the sugar mixture into the flesh, then sprinkle on half the dill. Sprinkle the remaining vodka over the second salmon fillet and rub the remaining sugar mixture into the flesh. Lay it flesh-side-down on top of the dill-coated salmon. Cover with plastic wrap and place a heavy board on top, then weigh this down with 3 heavy cans or a foil-covered brick.

2 Place the wrapped salmon in the refrigerator for 24 hours, turning it over after 12 hours.

3 To make the mustard sauce, whisk together the ingredients, then cover until needed.

4 When the salmon is ready, take off the weights and remove the plastic wrap. Lift off the top fillet and lay both fillets on a wooden board. Brush off all the dill and any seasoning mixture with a stiff pastry brush. Sprinkle with the remaining fresh dill and press it onto the salmon flesh, shaking off any excess.

5 Serve whole on the serving board or very thinly sliced on an angle towards the tail, with the sauce.

NUTRITION PER SERVE
Protein 22.5 g; Fat 15 g; Carbohydrate 3 g; Dietary Fibre 0 g; Cholesterol 37.5 mg; 1234 kJ (294 cal)

Rub the sugar mixture into the second salmon fillet.

Whisk all the ingredients of the mustard sauce together.

The salmon can be served sliced thinly on an angle towards the tail.

SEAFOOD TREATS

Melt-in-the-mouth delicious, shellfish are one of nature's delights. And you can indulge with a clear conscience knowing that they are an excellent source of vitamins and minerals.

Oysters with toasted sesame seed mayonnaise

Remove 2 dozen rock oysters from their shells and wipe them with a damp cloth to remove any grit. Wash the shells thoroughly. Put the oysters back in their shells, cover with a damp cloth and refrigerate. Add 1 crushed garlic clove, 1 tablespoon sesame oil and 2 tablespoons toasted sesame seeds to ⅓ cup (80 g) whole-egg mayonnaise, and stir well to combine. Season well. Arrange the oysters on a serving platter and top each with a dollop of mayonnaise and a sprig of dill. Serve with lime wedges. *Serves 6*

Mussels in ratatouille

Cover 1 kg scrubbed and debearded black mussels with a damp cloth and refrigerate. (Discard any open ones.) Heat 2 tablespoons olive oil in a pan and cook 1 finely chopped onion and 2 crushed garlic cloves for 5 minutes, or until softened. Dice 2 baby eggplants, 2 zucchini, 1 red and 1 green capsicum, and add to the onion, continuing to cook for 10 minutes. Increase the heat to high and add a 420 g can chopped tomatoes and 1 cup (250 ml) red wine. Bring to the boil, then reduce the heat and simmer for 30 minutes. Add the mussels to the sauce and cover with a lid. Shake the pan occasionally for even cooking and remove the mussels as soon as they open to avoid overcooking. This may take 5–10 minutes, though some will open a lot quicker than others. Discard any that do not open. Remove the lid and stir until the sauce has thickened slightly. Spoon the sauce over the mussels and sprinkle liberally with ¼ cup (7 g) chopped fresh flat-leaf parsley. *Serves 6*

Scallops with honeydew and mint chutney

Remove 2 dozen scallops from their shells, clean with a damp cloth, and wash the shells. Put the scallops in a bowl with the juice of 2 limes, cover and refrigerate. To make the chutney, combine 1 tablespoon white wine vinegar, 1 tablespoon finely chopped fresh mint, 2 tablespoons toasted flaked coconut and ½ cup finely diced honeydew melon. Cook the scallops on a char-grill or barbecue plate for 1–2 minutes each side, or until just tender. Put them back into the cleaned shells and top with a generous spoonful of the chutney. Serve warm or at room temperature. *Serves 6*

Left to right: Oysters with toasted sesame seed mayonnaise; Mussels in ratatouille; Scallops with honeydew and mint chutney; Barbecued prawns with sweet cucumber vinegar; Herbed scampi with butter and sweet cider sauce.

Barbecued prawns with sweet cucumber vinegar

Cook 24 raw prawns in their shells on a chargrill or barbecue plate over medium heat for 1–2 minutes on each side, or until pink. Remove from the heat and cover. Combine ¼ cup (60 ml) white wine vinegar and ⅓ cup (90 g) caster sugar in a pan and bring to the boil. Stir and remove from the heat. Allow to cool. Add 2 tablespoons lime juice, 2 tablespoons fish sauce, 1 seeded, thinly sliced, long red chilli, 1 seeded, thinly sliced, long green chilli, 2 diagonally sliced spring onions, 1 Lebanese cucumber, peeled, halved, seeded and thinly sliced, and ¼ cup (15 g) chopped fresh coriander. Combine well and pour over the cooked prawns. Serve warm. *Serves 4–6*

Herbed scampi with butter and sweet cider sauce

Twist and remove the heads from 12 scampi or langoustines. Cut the scampi in half lengthways. Combine ¼ cup (60 ml) olive oil, the juice of 2 lemons, 2 crushed garlic cloves, ½ cup (15 g) firmly packed finely chopped fresh flat-leaf parsley and ½ cup (30 g) finely chopped fresh dill and pour over the scampi. Cover and refrigerate for at least 1 hour. Cook the scampi, shell-side-down, on a char-grill or barbecue plate for 2 minutes. Turn and cook for a further 2 minutes, or until tender. Meanwhile, simmer ¼ cup (60 ml) alcoholic cider until it has reduced by two-thirds. Lower the temperature and add 25 g butter, stirring until melted. Remove from the heat and pour over the scampi. Serve immediately. *Serves 6*

BAKED RICOTTA

Preparation time: 15 minutes +
  overnight draining
Total cooking time: 30 minutes
Serves 8–10 as an appetiser

1 whole fresh ricotta (2 kg)
3/4 cup (185 ml) olive oil
3/4 cup (185 ml) lemon juice
2 tablespoons julienned lemon rind
2 cloves garlic, crushed
1/2 cup (20 g) fresh basil leaves,
  finely shredded
1/2 cup (50 g) semi-dried tomatoes,
  roughly chopped

1 Put the ricotta in a plastic
colander, place over a bowl, cover
with plastic wrap and leave to drain
in the refrigerator overnight.

2 Preheat the oven to very hot
250°C (500°F/Gas 10). Line a

baking tray with baking paper. Place
the ricotta on the tray and brush with
a little of the olive oil. Cook in the
oven for 30 minutes, or until golden
brown. Allow to cool slightly.

3 Place the olive oil, lemon juice
and rind, garlic and basil in a
bowl. Mix well and season to taste
with salt and pepper.

4 Place the whole ricotta on a serving
platter, pour on the dressing and
scatter with the semi-dried tomatoes.

*Bake the ricotta in a very hot oven until
it is golden brown.*

Serve with thin slices of Italian-style
bread or bruschetta.

NUTRITION PER SERVE (10)
Protein 20 g; Fat 40 g; Carbohydrate
3.5 g; Dietary Fibre 0 g; Cholesterol
95 mg; 1917 kJ (458 cal)

NOTE: If your ricotta comes in a
basket, it may have a piece of paper
in the base. Make sure you remove
this before draining.

*Combine all the dressing ingredients and
season well with salt and black pepper.*

SALMON AND FENNEL FRITTATA

Preparation time: 35 minutes
Total cooking time:
   1 hour 15 minutes
Serves 8

1½ tablespoons olive oil
1 onion, finely chopped
1 fennel bulb (280 g), finely
   chopped
¼ cup (60 ml) white wine
2 cups (60 g) watercress sprigs
12 eggs
1¾ cups (440 ml) cream
¼ cup (15 g) chopped fresh dill
½ cup (50 g) grated Parmesan
300 g smoked salmon,
   cut into strips

1 Preheat the oven to moderate 180°C (350°F/Gas 4). Lightly grease a 22 cm springform tin and line the base and side with baking paper, making sure you have a tight seal all the way around the tin. Heat the olive oil in a heavy-based pan and add the onion, fennel and a pinch of salt. Cook over low heat for 5 minutes, stirring occasionally. Add the white wine and cook for another 5 minutes, or until the vegetables are tender. Remove from the heat and leave to cool.

2 Finely chop half the watercress and divide the remainder into small sprigs. Beat the eggs lightly and add the cream, dill, Parmesan, chopped watercress, and the onion and fennel mixture. Season with plenty of salt and black pepper.

3 Pour half of the egg mixture into the prepared tin, sprinkle with 200 g smoked salmon and pour in the remaining egg mixture. Place the tin on a baking tray in case it leaks and bake for 65 minutes, or until the frittata is set, cooked in the centre and golden on the surface. Remove from the pan and peel off the baking paper from the side. Flip over onto a plate and remove the baking paper from the base, flip over again onto a serving dish and arrange the remaining salmon and watercress on top. Cut into slices and serve warm.

NUTRITION PER SERVE
Protein 20 g; Fat 15 g; Carbohydrate 2 g; Dietary Fibre 1.5 g; Cholesterol 295 mg; 956 kJ (228 cal)

Add the white wine to the onion and fennel and cook until tender.

Finely chop half the watercress, leaving the remainder as small sprigs.

Pour half the egg mixture into the tin and sprinkle with some smoked salmon.

HONEY MUSTARD CHICKEN DRUMETTES

Preparation time: 20 minutes +
  2 hours marinating
Cooking time: 45 minutes
Makes 24

⅓ cup (80 ml) oil
¼ cup (90 g) honey
¼ cup (60 ml) soy sauce
¼ cup (60 g) Dijon mustard
¼ cup (60 ml) lemon juice
4 cloves garlic, crushed
24 chicken drumettes (see Note)

1 To make the marinade, place the oil, honey, soy sauce, mustard, lemon juice and garlic in a large non-metallic dish and mix together thoroughly.

2 Trim the chicken of any excess fat, then place the drumettes in the dish with the marinade and toss until they are well coated. Cover and refrigerate them for at least 2 hours, or preferably overnight, turning them over 2–3 times to make sure the marinade covers every part of the chicken pieces.

3 Preheat the oven to moderately hot 200°C (400°F/Gas 6). Place the drumettes on a wire rack over a foil-lined baking tray. Bake them, turning and brushing them with the marinade 3–4 times, for 45 minutes, or until they are golden brown and cooked. Serve them immediately along with serviettes as people's fingers will get very sticky.

NOTE: Drumettes are the chicken wing with the wing tip removed. You can cook them a day in advance and reheat in a warm (160°C/315°F/ Gas 2–3) oven for 10–12 minutes.
VARIATION: For a teriyaki marinade, combine ½ cup (125 ml) teriyaki sauce, ¼ cup (60 ml) pineapple juice, 2 tablespoons honey, 1 tablespoon grated fresh ginger, 2 cloves crushed garlic and 1 teaspoon sesame oil in a bowl and mix well.

Trim the excess fat from the chicken drumettes.

Lay the chicken on a wire rack over a foil-lined baking tray to catch the drips.

THAI CHICKEN BALLS

Preparation time: 20 minutes
Total cooking time: 40 minutes
Serves 6

1 kg (2 lb) chicken mince
1 cup (80 g/2¾ oz) fresh
   breadcrumbs
4 spring onions, sliced

1 tablespoon ground coriander
1 cup (50 g/1¾ oz) chopped fresh
   coriander
3 tablespoons sweet chilli sauce
1–2 tablespoons lemon juice
oil, for frying

1 Preheat the oven to 200°C (400°F/Gas 6). Mix the mince and breadcrumbs in a large bowl.

2 Add the spring onion, ground and fresh coriander, chilli sauce and lemon juice and mix well. Using damp hands, form the mixture into evenly shaped balls that are either small enough to eat with your fingers or large enough to use as burgers.

3 Heat the oil in a deep frying pan, and shallow-fry the chicken balls in batches until browned all over. Place them on a baking tray and bake until cooked through. (The small chicken balls will take 5 minutes to cook and the larger ones will take 10–15 minutes.)

NUTRITION PER SERVE
Protein 40 g; Fat 8 g; Carbohydrate 10 g; Dietary Fibre 1 g; Cholesterol 85 mg; 1160 kJ (275 cal)

Mix the spring onion, coriander, chilli sauce and lemon juice into the mixture.

With damp hands, form the mixture into evenly shaped balls.

Fry the chicken balls in oil until they are browned on both sides.

VEGETABLE SHAPES WITH CREME FRAICHE AND FRIED LEEK

Preparation time: 25 minutes
Total cooking time: 45 minutes
Makes 35

2 (850 g in total) long thin orange
    sweet potatoes
5 beetroots
½ cup (125 g) crème fraîche
1 clove garlic, crushed
¼ teaspoon grated lime rind
oil, for deep-frying
2 leeks, cut lengthways into very fine
    slices

1 Bring two large saucepans of water to the boil over high heat and place the sweet potatoes in one saucepan and the beetroots in the other. Boil, covered, for 30–40 minutes, or until tender, adding more boiling water if it starts to evaporate. Drain separately and set aside until cool enough to touch. Remove the skins from the beetroots. Trim the ends from the beetroots and sweet potatoes and cut both into 1 cm slices. Using a biscuit cutter, cut the thin slices into shapes. Leave to drain on paper towels.

2 Place the crème fraîche, garlic and lime rind in a bowl and mix together well. Refrigerate until ready to use.

3 Fill a deep heavy-based saucepan one third full of oil and heat until a cube of bread dropped into the oil browns in 10 seconds. Cook the leek in four batches for 30 seconds, or until golden brown and crisp. Drain on crumpled paper towels and season with salt.

4 To assemble, place a teaspoon of the crème fraîche mixture on top of each vegetable shape and top with some fried leek.

NUTRITION PER VEGETABLE SHAPE
Protein 1 g; Fat 2 g; Carbohydrate 5.5 g; Dietary Fibre 1 g; Cholesterol 2.5 mg; 180 kJ (43 cal)

NOTE: You can make the crème fraîche mixture and deep-fry the leek a day before and keep them in separate airtight containers. Refrigerate the crème fraîche mixture to allow the flavours to infuse. If the leek softens, place on a baking tray and crisp in a hot oven for 5 minutes. Assemble at the last minute to prevent the crème fraîche running.

Using a biscuit cutter, cut the beetroot and sweet potato into shapes.

Cook the leek in batches until golden brown and crisp.

SWEET POTATO AND LENTIL PASTRY POUCHES

Preparation time: 45 minutes
Total cooking time: 55 minutes
Makes 32

2 tablespoons olive oil
1 large leek, finely chopped
2 cloves garlic, crushed
125 g button mushrooms, roughly
    chopped
2 teaspoons ground cumin
2 teaspoons ground coriander
1/2 cup (95 g) brown or green lentils
1/2 cup (125 g) red lentils
2 cups (500 ml) vegetable stock
300 g sweet potato, diced
4 tablespoons finely chopped fresh
    coriander leaves
8 sheets ready-rolled puff pastry
1 egg, lightly beaten
1/2 leek, extra, cut into 5 mm wide
    strips
200 g plain yoghurt
2 tablespoons grated Lebanese
    cucumber
1/2 teaspoon soft brown sugar

1 Preheat oven to 200°C (400°F/ Gas 6). Heat the oil in a saucepan and cook the leek for 2–3 minutes, or until soft. Add the garlic, cumin, mushrooms, and ground coriander and cook for 1 minute, or until fragrant.

2 Add the combined lentils and stock and bring to boil. Reduce heat and simmer for 20–25 minutes, or until the lentils are cooked, stirring occasionally. Add the sweet potato in the last 5 minutes.

3 Transfer to a bowl and stir in the coriander. Season to taste. Cool.

4 Cut the pastry sheets into four even squares. Place 1 1/4 tablespoons of filling into the centre of each square and bring the edges together to form a pouch. Pinch together, then tie each pouch with string. Lightly brush with egg and place on lined baking trays. Bake for 20–25 minutes, or until pastry is puffed and golden.

5 Soak the leek strips in boiling water for 30 seconds. Remove the string and re-tie with a piece of blanched leek. Put the yoghurt, cucumber and sugar in a bowl and mix well. Serve with the pouches.

NUTRITION PER PASTRY POUCH
Protein 5 g; Fat 11 g; Carbohydrate 20 g; Dietary Fibre 2 g; Cholesterol 17 mg; 835 kJ (200 cal)

Transfer to a bowl and stir in the coriander leaves.

Put the filling in the centre of each square, form a pouch and tie with string.

Blanch the long strips of leek by soaking them for 30 seconds in boiling water.

VEGETABLE FRITTATA WITH HUMMUS AND BLACK OLIVES

Preparation time: 35 minutes +
cooling time
Total cooking time: 40 minutes
<u>Makes:</u> 30 pieces

2 large red capsicums
600 g orange sweet potato,
cut into 1 cm slices
¼ cup (60 ml) olive oil
2 leeks, finely sliced
2 cloves garlic, crushed
250 g zucchini, thinly sliced
500 g eggplant, cut into 1 cm slices
8 eggs, lightly beaten
2 tablespoons finely chopped fresh
basil
1¼ cups (125 g) grated Parmesan
200 g ready-made hummus
black olives, pitted and halved, to
garnish

1 Cut the capsicums into large pieces, removing the seeds and membrane. Place, skin-side-up, under a grill until skin blackens and blisters. Cool in a plastic bag, then peel.

2 Cook the sweet potato in a saucepan of boiling water for 4–5 minutes, or until just tender. Then drain.

3 Heat 1 tablespoon of the oil in a deep round 23 cm frying pan and stir the leek and garlic over medium heat for 1 minute, or until soft. Add the zucchini and cook for 2 minutes, then remove from the pan.

4 Heat the remaining oil in the same pan and cook the eggplant in batches for 2 minutes each side, or until golden. Line the base of the pan with half the eggplant and spread with the leek mixture. Cover with the roasted capsicum, then the rest of the eggplant and the sweet potato.

5 Put the eggs, basil, Parmesan and pepper in a jug, mix and pour over the vegetables. Cook over low heat for 15 minutes, until almost cooked. Place the pan under a grill for 2–3 minutes, or until golden and cooked. Cool before inverting onto a board. Trim the edges and cut into 30 squares. Top each with hummus and half an olive.

NUTRITION PER PIECE
Protein 4.5 g; Fat 6 g; Carbohydrate 5 g; Dietary Fibre 2 g; Cholesterol 52 mg; 387 kJ (92 cal)

Lay the roasted capsicum pieces over the leek and zucchini mixture.

Pour the egg mixture over the vegetables so that they are covered.

Cook the frittata under a hot grill until it is golden brown on top.

ROSTI WITH SMOKED TROUT AND SALSA VERDE

Preparation time: 15 minutes
Cooking time: 30 minutes
Makes 32

1 small smoked trout
450 g floury potatoes (e.g. russet, King Edward or pontiac)
2 spring onions, thinly sliced
⅓ cup (80 ml) olive oil

SALSA VERDE
1½ cups (30 g) fresh flat-leaf parsley
1 cup (30 g) fresh basil
1 tablespoon capers, drained
1 tablespoon chopped gherkin or 4 cornichons (baby gherkins)
2 anchovies, drained
1 clove garlic, chopped
2 teaspoons Dijon mustard
¼ cup (60 ml) olive oil
1 tablespoon lemon juice

1 Remove the skin from the trout, pull the flesh from the bones and flake into pieces.

2 To make the salsa verde, place the parsley, basil, capers, gherkin, anchovies, garlic and mustard in a food processor and blend until finely chopped. While the motor is running, blend in the oil and lemon juice until mixed together. Season with pepper.

3 To make the rösti, peel and coarsely grate the potatoes. Squeeze out as much liquid as possible. Put the flesh in a bowl with the spring onion and mix together. Heat the oil in a large heavy-based frying pan over medium–high heat. To cook the rösti, take heaped teaspoons of the potato mixture, add to the pan in batches and press down with an egg flip to help the potato stay together. Cook for 2–3 minutes each side, or until crisp and golden. Drain on crumpled paper towels.

4 Top each rösti with a teaspoon of salsa verde then some flakes of trout. Serve the dish either warm or at room temperature.

NOTE: The rösti can be made 8 hours in advance as long as it is kept in an airtight container that has been lined with paper towels. Reheat for 5 minutes in a moderate 180°C (350°F/Gas 4) oven before serving.

Remove the flesh from the smoked trout, being careful to throw out any bones.

Blend the salsa verde ingredients together until they are finely chopped.

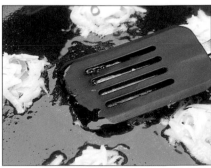

Cook the rösti in batches, slightly flattening each one with an egg flip.

PUMPKIN AND PESTO CHICKEN IN FILO PASTRY

Preparation time: 30 minutes
Total cooking time: 50 minutes
Serves 4

4 chicken breast fillets
1 tablespoon oil
250 g (8 oz) pumpkin
1 bunch English spinach
12 sheets filo pastry
100 g (3½ oz) butter, melted
¼ cup (25 g/¾ oz) dry
   breadcrumbs
100 g (3½ oz) ricotta
⅓ cup (90 g/3 oz) pesto
   (see Note)
1 tablespoon pine nuts, chopped

1 Preheat the oven to moderately hot 200°C (400°F/Gas 6). Season the chicken fillets with salt and pepper. Heat half the oil in a frying pan and fry the chicken until browned on both sides, then remove from the pan.

2 Cut the peeled pumpkin into 5 mm (¼ inch) slices. Heat the remaining oil in the same pan and fry the pumpkin until lightly browned on both sides. Allow to cool.

3 Put the spinach leaves into a pan of boiling water and stir until just wilted. Drain well and pat dry with paper towels. Layer 3 sheets of filo pastry, brushing each with some of the melted butter, sprinkling between layers with some of the breadcrumbs.

4 Wrap each chicken breast in a quarter of the spinach and place on one short side of the filo, leaving a gap of about 2 cm (¾ inch). Top the chicken with a quarter of the pumpkin slices, then spread a quarter of the ricotta down the centre of the pumpkin. Top with a tablespoon of the pesto.

5 Fold the sides of the pastry over the filling, then roll the parcel up until it sits on the unsecured end. Repeat with the remaining ingredients. Place the parcels on a lightly greased baking tray, brush with any remaining butter and sprinkle with the pine nuts. Bake for 15 minutes, cover loosely with foil and bake for a further 20 minutes, or until the pastry is golden brown.

NUTRITION PER SERVE
Protein 35 g; Fat 40 g; Carbohydrate 30 g; Dietary Fibre 2.5 g; Cholesterol 132 mg; 2635 kJ (630 cal)

NOTE: Bottled pesto is not suitable for this recipe—you can either make your own (see page 56) or use fresh pesto from a deli.

Remove the spinach from the boiling water and drain well.

Top the chicken with a quarter of the pumpkin slices.

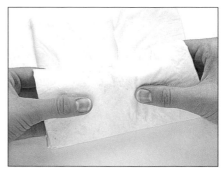

Roll the parcel up until it sits on the unsecured end.

TARTLETS

The beauty of these tartlets is that the pastry cases can be made ahead of time, so that you just need to make the toppings on the day. Each recipe makes 30 delicious tartlets.

Basic pastry cases

2 cups (250 g) plain flour
125 g chilled butter, chopped
1 egg

Preheat the oven to moderately hot 200°C (400°F/Gas 6). Lightly grease 30 mini muffin holes. Sift the flour into a large bowl and rub the butter in with your fingertips until the mixture resembles fine breadcrumbs. Make a well in the centre, add the egg and mix with a flat-bladed knife, using a cutting action until it comes together in beads. If the dough seems to be too dry, add a little cold water. Press the dough into a ball on a lightly floured surface, then wrap it in plastic wrap and refrigerate it for 30 minutes.

Roll out the dough between two sheets of baking paper to 2 mm thick and cut out 30 rounds with a 6 cm cutter. Press a round into each muffin hole. Prick the bases with a fork and bake for 6–8 minutes, or until dry and golden. If they puff up, use a clean tea towel to press out any air pockets. Cool the cases before filling with the topping of your choice. Makes 30.

NOTE: The pastry cases can be made 2–3 days early and then be kept in an airtight container. If they go soft, crispen them on a baking tray in a warm 170°C (325°F/Gas 3) oven for 5 minutes.

Cherry tomato and bocconcini

Ready in about 1 hour 30 minutes.

300 g cherry tomatoes, quartered
2 tablespoons olive oil
1 clove garlic, crushed
200 g bocconcini, quartered
80 g chopped Kalamata olives
1 tablespoon extra virgin olive oil
1 tablespoon torn fresh basil

oil, for deep-frying
30 small fresh basil leaves
30 cooked tartlet cases

Preheat the oven to moderately hot 200°C (400°F/Gas 6). Combine the tomatoes, olive oil and garlic in a roasting tin and bake for 15 minutes, or until golden. Cool, then transfer to a bowl and add the bocconcini, olives, extra virgin olive oil and torn basil, then season and gently toss.

Fill a small saucepan one third full of oil and heat to 180°C (350°F), or until a cube of bread browns in 15 seconds. Deep-fry the basil in batches for 30 seconds, or until crisp. Drain. Spoon the mixture into the cases and top with a basil leaf.

Creamed egg with roe
Ready in under 1 hour.

4 eggs and 4 egg yolks
75 g unsalted butter
4 tablespoons roe
30 cooked tartlet cases

Lightly beat the eggs and egg yolks together. Melt the butter in a small saucepan over very low heat, then add the eggs and whisk slowly and constantly for 5–6 minutes, or until the mixture is thick and creamy but the eggs are not scrambled. Remove from the heat straight away and season to taste with salt and cracked black pepper. Fill each pastry case with 1 teaspoon of the creamed egg mixture, then top with ¼ teaspoon of roe before serving.

Mushroom ragout
Ready in about 1 hour 15 minutes.

50 g butter
4 spring onions, chopped
2 cloves garlic, chopped
150 g small Swiss brown or shiitake mushrooms, thinly sliced
100 g oyster mushrooms, cut into eighths
50 g enoki mushrooms, trimmed, pulled apart, sliced lengthways
3 teaspoons plain flour
2 tablespoons chicken stock or water
2 tablespoons sake
⅓ cup (80 ml) thick cream
snow pea sprouts, stalks removed
30 cooked tartlet cases

Melt the butter in a large frying pan over medium heat, add the spring onion and garlic and cook for 1 minute. Add the mushrooms and cook, stirring, for 3–4 minutes, or until soft. Add the flour and stir for another minute. Pour in the stock and sake and stir for 1 minute, or until evaporated, then add the cream and cook for 1 minute, or until thickened. Season. Spoon into the prepared pastry cases and top each one with a snow pea sprout leaf.

Asian-flavoured crab
Ready in under 1 hour.

¼ cup (60 ml) lime juice
1 tablespoon fish sauce
1 tablespoon grated palm sugar or soft brown sugar
300 g fresh crab meat, shredded and well drained
2 tablespoons chopped fresh coriander leaves
1 tablespoon chopped fresh Vietnamese mint
1 small fresh red chilli, finely chopped
2 kaffir lime leaves, finely shredded
30 cooked tartlet cases

Combine the lime juice, fish sauce and sugar in a bowl and stir until the sugar is dissolved. Mix in the rest of the ingredients, then spoon into the prepared pastry cases and serve.

From left: Cherry tomato and bocconcini, Creamed egg with roe, Mushroom ragout, Asian-flavoured crab.

ROAST VEGETABLE AND GOAT'S CHEESE ROULADE

Preparation time: 1 hour +
    2 hours refrigeration
Cooking time: 30 minutes
Makes 48

PESTO
2 cups (60 g) fresh basil
30 g pine nuts, toasted
1 clove garlic
50 ml olive oil
1/4 cup (25 g) finely grated
    Parmesan

4 RED CAPSICUMS
1 eggplant, sliced lengthways into
    5 mm slices
1/4 cup (60 ml) olive oil, plus extra
    for brushing
100 g soft goat's cheese, lightly
    beaten until smooth
15 large fresh basil leaves
1 loaf olive bread, crusts removed
    and cut into 5 mm thick slices

1 To make the pesto, place the basil, pine nuts and garlic in a food processor and process until finely chopped. With the motor running, add the olive oil in a thin stream until well combined. Transfer to a bowl, add the Parmesan, season and mix well. Place plastic wrap directly onto the surface of the pesto and refrigerate until needed.

2 Cut the capsicums into halves, removing the seeds and membrane. Place, skin-side-up, under a hot grill and cook for 10 minutes, or until the skin blackens and blisters. Place in a plastic bag, leave to cool, then peel away the skin, leaving the capsicum as intact as possible. Trim the ends so that the pieces are even and flat.

3 Brush the eggplant slices with olive oil and cook on a very hot chargrill pan for 3–5 minutes each side, or until cooked.

4 To assemble sprinkle a flat work surface with water and place a 50 cm long piece of plastic wrap on top (the water helps secure the plastic).

Lay half the capsicum strips on the plastic to form a rectangle 30 cm x 13 cm. Lightly season the capsicum. Layer half the eggplant over the capsicum, then spread with half the cheese to cover the entire rectangle. Season. Lay half the basil leaves in a single layer over the cheese. Using the plastic wrap, tightly roll up the capsicum lengthways, sealing the ends. Wrap tightly in foil and twist the ends firmly. Repeat with the remaining ingredients to make another roll, then refrigerate for at least 2 hours.

5 Preheat the oven to a moderate 180°C (350°F/Gas 4). Stamp out 48 rounds from the olive bread using a cutter that is the same width as the roulade, which should ideally be 4 cm diameter. Next, brush the rounds lightly with olive oil and bake them for 5–10 minutes, or until they are crisp and lightly browned. Then spread 1/2 teaspoon of pesto on each crouton. Remove the plastic from the roulade and, using a very sharp knife, slice it into 5 mm thick slices and finish off by placing one slice onto each croûton.

Lay the strips of chargrilled eggplant over the capsicum slices.

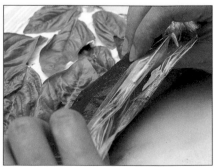

Use the plastic wrap to help you tightly roll up the vegetables.

GOAT'S CHEESE, WALNUT AND BEETROOT CREPE ROLLS

Preparation time: 20 minutes +
30 minutes standing
Cooking time: 1 hour 50 minutes
Makes 48

2 small or 1 medium beetroot
2 cloves garlic, unpeeled
1 teaspoon olive oil
1 cup (125 g) plain flour
2 eggs
1½ cups (375 ml) milk
30 g butter, melted and cooled
1 cup (100 g) walnut halves
40 g butter, extra
150 g soft goat's cheese
48 fresh basil leaves

1 Preheat the oven to moderately hot 200°C (400°F/Gas 6). Scrub the beetroot clean. Sit the beetroot and garlic on a piece of foil, add the oil, season with salt and pepper, then wrap up in the foil. Place on a baking tray and roast for 1–1¼ hours, or until tender. Remove from the oven, and when cool enough to handle, peel the skin from the beetroot and garlic. Place the flesh in a food processor and blend until finely chopped. Reduce the oven to moderate 180°C (350°F/Gas 4).

2 Sift the flour into a large bowl and make a well in the centre. Gradually add the combined eggs, milk and melted butter, whisking the mixture to a smooth batter. Add the beetroot mixture, cover and leave for 30 minutes.

3 Spread the walnuts on a baking tray and roast for 5–10 minutes, or until lightly golden. Finely chop.

4 Transfer the beetroot mixture to a jug for easier pouring. Melt 1 teaspoon of the extra butter in a crepe pan or frying pan. Pour one eighth of the mixture into the pan, shaking the pan gently to spread the mixture out thinly. Cook for 1–2 minutes, or until bubbles appear around the edges. Flip gently with a palette knife or spatula and cook the other side for 1 minute, or until just set. Transfer to a plate and repeat with the remaining ingredients to make eight crepes.

5 Beat the goat's cheese in a bowl until it becomes smooth then season to taste.

6 Lay one crepe out on a work surface and gently spread it with one eighth of the cheese. Sprinkle with one eighth of the walnuts and 6 basil leaves. Roll up gently, but firmly, then repeat with the remaining ingredients to make eight rolls. Remove the ends and slice each roll into six 2 cm slices.

NOTE: The crepes can be made up to 2 days in advance. Store in the fridge with a piece of plastic wrap between each one. Assemble up to 2 hours before serving and keep in the fridge until ready to serve.

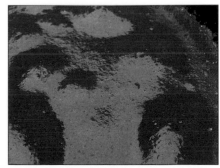
When the beetroot and garlic are cool enough to touch, peel off the skins.

Cook the beetroot batter until bubbles start to appear around the edges.

FINGER FOOD

It is difficult to predict how much finger food to serve at a party, but as a general rule, allow 4–6 pieces per person per hour.

Turkey meatballs

Combine 600 g turkey mince, 2 crushed garlic cloves, 2 tablespoons finely chopped fresh mint, 2 teaspoons finely chopped fresh rosemary and 2 tablespoons mango lime chutney. With wetted hands, roll tablespoons of the mixture into balls. Heat 1 tablespoon oil in a large frying pan over medium heat and cook the turkey balls for 5 minutes, or until cooked through. Combine 200 g plain yoghurt, 2 tablespoons finely chopped fresh mint and 2 teaspoons mango lime chutney. Serve with the turkey balls.
Makes 30

Left to right: Turkey meatballs; Cucumber rounds with avocado and turkey; Pesto dip; Mini egg florentines; Noodle nests with smoked salmon tartare; Steamed prawn wontons.

Cucumber rounds with avocado and turkey

Slice 3 Lebanese cucumbers into 1.5 cm rounds to make 30 pieces. Cut 30 rounds from 100 g sliced smoked turkey using a 3 cm cutter. Combine half a mashed avocado with 1 crushed garlic clove, 2 tablespoons cranberry sauce and 2 tablespoons sour cream. Spoon 1 teaspoon of avocado mixture onto each cucumber round and top with a round of turkey. Spoon a little cranberry sauce on top and garnish with a snow pea sprout.
Makes 30

Pesto dip

Process 2 cups (100 g) firmly packed fresh basil leaves, ½ cup (50 g) freshly grated Parmesan, ½ cup (80 g) toasted pine nuts and 1 crushed garlic clove in a food processor until smooth. With the motor running, gradually add ¼ cup (60 ml) olive oil. Add 1 cup (250 g) ricotta cheese and ½ cup (125 g) sour cream, and process until smooth. Season with salt and pepper. Serve with crackers.
Makes 2 cups (500 ml)

Mini egg florentines

Preheat the oven to moderate 180°C (350°F/Gas 4). To make the hollandaise sauce, process 2 egg yolks and 2 teaspoons lemon juice in a food processor for 10 seconds. With the motor running, add 85 g melted butter in a thin stream. Add 2 teaspoons finely chopped fresh basil and process until combined. Using a 4 cm cutter, cut out 24 rounds from 8 slices of white bread. Brush the rounds with oil and bake for 10–15 minutes, or until golden brown. Melt 20 g butter in a pan, add 50 g baby English spinach leaves and toss until just wilted. Place a little spinach on each bread round, top with ½ hard-boiled quail egg and drizzle with hollandaise sauce and freshly ground black pepper. *Makes 24*

Noodle nests with smoked salmon tartare

Preheat the oven to moderately hot 200°C (400°F/Gas 6). Pour boiling water over 200 g fresh flat egg noodles, soak for 5 minutes, then drain well and pat dry. Divide the noodles among 30 greased mini muffin holes, pressing down to form 'nests'. Brush lightly with olive oil and bake for 15 minutes. Remove from the oven, turn out onto a wire rack and return to the oven for 5 minutes to crisp. Combine 200 g diced smoked salmon, 1 tablespoon extra virgin olive oil, 3 teaspoons white wine vinegar, 1½ cup (125 g) whole-egg mayonnaise, 1 crushed garlic clove and 1 tablespoon finely chopped fresh dill. Place 1 heaped teaspoon of the mixture into each noodle basket and garnish with fresh dill and pepper. *Makes 30*

Steamed prawn wontons

Pour boiling water over ¾ cup (15 g) sliced dried Chinese mushrooms and stand for 5 minutes. Drain well and finely chop. Combine with 1 tablespoon sake, 1 tablespoon grated fresh ginger, 1 teaspoon sesame oil and 2 teaspoons sweet chilli sauce. Peel and devein 24 raw prawns, leaving the tails intact. Cut the prawns in half, and set aside the tail end of the prawn. Finely chop the remaining prawns and add to the mushroom mixture. Put a heaped teaspoon of the mixture in the centre of a gow gee wrapper. Place the prawn tail in the centre, standing up. Brush the edges of the wrapper with water and gather up to form a parcel, leaving the prawn tail exposed. Steam in a bamboo steamer for 5 minutes, or until cooked. Combine ¼ cup (60 ml) soy sauce, 1 tablespoon fish sauce, 1 tablespoon lime juice and ¼ cup (60 ml) sweet chilli sauce for a dipping sauce. *Makes 24*

Seafood pyramids with Asian sauce

Combine 200 g chopped scallops (roe removed), 8 finely chopped spring onions, 4 tablespoons Japanese breadcrumbs, 1/3 cup (20 g) finely chopped fresh coriander, 2 crushed garlic cloves, 1 teaspoon finely chopped kaffir lime leaves and 1/2 teaspoon sesame oil. Place 2 teaspoons of the mixture in the centre of each of 24 won ton wrappers. Brush the edges with water and bring the corners up to meet, pushing the edges together to form a pyramid shape. Deep-fry in hot oil until crisp and golden. Drain well. For the dipping sauce, combine 2 tablespoons lime juice, 1 tablespoon sake, 2 teaspoons soy sauce, 1/4 teaspoon sesame oil and 1 teaspoon grated fresh ginger and serve with the pyramids. *Makes 24*

Left to right: Seafood pyramids with Asian sauce; Black sesame seed tarts with marinated feta; Tex Mex cheese crisps; Roasted capsicum and olive pâté

Black sesame seed tarts with marinated feta

Preheat the oven to moderately hot 200°C (400°F/Gas 6). Combine 200 g diced feta, 1 1/2 cups (300 g) peeled, seeded and diced tomatoes, 1/2 cup (75 g) pitted and diced black olives, 1 teaspoon finely chopped fresh thyme, 2 crushed garlic cloves and 1 tablespoon extra virgin olive oil. Set aside. Add 125 g chopped butter to 2 cups (250 g) sifted plain flour in a large bowl and rub together with your fingertips until it resembles fine breadcrumbs. Stir in 1/2 cup (50 g) finely grated fresh Parmesan and 1 tablespoon black sesame seeds. Make a well in the centre, add 1 egg and mix with a flat-bladed knife, using a cutting action until the mixture comes together in beads (add a little cold water if it is too dry). On a lightly floured surface, press together into a ball, then wrap in plastic wrap and refrigerate for 10 minutes. Roll the dough out to 2 mm thick between two sheets of baking paper. Remove the paper and cut out 30 rounds using a 6 cm cutter. Gently press into two lightly greased mini muffin tins and bake for 10 minutes, or until dry and golden. Cool and place 1 heaped teaspoon feta filling into each pastry shell. Garnish with fresh thyme leaves and serve immediately. *Makes 30*

Tex Mex cheese crisps

Preheat the oven to hot 210°C (415°F/Gas 6–7) and brush two baking trays with melted butter. Mix 1¾ cups (220 g) plain flour, ½ teaspoon chilli powder, 1 teaspoon garlic salt, ½ teaspoon ground paprika and 200 g chopped butter in a food processor for 30 seconds, or until the mixture is fine and crumbly. Add 1 lightly beaten egg and 1½ cups (185 g) grated Cheddar, and process for a further 10 seconds, or until the ingredients are just combined. Turn the dough onto a lightly floured surface. Knead for 1 minute, or until smooth, and shape into a ball. Cover with plastic wrap and refrigerate for 20 minutes. Roll out the dough to a 3 mm thickness on a lightly floured surface and cut into shapes using a 5 or 6 cm star-shaped biscuit cutter. Place on the baking trays, allowing room for spreading. Refrigerate any stars which do not fit on the trays until you have a spare tray. Bake for 12–14 minutes, or until crisp. Leave the biscuits on the tray for 2 minutes before transferring to a wire rack to cool. *Makes 95*

Roasted capsicum and olive pâté

Process 2 (600 g) oven-roasted and peeled capsicums, 1 tablespoon finely chopped fresh basil, 1 tablespoon finely chopped fresh flat-leaf parsley, 1 crushed garlic clove and 1 teaspoon lemon juice in a food processor until smooth. Add 1 cup (250 g) softened cream cheese and ½ cup (125 g) ricotta cheese and process until combined. In a small bowl, sprinkle 2 teaspoons gelatine over 1 tablespoon warm water and stir until dissolved. Stir through the capsicum mixture with ⅓ cup (50 g) chopped pitted black olives. Season well. Spoon into an oval bowl and refrigerate overnight. Sprinkle with 2 tablespoons toasted chopped pistachio kernels. Serve with crackers. *Makes 2½ cups (600 ml)*

BREAD TREE

Preparation time: 30 minutes +
1 hour 30 minutes proving
Total cooking time: 30 minutes
Makes 16 rolls

7 g sachet dried yeast
1 teaspoon sugar
2 tablespoons plain flour
2/3 cup (170 ml) lukewarm milk
3 cups (375 g) plain flour, extra
1/3 cup (50 g) polenta
2 tablespoons olive oil
1 clove garlic, crushed
1/4 cup (15 g) finely chopped
    fresh basil
1/4 cup (15 g) finely chopped
    fresh parsley
2 tablespoons finely chopped
    fresh tarragon
2 tablespoons finely chopped
    fresh coriander
2 tablespoons pepitas
    (pumpkin seeds)
1/3 cup (35 g) grated Parmesan
2 teaspoons milk, extra
extra pepitas, to garnish

1 Combine the dried yeast, sugar and flour in a bowl. Add the milk gradually and mix until smooth. Stand, covered, in warm place for 10 minutes, or until foamy. Sift the extra flour, polenta and 1 teaspoon salt into a bowl. Make a well in the centre, add the oil, garlic, herbs, pepitas, yeast mixture and 2/3 cup (170 ml) lukewarm water. Using a flat-bladed knife, mix to a soft dough.

2 Turn the dough onto a lightly floured surface and knead for 3 minutes, or until smooth. Shape into a ball. Cover and leave in a large, lightly oiled bowl in a warm place for 1 hour, or until well risen, then return to the lightly floured work surface and knead for 2 minutes. Preheat the oven to hot 210°C (415°F/Gas 6–7).

3 Divide the dough evenly into 17 pieces. Knead one portion at a time on a floured surface until smooth. Flatten and sprinkle a little Parmesan in the centre and fold the dough over to form a ball. Repeat with the remaining dough.

4 To assemble the tree, place the bread on a greased baking tray in a tree shape, beginning with a row of five balls, followed by a row of four, then three, two and one balls. Knead the remaining two balls together and shape into an oval, flatten slightly and place at the base of the tree. Leave, covered with plastic wrap, in a warm place for 20 minutes, or until well risen. Brush the tree with milk, decorate with extra pepitas, then score the base with a sharp knife or scalpel. Bake for 30 minutes, or until browned and cooked through. Stand for 5 minutes before transferring to a wire rack to cool.

NUTRITION PER ROLL
Protein 2.5 g; Fat 3.5 g; Carbohydrate 8 g; Dietary Fibre 0.5 g; Cholesterol 3.5 mg; 307 kJ (75 cal)

Use a flat-bladed knife to combine the mixture to a soft dough.

Sprinkle a little Parmesan in the centre of each portion and fold over to form a ball.

Decorate the tree with pepitas and score the base with a sharp knife.

DRESSED-UP BABY POTATOES

Preparation time: 25 minutes
Cooking time: 45 minutes
Makes 24

24 even bite-sized new potatoes,
    washed and dried
1/3 cup (80 ml) olive oil
1 tablespoon capers, patted dry
1 rasher bacon
1 tablespoon cream
10 g butter
1/2 cup (125 g) sour cream
1 tablespoon chopped fresh chives
1 tablespoon red or black caviar

1 Preheat the oven to moderate 180°C (350°F/Gas 4). Line a baking tray with baking paper. Place the potatoes in a bowl and toss with half the olive oil. Sprinkle with salt and black pepper, then put on the baking tray and bake for 40 minutes, or until cooked through, rotating them 2–3 times so that they brown off evenly.

2 Meanwhile, heat the remaining oil in a frying pan and cook the capers over high heat, or until they open into small flowers. Drain on paper towels. Cook the bacon under a hot grill until crispy. Cool, then finely chop.

3 Remove the potatoes from the oven. When cool enough to handle, cut a thin lid from each potato. Discard the lids. Use a melon baller or small teaspoon to scoop out the flesh from the middle of the potatoes, leaving a 1 cm border. Put the potato flesh in a bowl and mash thoroughly with the cream, butter and salt and black pepper. Spoon the mash back into the potatoes.

4 Top each potato with a small dollop of sour cream. Divide the potatoes into four groups of six and then use a separate topping for each group: so the capers, bacon, chives and caviar.

NOTE: The potatoes can even be pre-prepared up to the stage when they are filled with mash. To reheat, place them, covered, in a warm 160°C (315°F/Gas 2–3) oven for 10 minutes, cool them slightly, then add the toppings.

Turn the potatoes once or twice during cooking so they brown evenly.

Scoop out a small amount of flesh from the potatoes, reserving the flesh.

SAVOURY SHORTBREAD WITH TOMATO JAM

Preparation time: 30 minutes +
  2 hours refrigeration
Cooking time: 3 hours
Makes 48

TOMATO JAM
5 vine-ripened tomatoes, quartered
1 teaspoon fennel seeds
1/2 teaspoon cumin seeds
1 small red onion
2 cloves garlic
100 ml olive oil
1 1/2 tablespoons soft brown sugar
1 1/2 tablespoons red wine vinegar

SHORTBREAD
250 g butter, at room temperature
1 tablespoon hot water
3 1/4 cups (405 g) plain flour
1/2 teaspoon sweet paprika
300 g bacon, finely chopped
1 1/4 cups (125 g) grated Parmesan
60 g poppy seeds
small fresh basil leaves, to garnish

1 Preheat the oven to moderate 180°C (350°F/Gas 4). Place the tomatoes on a roasting tray and roast for 30 minutes. Cool slightly, then purée in a blender or food processor until just smooth. Toast the fennel and cumin seeds in a dry frying pan for 1–2 minutes, or until fragrant. Cool slightly, then grind the seeds to a powder.

2 Purée the onion, garlic, ground spices and half the olive oil in a food processor until the mixture is well combined.

3 Heat the remaining olive oil in a large saucepan and cook the onion mixture over low heat for 25–30 minutes, or until the onion is just beginning to caramelise. Add the sugar and vinegar and cook for a further 2 minutes, then stir in the tomato mixture. Cook over very low heat, stirring occasionally, for 1–1 1/2 hours, or until the paste is thick and there is very little liquid remaining. Remove from the heat and allow to cool.

4 To make the shortbread, beat the butter in a bowl until pale. Gradually add the hot water. Sift the flour and paprika into the bowl and mix with a wooden spoon until smooth. Stir in the bacon, Parmesan and 1/4 cup (60 ml) water, then season well with cracked black pepper, adding more water if necessary. Roll into four logs 3 cm thick. Wrap in plastic wrap and refrigerate for 2 hours. Spread the poppy seeds out on a clean work surface and roll the logs in them until evenly coated.

5 Preheat the oven to warm 170°C (325°F/Gas 3) and lightly grease

two baking trays. Slice the logs into 5 mm thick slices. Place on the prepared trays and bake for 15–18 minutes, or until pale and crisp. Then cool them completely.

6 To serve the shortbread, top with 1 teaspoon tomato jam and a small basil leaf.

NOTE: The jam will keep for up to 4 weeks in the refrigerator. The shortbread can be made up to 1 week in advance and stored in single layers in an airtight container. Variations: Grated Cheddar, chopped fresh herbs, finely chopped nuts or a spice mix can be added for flavour.

Cook the tomato jam until it is thick and most of the liquid has evaporated.

Roll each of the shortbread logs in the poppy seeds.

MINI CHERRY GALETTES

Preparation time: 30 minutes
Cooking time: 30 minutes
Makes 30

670 g jar pitted morello cherries, drained
30 g unsalted butter
1 1/2 tablespoons caster sugar
1 egg yolk
1/2 teaspoon vanilla essence
1/2 cup (95 g) ground almonds
1 tablespoon plain flour
2 sheets ready-rolled puff pastry, thawed

icing sugar, for dusting
1/2 cup (160 g) cherry jam

1 Preheat the oven to moderate 180°C (350°F/Gas 4). Line a baking tray with baking paper. Spread the cherries onto several sheets of paper towel to absorb any excess liquid. Combine the butter and sugar in a bowl and beat until creamy. Add the egg yolk and vanilla, then stir in the combined almonds and flour and refrigerate until they are required.

2 Cut 30 rounds from the pastry sheets using a 5 cm round cutter. Place half the rounds on the prepared tray and lightly prick them all over with a fork. Cover with another sheet of baking paper and weigh down with another baking tray—this prevents the pastry from rising during cooking. Cook for 10 minutes, remove from the oven and allow to cool on the trays. Repeat with the remaining rounds. Leave the oven on.

3 Place 1 level teaspoon of almond mixture in the centre of each cooled pastry round, then press three cherries onto the almond mixture.

4 Bake for another 10 minutes or until lightly browned. Cool slightly then dust lightly with icing sugar. Place the jam in a cup, stand in a saucepan of hot water and stir until melted. Glaze the cherries by brushing them with the warmed jam.

NOTE: The almond topping can be prepared up to 4 days in advance. Assemble on the day of the party so that they don't go soggy.

Beat the butter and sugar together until a creamy consistency is reached.

Prick each of the pastry rounds with the tines of a fork.

Firmly press three cherries onto the almond mixture.

MINI MUD CAKES

Preparation time: 1 hour
Cooking time: 35 minutes
Makes 30

¾ cup (185 g) caster sugar
175 g dark chocolate, chopped
90 g unsalted butter, chopped
2 eggs, lightly beaten
2 tablespoons brandy
½ cup (60 g) plain flour
½ cup (60 g) self-raising flour
¼ cup (30 g) cocoa powder
50 g milk chocolate melts
200 g dark chocolate melts, chopped
½ cup (125 ml) cream

1 Preheat the oven to moderate 180°C (350°F/Gas 4). Lightly grease the base and sides of a 20 cm x 30 cm baking tin. Cover the base and two long sides with baking paper. Place the sugar, chocolate, butter and ½ cup (60 ml) water in a small saucepan and stir over low heat for about 5 minutes, or until the chocolate has melted completely. Then remove from the heat, cool to room temperature then stir in the eggs and brandy.

2 Sift the flours and cocoa into a bowl and make a well in the centre. Pour the chocolate mixture into the well. Mix and pour into the prepared tin. Bake for about 20–25 minutes, or until a skewer inserted into the centre comes out clean. Cool in the tin for 5 minutes before inverting onto a wire cake rack to cool.

3 Dip a 3 cm round cutter in hot water and cut out 30 rounds of cake, re-dipping the cutter between each round (this makes a neater edge). Roll the cut surface gently on the bench to press in any crumbs. Place the little cakes, top-side-down, on a wire cake rack over an oven tray.

4 To make chocolate curls, place the milk chocolate melts in a heatproof bowl. Bring a saucepan of water to the boil, then remove the pan from the heat. Sit the bowl over the pan, making sure the base of the bowl does not sit in the water. Stir occasionally until the chocolate has melted. Spread the chocolate fairly thinly over a marble board or cool baking tray and leave at room temperature until just set. Using the edge of a sharp knife at a 45 degree angle, scrape over the top of the chocolate. The strips will curl as they come away—don't press too hard. If the chocolate has set too firmly, the curls will break. Leave in a warm place and try again.

5 Place the dark chocolate melts in a bowl. Heat the cream until almost boiling and pour over the chocolate; leave for 2 minutes, then stir until the chocolate melts and is smooth. Spoon the chocolate mixture evenly over the cakes, reheating gently if it becomes too thick. Tap the tray gently to settle the chocolate, top each cake with a chocolate curl and allow to set. Use a palette knife to remove from the cake rack.

NOTE: Un-iced mud cakes will keep in an airtight container for 3 days in a cool place or for 2 months in the freezer.

Roll the cake rounds on the bench so that the crumbs are pushed in.

Scrape the chocolate with a sharp knife at a 45 degree angle.

CHOC-DIPPED ICE CREAM BALLS

Preparation time: 30 minutes + freezing
Cooking time: 10 minutes
<u>Makes 36</u>

500 g good-quality ice cream (use vanilla or a mixture of vanilla, pistachio and chocolate)
150 g dark chocolate
150 g white chocolate
150 g milk chocolate
2 tablespoons toasted shelled walnuts, roughly chopped
2 tablespoons shelled pistachios, roughly chopped
2 tablespoons toasted shredded coconut

1 Line two large baking trays with baking paper and place in the freezer to chill. Working quickly, use a melon baller to form 36 balls of ice cream and place on the chilled baking trays. Place a cocktail stick in each ice cream ball. Return to the freezer for 1 hour to freeze hard.

2 Place the chocolate in three separate heatproof bowls. Bring a saucepan of water to the boil, then remove the pan from the heat. Sit one bowl at a time over the pan, making sure the base of the bowl does not sit in the water. Stir occasionally until the chocolate has melted. Remove the bowl from the heat and set aside to cool; the chocolate should remain liquid; if it hardens, repeat.

3 Put the walnuts, pistachios and coconut in three separate small bowls. Working with 12 of the ice cream balls, dip one at a time quickly in the dark chocolate, then into the bowl with the walnuts. Return to the freezer. Repeat the process with another 12 balls, dipping them in the melted white chocolate and the pistachios. Dip the last 12 balls in the milk chocolate, then the toasted coconut. Freeze all the ice cream balls for 1 hour.

NOTE: Storage: Ice cream balls can be prepared up to 2 weeks in advance and kept in a single layer in an airtight container.

Scoop ice cream balls with a melon baller and place on chilled baking trays.

Dip the ice cream balls in the melted dark chocolate.

Dip the chocolate-covered balls in the toasted walnuts.

WARM DRINKS

Steaming hot chocolate drinks, mulled wine and hot toddies bring out the Christmas traditionalist in us all. What an ideal way to warm the body and the soul!

Chocolate hazelnut drink

Place 2 cups (500 ml) milk, ¼ cup (80 g) chocolate hazelnut spread and 50 g finely chopped dark chocolate in a pan and heat slowly, without boiling. Stir constantly for 5 minutes, or until the chocolate has melted. Divide between 2 mugs and top with whipped cream and roughly chopped roasted hazelnuts. *Serves 2*

Brandied apple cider

Thinly slice an apple into discs, discarding the ends—do not core. Place the apple in a large heavy-based pan and add 1 bottle (375 ml) alcoholic cider and ½ cup (125 ml) brandy or Calvados. Heat until almost boiling—do not boil. Serve in heatproof glasses. *Serves 2*

Hot toddy

Put 2 teaspoons soft brown sugar, 2 slices of lemon, 2 cinnamon sticks, 6 whole cloves, ¼ cup (60 ml) whisky and 2 cups (500 ml) boiling water in a heatproof jug. Stir to combine and leave to infuse for a few minutes, then strain through a sieve. Add more sugar, if desired. *Serves 2*

*Left to right: Chocolate hazelnut drink;
Brandied apple cider; Hot toddy;
Hot buttered rum; Hot caramel and
vanilla milkshake; Mulled wine.*

Hot buttered rum

Place 2 teaspoons sugar, 1/2 cup
(125 ml) rum and 1 cup (250 ml)
boiling water in a heatproof jug.
Stir to dissolve the sugar, then
divide between 2 mugs. Stir
1–2 teaspoons softened unsalted
butter into each mug and serve.
Serves 2

Hot caramel and vanilla milkshake

Slowly heat 2 cups (500 ml)
milk in a pan—be careful not
to boil. Add 50 g hard caramels
and heat until melted, stirring
occasionally. Place in a blender
with 1–2 scoops vanilla ice
cream, and blend briefly until
smooth. Pour the mixture into
2 tall glasses. *Serves 2*

Mulled wine

Stick 12 cloves into 2 oranges
and place in a pan with 1/4 cup
(60 g) sugar, 1/2–1 whole nutmeg,
grated, 4 cinnamon sticks and
2 sliced lemons. Add 2 cups
(500 ml) water and bring to
the boil, then reduce the heat
and simmer for 20 minutes. Cool,
then strain. Place the mixture
in a pan and add 3 cups (750 ml)
full-bodied red wine and heat
until almost boiling—do not boil
or the alcohol will evaporate off.
Serve in heatproof glasses. *Serves 6*

CHILLED DRINKS

To set the party mood, the look of a cocktail is almost as important as the taste. Serve strong alcoholic drinks in small tumblers or glasses, and mixed and non-alcoholic drinks in goblets or highball glasses.

Pineapple crush

Peel and cube a fresh pineapple and place it in a blender with 2 cups (270 g) crushed ice. Blend until smooth and then add to a bowl with 1 litre ginger beer and stir to mix. Serve with a fresh piece of pineapple for garnish. *Serves 4*

Frozen passionfruit margarita

Put 80 ml tequila, 30 ml Cointreau, 40 ml lime juice and the sieved pulp and juice of 6 passionfruit in a blender with 1 cup (135 g) crushed ice in a blender and whizz together. Dip the rim of 2 glasses in lemon juice and salt, then pour in the margarita. Garnish with lime slices. *Serves 2*

Peach cup

Cut 2 ripe peaches in half, remove the stones and slice thinly. Put these in a bowl with 1 bottle (750 ml) peach brandy, 750 ml peach juice, 1 bottle sparkling rosé and 1 bottle soda water. Stir together and serve garnished with mint sprigs. *Serves 12*

Left to right: Pineapple crush,
Frozen passionfruit margarita;
Peach cup; Strawberry Champagne punch;
Watermelon cooler, Mint julep.

Strawberry Champagne punch

Hull and slice 250 g strawberries and place them in a punch bowl. Add 50 g caster sugar, 1/2 cup (125 ml) Grand Marnier or Cointreau and 30 ml Grenadine and leave to stand. Just before serving, add 2 bottles chilled Champagne and 1 bottle soda water. *Serves 12*

Watermelon cooler

Cut 1/2 large or 1 small watermelon into pieces and remove the seeds. Put in a blender with 1–2 cm fresh ginger and 1 cup (250 ml) orange juice and blend until smooth. Pour over crushed ice to serve. (For a decorative effect, cut a slice off the top of the watermelon and scoop out the inside, and use this as a serving bowl for the finished drink.) Serve in highball glasses. *Serves 4*

Mint julep

Place the rind of 3 lemons in a pan with 1 cup (250 g) sugar and 1 cup (250 ml) water. Dissolve the sugar slowly and bring to the boil. Reduce the heat and simmer for 5 minutes, then strain and leave to cool. Juice the lemons, as well as another 2 lemons. Place 4 cups (540 g) crushed ice and 1 cup (20 g) mint leaves in a food processor and whizz briefly to crush the mint. Tip into a large chilled bowl and add the lemon syrup, lemon juice and 1/2 cup (125 ml) whisky. Dip the rims of martini glasses in lemon juice and sugar, pour in the julep and garnish with mint sprigs. *Serves 8–10*

GIFTS AND SWEETS

HANDMADE JAMS, sweets and biscuits are personal gifts which no store-bought presents can ever match. They're practical, cost-effective, individual and come from the heart. You can always make a few more for those unexpected guests who arrive on the doorstep, gift in hand. And as for the gingerbread house—such design, such engineering— who could fail to be impressed?

PINEAPPLE AND MANGO JAM

Preparation time: 30 minutes
Total cooking time: 40 minutes
Makes 1 litre

1 ripe pineapple
2 large mangoes
1 teaspoon grated lemon rind
⅓ cup (80 ml) lemon juice, reserving the pips and rind of
  1 lemon
1.2 kg sugar, warmed (see Note)

1 Place two plates in the freezer. Remove the skin and the tough eyes from the pineapple. Cut into quarters lengthways, remove the core and cut the flesh into 1 cm pieces. Peel the mangoes and cut each mango cheek from the stone. Cut into 1 cm pieces. Place the pineapple, mango, any juices, lemon rind and juice, and sugar in a large pan. Stir until all the sugar has dissolved.

2 Place the reserved pips and skin onto a square of muslin and tie securely with string. Add to the pan.

3 Bring to the boil, then reduce the heat and simmer, stirring, for 30–40 minutes, or until setting point is reached. Remove any scum with a skimmer or slotted spoon. Stir across the base of the pan to check that the jam is not sticking or burning. Be careful, the jam will froth. When the jam falls from a tilted wooden spoon in thick sheets without dripping, start testing for setting point.

4 Remove from the heat and test for setting point by placing a little jam on one of the plates. A skin will form on the surface and the jam will wrinkle when pushed with your finger when setting point is reached. Remove any scum from the surface.

5 Pour into clean, warm jars and seal. Turn the jars upside down for 2 minutes, then invert and cool. Label and date. Store in a cool, dark place for 6–12 months. Refrigerate after opening for 6 weeks.

NUTRITION PER TABLESPOON
Protein 0.5 g; Fat 0 g; Carbohydrate 30 g; Dietary Fibre 1 g; Cholesterol 0 mg; 497 kJ (120 cal)

NOTE: To warm the sugar, place it in a baking tray in a slow oven (150°C/ 300°F/Gas 2) for 10–15 minutes, or until warmed through. Warming the sugar speeds up the cooking process.

Simmer until setting point is reached, stirring occasionally to prevent burning.

Setting point is reached when the jam wrinkles when pushed with your finger.

Remove any scum from the surface before pouring the jam into clean, warm jars.

FIG AND ORANGE JAM

Preparation time: 20 minutes
Total cooking time: 50 minutes
<u>Makes</u> 1.5 litres (48 fl oz)

1.5 kg (3 lb) fresh figs, chopped
¾ cup (185 ml/6 fl oz) orange juice
¼ cup (60 ml/2 fl oz) lemon juice
2 tablespoons sweet sherry
1 kg (2 lb) sugar, warmed
   (see page 166)

1 Put two small plates in the freezer. Place the figs in a large pan with the orange and lemon juice, and the sherry. Bring to the boil, then reduce the heat and simmer for 20 minutes, or until the figs are soft.

2 Add the sugar and stir over low heat, without boiling, until all the sugar dissolves. Return to the boil for 20–25 minutes, stirring often. Remove any scum during cooking with a skimmer or slotted spoon. When the jam falls from a tilted wooden spoon in thick sheets without dripping, start testing for setting point.

3 Remove from the heat, place a little jam onto one of the cold plates and place in the freezer for 30 seconds. A skin will form on the surface and the jam will wrinkle when pushed with your finger when setting point is reached. Remove any scum from the surface with a skimmer or slotted spoon.

4 Pour immediately into clean, warm jars and seal. Turn them upside down for 2 minutes, then invert and leave to cool. Label and date. Store in a cool, dark place for 6–12 months. Refrigerate after opening for up to 6 weeks.

NOTE: Either dark- or green-skinned figs can be used.

Reduce the heat and simmer for 20 minutes, or until the figs are tender.

Test for setting point when the jam falls in sheets from a spoon without dripping.

Setting point is reached when the jam wrinkles when pushed with your finger.

RHUBARB AND GINGER JAM

Preparation time: 15 minutes +
 overnight soaking
Total cooking time: 35 minutes
Makes 1.5 litres (48 fl oz)

1.5 kg (3 lb) trimmed rhubarb
 (leaves and ends removed)
1.5 kg (3 lb) sugar, warmed
1/2 cup (125 ml/4 fl oz) lemon juice
4 cm (11/2 inch) piece fresh ginger,
 bruised and halved
100 g (31/2 oz) glacé ginger

1 Chop the rhubarb into small pieces. Layer the rhubarb, sugar and lemon juice in a non-metallic bowl. Cover and leave overnight.

2 Put two small plates in the freezer. Place the rhubarb mixture in a large pan. Finely chop the fresh ginger and place on a square of muslin, tie securely with string and add to the pan. Stir over low heat for 5 minutes, or until all the sugar has dissolved. Bring to the boil and boil rapidly for 20–30 minutes, stirring often. Remove any scum during cooking with a skimmer or slotted spoon. When the jam falls from a tilted wooden spoon in thick sheets without dripping, start testing for setting point.

3 Remove from the heat, place a little jam onto one of the cold plates and place in the freezer for 30 seconds. When setting point is reached, a skin will form on the surface and the jam will wrinkle when pushed with your finger. Remove any scum and discard the muslin bag. Finely chop the glacé ginger and add to the pan.

4 Spoon immediately into clean, warm jars, and seal. Turn upside down for 2 minutes, then invert and cool. Label and date. Store in a cool, dark place for 6–12 months. Refrigerate after opening for up to 6 weeks.

NOTE: The amount of ginger can be varied, according to taste.

Discard the leaves and ends from the rhubarb and chop the stalks into pieces.

When the jam has thickened, start testing for setting point.

Remove any scum from the surface and stir in the glacé ginger.

LIME MARMALADE

Preparation time: 20 minutes +
  overnight soaking
Total cooking time: 1 hour 10
  minutes
Makes 2.25 litres (72 fl oz)

1 kg (2 lb) limes
2.25 kg (4¹/₂ lb) sugar, warmed

1 Scrub the limes under warm, running water with a soft bristle brush to remove the wax coating. Cut in half lengthways, reserving any pips, slice thinly and place in a large non-metallic bowl with 2 litres (64 fl oz) water. Tie any lime pips securely in a square of muslin and add to the bowl. Cover and leave overnight.

2 Put two small plates in the freezer. Place the fruit and water in a pan. Bring slowly to the boil, then reduce the heat and simmer, covered, for 45 minutes, or until the fruit is tender. Add the sugar and stir over low heat, without boiling, for 5 minutes, or until all the sugar dissolves. Return to the boil and boil rapidly, stirring often, for 20 minutes. Remove any scum during cooking with a skimmer or slotted spoon. When the marmalade falls from a tilted wooden spoon in thick sheets without dripping, start testing for setting point.

3 Remove from the heat, place a little marmalade onto one of the cold plates and place in the freezer for 30 seconds. A skin will form on the surface and the marmalade will wrinkle when pushed with your finger when setting point is reached. Discard the muslin bag. Remove any scum from the surface.

4 Spoon immediately into clean, warm jars. Turn upside down for 2 minutes, then invert and leave to cool. Label and date. Store the jars in a cool, dark place for 6–12 months. Refrigerate the marmalade after opening for up to 6 weeks.

NOTE: Look for brightly coloured limes that feel heavy for their size.

Scrub the limes with a soft bristle brush under warm, running water.

Stir the mixture over low heat, without boiling, until the sugar has dissolved.

Test a little marmalade on a plate to see if setting point has been reached.

PEACH CONSERVE

Preparation time: 20 minutes
Total cooking time: 1 hour 5 minutes
Makes 1.25 litres (40 fl oz)

1.5 kg (3 lb) peaches (about
   9 large peaches)
1 green apple
1 lemon
1 kg (2 lb) sugar, warmed

1 Put two small plates in the freezer. Score a cross in the base of the peaches. Place them in a heatproof bowl and cover with boiling water. Leave for 1–2 minutes, then remove with a slotted spoon, cool slightly and peel. Halve, remove the stone and chop into 2 cm (1 inch) pieces.

2 Chop the apple, including the peel and core, into 1 cm (½ inch) pieces. Peel thin strips of rind from the lemon, then cut it in half and juice. Place the apple and lemon rind onto a square of muslin and tie securely with string.

3 Place the chopped peaches, muslin bag and 1¼ cups (310 ml/10 fl oz) water into a pan. Bring slowly to the boil, then reduce the heat and simmer for 30 minutes, or until the peaches are tender. Remove any scum from the surface during cooking with a skimmer or slotted spoon. Squeeze excess juice from the muslin bag by pushing against the side of the pan, then discard the bag.

4 Add the sugar and stir over low heat for 5 minutes, or until all the sugar dissolves. Add the lemon juice, return to the boil and boil rapidly for 30 minutes, stirring often. Stir across the pan's base to check the conserve is not sticking or burning. When the conserve falls from a tilted wooden spoon in thick sheets without dripping, test for setting point.

5 Remove from the heat, place a little conserve onto one of the cold plates and place in the freezer for 30 seconds. When setting point is reached, a skin will form on the surface and the conserve will wrinkle when pushed with your finger. Remove any scum from the surface.

6 Spoon into clean, warm jars and seal. Turn the jars upside down for 2 minutes, then invert and cool. Label and date. Store in a cool, dark place for 6–12 months. Refrigerate after opening for up to 6 weeks.

Score a cross in the base of the peaches, cover in boiling water, cool and peel.

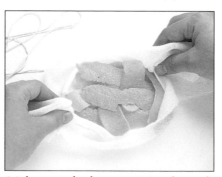

Make a muslin bag containing the apple and lemon rind and tie with string.

Remove excess juice from the muslin bag by pushing against the side of the pan.

QUINCE CONSERVE

Preparation time: 20 minutes
Total cooking time: 1 hour
    30 minutes
Makes 2 litres (64 fl oz)

2 kg (4 lb) quinces (about 5)
¾ cup (185 ml/6 fl oz) lemon juice
1.5 kg (3 lb) sugar, warmed

1 Put two small plates in the freezer. Cut each quince into quarters then peel, core and cut into small cubes. Place the fruit in a pan with 2 litres (64 fl oz) water and the lemon juice. Bring slowly to the boil, then reduce the heat and simmer, covered, for 1 hour, or until the fruit is soft.

2 Add the sugar and stir over low heat, without boiling, for 5 minutes, or until the sugar dissolves.

3 Return to the boil and boil, stirring often, for 25 minutes. Remove any scum during cooking with a skimmer or slotted spoon. When the conserve falls from a tilted wooden spoon in thick sheets without dripping, test for setting point.

4 Remove from the heat, place a little conserve onto one of the cold plates and place in the freezer for 30 seconds. A skin will form on the surface and the conserve will wrinkle when pushed with your finger when setting point is reached. Remove any scum from the surface with a skimmer or slotted spoon.

5 Spoon immediately into clean, warm jars and seal. Turn upside down for 2 minutes, then invert and leave to cool. Label and date. Store the jars in a cool, dark place for 6–12 months. Refrigerate after opening for up to 6 weeks.

NOTE: The quinces will turn from their natural yellow to a beautiful, rich red during cooking.

Using a sharp knife, cut the peeled and cored quinces into small cubes.

After the sugar has dissolved, return the mixture to the boil for 25 minutes.

Remove any scum from the surface before spooning into clean, warm jars.

PASSIONFRUIT CURD

Preparation time: 15 minutes
Total cooking time: 20 minutes
Makes 3 cups (750 ml)

4 eggs
3/4 cup (185 g) caster sugar
1/3 cup (80 ml) lemon juice

3 teaspoons finely grated lemon rind
1/2 cup (125 g) passionfruit pulp
200 g unsalted butter, chopped

1 Beat the eggs well, then strain into a heatproof bowl and stir in the remaining ingredients.

2 Place the bowl over a pan of simmering water and stir with a wooden spoon for 15–20 minutes, or until the butter has melted and the mixture coats the back of the spoon.

3 Transfer the curd to a heatproof jug and pour into clean, warm jars.

Seal while hot. Turn the jars upside down for 2 minutes, invert and leave to cool, then refrigerate. Store in the refrigerator for up to 2 weeks.

NUTRITION PER TABLESPOON
Protein 1 g; Fat 5 g; Carbohydrate 5.5 g; Dietary Fibre 0.5 g; Cholesterol 35 mg; 293 kJ (70 cal)

NOTE: For a quick and delicious dessert, fill ready-made tartlet shells with the passionfruit curd and serve with whipped cream.

Strain the beaten eggs into a heatproof bowl before adding the rest of the ingredients.

Stir the mixture constantly until it thickly coats the back of a wooden spoon.

Carefully pour the curd into clean, warm jars and seal while hot.

ROSEMARY WINE JELLY

Preparation time: 30 minutes + overnight draining
Total cooking time: 1 hour 15 minutes
Makes 3 cups (750 ml/24 fl oz)

2 kg (4 lb) green apples
3 cups (750 ml/24 fl oz) dry white wine
3½ cups (875 g/11 lb 12 oz) sugar, approximately
2 tablespoons roughly chopped fresh rosemary leaves
large sprigs of rosemary, for each jar

1 Wash the apples well and discard the stalks. Cut into chunks and place in a large pan, skins and seeds included. Add the wine and bring to the boil. Reduce the heat and simmer, covered, for 1 hour. Stir a couple of times during cooking to make sure the apples cook evenly.

2 Place a jelly bag in a bowl, cover with boiling water, drain and suspend the bag over a large heatproof bowl.

3 Ladle the fruit and liquid into the bag. Do not push the fruit through the bag or the jelly will become cloudy. Cover the top of the bag loosely with a clean tea towel, without touching the mixture. Allow the mixture to drip through the bag overnight, or until there is no liquid dripping through the cloth.

4 Place two small plates in the freezer. Discard the pulp, and measure the liquid. For each cup (250 ml/8 fl oz) liquid, allow 1 cup (250 g/8 oz) sugar. Heat the liquid in a pan and add the sugar. Stir, without boiling, for 5 minutes, or until the sugar dissolves. Remove any scum with a skimmer or slotted spoon.

5 Place the rosemary leaves onto a square piece of muslin and tie securely with string, then add to the pan. Boil for 10 minutes, then remove from the heat and test for setting point.

6 Remove the pan from the heat and test for setting point by placing a little jelly on one of the plates. A skin will form on the surface and the jelly will wrinkle when pushed with your finger when setting point is reached. Discard the muslin bag.

7 Place a sprig of rosemary into each clean, warm jar, and immediately pour the jelly down the sides of the jar and seal. Turn upside down for 2 minutes, then invert and cool. Label and date. Store in a cool, dark place for 6–12 months. Refrigerate after opening for up to 6 weeks.

Pour the mixture into a suspended jelly bag and leave to strain through.

Remove any scum from the surface with a skimmer or slotted spoon.

Put a sprig of rosemary into each warm jar before pouring in the jelly.

BANANA, TAMARIND AND DATE CHUTNEY

Preparation time: 25 minutes
Total cooking time: 45 minutes
Makes 1.5 litres (48 fl oz)

125 g (4 oz) tamarind pulp
1/3 cup (90 g/3 oz) caster sugar
1 teaspoon ground cumin
1/2 teaspoon cayenne pepper
2 tablespoons grated fresh ginger
250 g (8 oz) pitted dates, chopped
1/2 cup (60 g/2 oz) slivered almonds
8 firm ripe bananas, chopped

1 Put the tamarind pulp in a bowl with 3 cups (750 ml/24 fl oz) boiling water. Cool, then break up with a fork. Pour into a sieve placed over a bowl and press out the liquid. Discard the seeds.

2 Put the liquid in a large pan with the sugar, cumin, cayenne pepper and 1 teaspoon salt. Stir over low heat until all the sugar has dissolved.

3 Add the ginger, almonds and dates. Bring to the boil, then reduce the heat and simmer for 10 minutes. Add the banana and cook, stirring, for 30 minutes, or until soft and pulpy.

4 Spoon immediately into clean, warm jars. Use a metal skewer to remove any air bubbles and seal. Turn upside down for 2 minutes, then invert and cool. Label and date. Leave for 1 month before opening to allow the flavours to develop. Store in a cool, dark place for up to 12 months. Refrigerate after opening for up to 6 weeks.

Put the tamarind pulp in a bowl with boiling water and leave to cool.

Put the strained liquid in a large pan with the sugar, cumin, salt and cayenne.

Cook the mixture until it is thick and pulpy, stirring frequently.

DRIED APRICOT CHUTNEY

Preparation time: 20 minutes +
2 hours soaking
Total cooking time: 50 minutes
Makes 1.75 litres (56 fl oz)

500 g (1 lb) dried apricots
1 large onion, chopped
3 cloves garlic, finely chopped
2 tablespoons grated fresh ginger
2 cups (500 ml/16 fl oz) cider
vinegar
1 cup (230 g/7½ oz) firmly packed
soft brown sugar
1 cup (125 g/4 oz) sultanas
2 teaspoons mustard seeds, crushed
(see Note)
2 teaspoons coriander seeds,
crushed
½ teaspoon ground cumin
⅓ cup (80 ml/2¾ fl oz) orange juice
½ teaspoon grated orange rind

1 Put the apricots in a bowl, cover with 2 litres (64 fl oz) water and leave to soak for 2 hours. Drain and put 1 litre (32 fl oz) of the water into a pan. Make up with fresh water if there isn't enough. Chop the apricots. Put them, and all other ingredients except the orange juice and rind, into the pan. Add 1 teaspoon salt.

2 Stir the mixture over low heat for 5 minutes, or until all the sugar has dissolved. Bring to the boil, cover and boil for 45 minutes, or until thick and pulpy. Stir often, especially towards the end of the cooking time so the mixture does not stick and burn. Remove any scum with the aid of a skimmer or slotted spoon.

3 Stir in the orange juice and rind. Spoon the chutney immediately into clean, warm jars. Use a skewer to remove air bubbles, then seal them. Turn each jar upside down for 2 minutes, then invert it and leave the chutney to cool. Label and date. Leave for 1 month to allow the flavours to develop. You can store the jars in a cool, dark place for up to 12 months. Refrigerate after opening but make sure you use it within 6 weeks.

NOTE: Crushing the mustard and coriander seeds helps to release their aroma. You can use the back of a large, heavy knife to crush the seeds, or a mortar and pestle, or put them in a thick plastic bag and crush them with a rolling pin.

Crush the mustard and coriander seeds to release their aroma.

When the apricots are plump, drain and reserve the soaking liquid.

Add the orange juice and rind to the chutney just before sealing it in the jars.

PRESERVED LEMONS

Preparation time: 20 minutes +
    6 weeks standing
Total cooking time: Nil
Fills: a 1-litre jar

6 thin-skinned lemons
    (see Note)
100 g (3½ oz) salt
2 cups (500 ml/16 fl oz)
    lemon juice

1 Wash and scrub the lemons well in warm water to remove any wax. Slice off the stems, then cut each lemon in half lengthways. Cut each half in half again without cutting all the way through, leaving the two pieces attached. Sprinkle some of the salt generously over each cut portion; then pack some more salt between the cut portions.

2 Rinse a wide-necked, clip-top, 1-litre jar with boiling water and dry in a warm oven (do not dry with a tea towel). Pack the lemons into the jar tightly and add the remaining salt. (The tighter you pack the jar, the less lemon juice you will use, and the fewer air gaps there will be, giving a better result.)

3 Pour the lemon juice into the jar until the lemons are covered. (It may not be necessary to use all the lemon juice.) Seal and gently turn the jar over to dissolve the salt. Leave in a cool, dark place for 6 weeks. Turn the jar over daily for the first 2 weeks.

4 Once opened, store the lemons in the refrigerator. To use, rinse with water to remove any excess salt and discard the flesh. Only the rind is used, which can be sliced or chopped and used in a variety of dishes. Alternatively, try stirring the lemons into a Moroccan-style couscous.

NOTE: For best results, check with your fruit and vegetable market for a variety of thin-skinned lemon, such as Meyer.

Variation: You could try adding a cinnamon stick, cloves and a bay leaf to the jar with the lemons.

Scrub the lemons thoroughly in warm water to remove any wax.

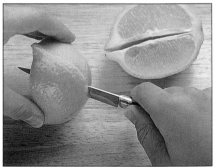

Cut each lemon half in half again, taking care not to cut all the way through.

Pack a generous amount of salt in-between the cut lemon portions.

Pour lemon juice into the jar until the lemons are fully covered.

WHITE CHRISTMAS

Preparation time: 15 minutes +
   30 minutes refrigeration
Total cooking time: 5 minutes
Makes 24

1½ cups (45 g) puffed rice cereal
1 cup (100 g) milk powder
1 cup (125 g) icing sugar

1 cup (90 g) desiccated coconut
⅓ cup (80 g) chopped red
   glacé cherries
⅓ cup (80 g) chopped green
   glacé cherries
⅓ cup (40 g) sultanas
250 g white vegetable shortening
   (copha)

1 Line a shallow 28 x 18 cm tin
   with foil.
2 Combine the puffed rice, milk
   powder, sugar, coconut, glacé cherries and sultanas in a large mixing
   bowl. Make a well in the centre.

3 Melt the shortening over low heat,
   cool slightly and add to the dry
ingredients. Stir the mixture with a
wooden spoon until all ingredients
are moistened and well combined.
4 Spoon into the prepared tin and
   smooth down the surface with
wetted hands or the back of a spoon.
Refrigerate for 30 minutes, or until
set. Cut into small triangles to serve.

NUTRITION PER PIECE
Protein 1.5 g; Fat 14 g; Carbohydrate
14 g; Dietary Fibre 0.5 g; Cholesterol
4.5 mg; 775 kJ (185 cal)

Combine all the dry ingredients in a bowl before adding the melted shortening.

Once the ingredients are moistened, spoon into the tin and smooth the surface.

When the mixture has set, cut it into small triangles to serve.

PANFORTE

Preparation time: 30 minutes
Total cooking time: 1 hour
Serves 10–12

edible rice paper
½ cup (60 g) walnuts
¾ cup (115 g) blanched almonds
¾ cup (105 g) hazelnuts
¼ cup (45 g) chopped dried figs
150 g glacé mixed peel, chopped
50 g glacé apricots, chopped
2 tablespoons finely grated
    orange rind
2 tablespoons cocoa powder
½ cup (60 g) plain flour
1 teaspoon ground cinnamon
1 teaspoon mixed spice
½ cup (175 g) honey
¼ cup (60 g) caster sugar
1 tablespoon plain flour, extra
¼ teaspoon ground cinnamon,
    extra

1 Preheat the oven to moderate 180°C (350°F/Gas 4). Line the base of a 22 cm round springform tin with rice paper trimmed to fit. Place the walnuts and almonds on a small baking tray and bake for about 8–10 minutes, or until fragrant and lightly toasted. Transfer to a plate to cool, then repeat with the hazelnuts. When cool, tip the hazelnuts onto a clean tea towel and rub vigorously to remove all the loose skin. Roughly chop all the nuts.

2 Combine the nuts, dried figs, glacé mixed peel, glacé apricots and orange rind in a bowl. Sift in the cocoa, flour, spices and ¼ teaspoon white pepper, stir to combine, then make a well in the centre. Combine the honey and sugar in a pan and stir over low heat without boiling until the sugar has dissolved.

3 Pour the honey mixture onto the dry ingredients, stirring until well combined. Transfer to the prepared tin and press in firmly. Smooth the surface with a wetted hand. Use a small sieve to dust the surface with the combined extra flour and the cinnamon. Bake for 35 minutes, then cool completely in the tin. Serve in thin wedges.

NUTRITION PER SERVE
Protein 6 g; Fat 15 g; Carbohydrate 37 g; Dietary Fibre 4 g; Cholesterol 0 mg; 1255 kJ (299 cal)

NOTE: Glacé citron (which can be used in place of mixed peel) and edible rice paper are available from delicatessens, speciality stores and health food shops. This recipe makes quite a large panforte, ideal for cutting into sections to give as gifts.

Line the base of the springform tin with rice paper trimmed to fit.

Rub the roasted hazelnuts vigorously in a tea towel to remove the loose skin.

Press down on the surface of the mixture with a wetted hand to smooth.

PEPPERMINT SLICE

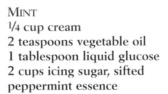

Preparation time: 45 minutes
Total cooking time: 30 minutes
Makes 24

2/3 cup self-raising flour
1/2 cup plain flour
1/4 cup cocoa powder
1/2 cup caster sugar
1 egg, lightly beaten
125 g unsalted butter, melted

MINT
1/4 cup cream
2 teaspoons vegetable oil
1 tablespoon liquid glucose
2 cups icing sugar, sifted
peppermint essence

ICING
100 g dark chocolate, chopped
1 tablespoon cream
40 g unsalted butter

Preheat oven to 180°C (350°F/ Gas 4). Line base and sides of shallow 27 x 18 cm rectangular tin with foil.

1 Sift flours with remaining dry ingredients into mixing bowl. Make a well in the centre. Pour the combined egg and butter in and use a wooden spoon to combine. Press into the base of the tin with hand. Bake for 15–20 minutes or until skewer inserted in centre comes out clean.

2 To make mint: Combine cream, oil, glucose and icing sugar in pan. Stir over low heat until mixture is smooth and creamy. Add a few drops of peppermint essence; mix well. Remove from heat. Pour mixture onto slice base. Smooth with flat-bladed knife and allow to set.

3 To make icing: Combine cream, chocolate and butter in pan and stir over low heat until smooth. Spread mixture over mint layer. Refrigerate for 5–10 minutes until set. Remove and cut into 24 squares.

1

2

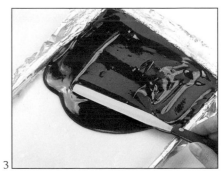

3

HANDMADE SWEETS

Handmade sweets and chocolates make ideal gifts for unexpected visitors, or decorations for your Christmas table setting.

Sesame caramel toffee

Mix 1 cup (250 g) caster sugar, 90 g butter, 1/2 cup (160 g) sweetened condensed milk, 1/3 cup (80 ml) glucose syrup and 2 tablespoons golden syrup together and cook over low heat, without boiling, until all the sugar has dissolved. Brush the side of the pan with a pastry brush dipped in warm water to prevent crystallisation. Bring to the boil, stirring constantly, and boil for 10 minutes. Stir in 1 cup (155 g) toasted sesame seeds and spread the mixture into a 20 cm square tin which has been coated with a non-stick spray. Cool for 15–20 minutes and turn out of the tin. Cut into finger-length pieces while still warm. *Makes 20*

Crunchy nuts

Preheat the oven to warm 170°C (325°F/Gas 3). Beat 2 egg whites in a dry, clean bowl with a pinch of salt until soft peaks form. Slowly add 1 cup (250 g) caster sugar and beat well until dissolved to form a meringue. Fold 3½ cups (420 g) whole toasted nuts (blanched almonds, hazelnuts, pecans, walnuts, cashews, brazils) and 1 teaspoon cinnamon into the meringue. Melt 125 g butter in a 15 x 10 x 3 cm baking tray. Spread the nut mixture over the butter and bake for 30 minutes, stirring every few minutes, or until the nuts and coating are browned and there is no butter remaining in the pan. Cool and break into pieces. *Makes 3½ cups (420 g)*

Rich almond rum balls

Melt 225 g chopped dark chocolate, then remove from the heat. Add 100 g diced butter and 2 teaspoons rum and beat until smooth. Beat in 175 g icing sugar, then refrigerate the mixture until firm. Shape 2 teaspoons of the mixture into balls with a 2.5 cm diameter. Finely chop 100 g slivered toasted almonds. Lay these out on a sheet of baking paper and roll the balls over them, coating them in almonds. Serve in gold paper cases. *Makes 35*

Left to right: Sesame caramel toffee; Crunchy nuts; Rich almond rum balls; Uncooked chocolate fudge; Lemon coconut truffles; Rich orange truffles.

Uncooked chocolate fudge

Break 225 g milk chocolate melts into small pieces and put into a bowl with 100 g unsalted butter. Place the bowl over a pan of hot water and heat gently until melted. In a separate bowl, beat 1 egg, then gradually add 450 g icing sugar, ½ cup (160 g) sweetened condensed milk and, finally, the chocolate mixture. Beat well and put into a lightly buttered 27.5 x 17.5 cm tin. Chill in the refrigerator for 3 hours, or until firm, then cut into squares. Chopped nuts, dried fruit or orange rind can also be added to the fudge. Store in the refrigerator. *Makes 20 squares*

Lemon coconut truffles

Heat ¼ cup (60 ml) cream and 250 g chopped white chocolate melts in a pan over low heat until the chocolate has just melted. Remove the pan from the heat and stir in 1 tablespoon grated lemon rind, 2 teaspoons lemon juice and ½ cup (45 g) desiccated coconut. Leave to cool for 30 minutes, then refrigerate for 1½ hours. Place teaspoonsful of the mixture onto a foil-lined tray and put back in the refrigerator for 45 minutes. Roll into balls and put back in the refrigerator for 10 minutes, then coat with toasted shredded coconut—you will need about ¾ cup (45 g). Keep refrigerated until ready to serve. *Makes 40*

Rich orange truffles

Combine 50 g chopped unsalted butter and 100 ml cream in a small pan. Heat gently until the butter has melted and the cream is bubbling. Remove from the heat and add 200 g milk chocolate melts, broken into pieces. Stir well until the chocolate melts. Stir in 1 egg yolk, 2 tablespoons finely chopped mixed peel, 2 tablespoons Grand Marnier and 1 teaspoon grated orange rind. Refrigerate for 3 hours, or until firm. Roll into small balls and coat lightly in cocoa powder. Return to the refrigerator until firm. Melt 140 g dark or milk chocolate melts. Using a fork or toothpick, dip each truffle in the chocolate, let the excess drip off and place on a tray lined with baking paper. Refrigerate to set and keep chilled until ready to serve. *Makes 30*

COGNAC TRUFFLES

Preparation time: 20 minutes +
    1 hour refrigeration
Total cooking time: 5 minutes
Makes about 20

150 g dark cooking chocolate,
    chopped
50 g butter
1/4 cup cream
1 tablespoon cognac or brandy
1/3 cup dark cocoa powder

1 Place chocolate in a medium mixing bowl. Combine butter and cream in a small pan; stir over a low heat until butter melts. Bring to the boil, remove from heat. Pour the mixture over the chocolate. Using a wooden spoon, stir until chocolate has melted and mixture is smooth. Stir in cognac or brandy.

2 Chill mixture in the refrigerator, stirring occasionally. When mixture is firm enough to handle, roll heaped teaspoons into balls; place on foil-lined tray. Refrigerate until firm.

3 Sift cocoa onto greaseproof paper. Roll each truffle in cocoa to generously coat; refrigerate until firm. Reserve remaining cocoa and re-roll truffles close to serving time. Serve in small foil confectionery cases.

NOTE: Powdered cocoa is a traditional coating for chocolate truffles, which gives them the appearance of the rare fungus they are named after. Storage: Truffles may be kept for up to 1 week in an airtight container in the refrigerator.

VARIATION: Rum or a liqueur can be used to flavour truffles instead.

TOFFEED PECANS

Preparation time: 15 minutes
Total cooking time: 15 minutes
Makes 1 cup

1 cup pecans
1 cup soft brown sugar

½ cup cream sherry
¼ teaspoon mixed spice
pinch salt

Line a flat oven tray with aluminium foil, brush lightly with oil.

1 Place nuts on a dry oven tray and place in a preheated 180°C (350°F/Gas 4) oven for 3–5 minutes, until lightly toasted; cool.

2 Combine sugar, sherry, spice and salt in a pan. Stir over medium heat without boiling until sugar has dissolved. Bring to boil, reduce heat slightly, and boil 12–15 minutes, or until the mixture reaches hard ball stage on a sugar thermometer.

3 Remove pan from heat and add pecans. Stir to coat nuts in syrup and, using forks, place them onto the tray. Set aside to cool completely.

STORAGE: Toffeed Pecans will keep for up to 2 days, stored between sheets of waxed paper in a single layer in an airtight container.

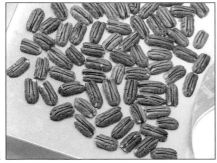

1

2

3

CHOCOLATE CLUSTERS

Preparation time: 25 minutes
Total cooking time: 3 minutes
Makes about 40

125 g dark choc melts

125 g white choc melts
125 g dried mixed fruit
125 g glacé ginger

Place dark and white choc melts separately into heatproof bowls.

1 Place each bowl over a pan of simmering water and stir gently until melted and smooth. Cool.

2 Stir mixed fruit into dark chocolate. Chop glacé ginger and combine with white chocolate.

3 Spoon mixtures into small paper confectionery cups, leave to set at room temperature.

NOTE: Use any single dried fruit, such as raisins or sultanas, instead of mixed fruit. Toasted chopped nuts—pecans, almonds, macadamia or brazil nuts—may also be used. Storage: Chocolate Clusters will keep for 4 weeks if stored in an airtight container in a cool, dark place.

1

2

3

MIXED FRUIT AND NUT BALLS

Preparation time: 30 minutes +
    1 hour soaking
Total cooking time: 7 minutes
Makes 35

¼ cup sultanas
¼ cup finely chopped pecan nuts
1 tablespoon mixed peel

2 tablespoons chopped glacé ginger
1 tablespoon brandy
1 tablespoon light olive oil
375 g dark chocolate, chopped
125 g toasted pecans, finely
    chopped

1 Place the sultanas, pecans, peel and ginger in medium bowl. Add brandy and oil, stir well and leave to soak for 1 hour.

2 Place the chocolate in a small heatproof bowl. Place bowl over a pan of simmering water and stir until chocolate has melted.

3 Add the fruit and nut mixture to the melted chocolate. Refrigerate the mixture until it is firm enough to handle.

4 Roll teaspoonfuls of the mixture into small balls. Roll each ball lightly in chopped nuts to coat. Place the balls in the refrigerator until they are firm. Serve in small paper confectionery cases.

NOTE: Mixed fruit and nut balls may be stored for up to 2 days in an airtight container in a cool, dark place.

1

2

3

RICH CHOCOLATE DIAMONDS

Preparation time: 40 minutes + overnight
Total cooking time: 45 minutes
Makes 12

¼ cup self-raising flour
¼ cup plain flour
1 tablespoon cocoa powder
60 g butter
50 g dark chocolate, chopped
½ cup caster sugar
1 tablespoon water
1 tablespoon oil
1 egg, lightly beaten
⅓ cup blackberry jam, warmed

TOPPING
150 g dark cooking chocolate, chopped
½ cup cream
50 g white chocolate melts, melted

Preheat the oven to 160°C (310°F/Gas 2). Brush a 26 x 8 x 4.5 cm bar tin with melted butter or oil; line the base and sides with baking paper.

1 Sift flours and cocoa into a mixing bowl; make a well in centre. Place butter, chocolate, sugar, water and oil in a small pan, stir over medium heat until melted and smooth.

2 Pour butter mixture onto dry ingredients. Add egg and stir until combined. Pour into prepared tin and bake for 40 minutes, until a skewer comes out clean when inserted into centre of cake. Leave in the tin for 5 minutes before turning onto a wire rack to cool. Place in an airtight container and leave overnight.

3 Trim top and sides from cake. Invert onto a board so that the smooth base becomes the top. Cut in half lengthways, then diagonally into 12 diamonds; discard ends.

4 Cut diamonds in half horizontally, spread each with blackberry jam

and sandwich together. Press all over lightly with fingers to smooth loose crumbs. Place on wire rack over tray.

5 Combine dark chocolate and cream in a heatproof bowl. Stand bowl over a pan of simmering water and stir until chocolate has melted and mixture is smooth. Spoon mixture over diamonds to cover the top and sides. Refrigerate until set.

6 Spoon melted white chocolate into a small paper piping bag and pipe small decorations onto a sheet of baking paper. When the chocolate has set, lift shapes from paper and place on the top of each diamond.

NOTE: The diamonds can be stored for up to 3 days in an airtight container in a cool dark place; refrigerate in warm weather.

PANETTONE

Preparation time: 30 minutes
+ soaking and rising
Total cooking time: 35 minutes
<u>Makes</u> 8

½ cup (95 g) chopped dried
  apricots
½ cup (75 g) currants
½ cup (60 g) sultanas
½ cup (125 ml) Marsala
2 x 7 g sachets dried yeast
¾ cup (185 ml) warm milk
½ cup (125 g) caster sugar
180 g unsalted butter, softened
2 teaspoons vanilla essence
3 eggs
2 egg yolks
4 cups (500 g) plain flour
1 teaspoon ground aniseed

1 Combine the dried apricots, currants, sultanas and Marsala in a bowl, cover with plastic wrap and leave to stand for 1 hour, or until most of the liquid is absorbed. Put the yeast, milk and 1 teaspoon of the sugar in a bowl and leave in a warm place until foamy.

2 Place the butter, vanilla and the remaining sugar in a bowl and beat with an electric mixer until light and fluffy. Add the eggs and the separated egg yolks one at a time, beating well after each addition.

3 Sift the flour and aniseed into a bowl, make a well in the centre and add the yeast mixture, butter mixture and fruit mixture. Mix with a flat-bladed knife, until the whole mixture forms a soft, sticky dough. Cover and leave in a warm place for 40 minutes, or until doubled in size.

4 Preheat the oven to moderately hot 200°C (400°F/Gas 6). Lightly oil the base and sides of eight ½ cup (125 ml) soufflé dishes. Cut a strip of brown paper long enough to fit around the inside of each dish and tall enough to come 10 cm above the edge. Fold down a cuff about 2 cm deep along the length of each strip. Make diagonal cuts up to the fold line on each strip, approximately 1 cm apart. Fit the strips around the inside of the dishes, pressing the cuts so they sit flat around the bottom edge of the dish. Cut circles

of brown paper using the dish as a guide, place in the base of each dish, and grease the paper.

5 Turn the dough out onto a floured surface and knead for 3 minutes, or until smooth. You will need more flour, up to ½ cup (60 g), and the dough should be soft but not sticky. Divide into eight equal portions and press into the dishes. Cover with a tea towel and place in a warm place for an hour, or until doubled in size.

Bake for 30–35 minutes, or until golden brown and cooked through when tested with a skewer. Remove from the soufflé dishes, leaving the paper attached. Dust with icing sugar, if desired. Serve warm, cold or sliced and toasted.

NUTRITION PER PANETTONE
Protein 13 g; Fat 25 g; Carbohydrate 80 g; Dietary Fibre 5 g; Cholesterol 170 mg; 2610 kJ (625 cal)

Mix the ingredients together with a flat-bladed knife to form a dough.

Divide the dough into eight portions and press into the paper-lined soufflé dishes.

CINNAMON PECAN BISCUITS

Preparation time: 20 minutes
Total cooking time: 15 minutes
Makes 40

100 g dark chocolate
125 g unsalted butter
1/2 cup caster sugar
1 egg, lightly beaten
3/4 cup finely chopped pecans
1/3 self-raising flour
2/3 cup plain flour
2 teaspoons ground cinnamon
1/2 cup (50 g) whole pecans,
   for decoration
1 tablespoon icing sugar, for dusting

Preheat oven to 180°C (350°F/ Gas 4). Line two 32 x 28 cm biscuit trays with baking paper.

1 Chop chocolate and place in a small heatproof bowl. Stand over a pan of simmering water. Stir until chocolate is melted and smooth. Allow to cool but not to rest.

2 Using electric beaters, beat butter and sugar in a small mixing bowl until light and creamy. Add egg gradually, beating thoroughly. Add cooled melted chocolate and beat until combined.

3 Transfer mixture to large mixing bowl; add pecans. Using a metal spoon, fold in sifted flours and cinnamon. Stir until ingredients are combined; do not overbeat. Lightly roll 2 teaspoonfuls of mixture onto oval shapes, place on prepared tray and press a pecan onto each. Bake for 10 minutes.

4 Transfer to wire rack to cool. Place icing sugar in a sieve, and lightly dust each biscuit.

NOTE: Biscuits may be stored for up to two days in an airtight container.

VARIATIONS: If liked, bake biscuits without the pecan on top. When baked and cooled, dip top of each biscuit in melted chocolate and press pecan on top. Use ground mixed spice or allspice in place of the cinnamon if preferred. Walnuts may be substituted for the pecans.

STAINED-GLASS WINDOW BISCUITS

Preparation time: 1 hour +
  15 minutes refrigeration
Total cooking time: 12 minutes
Makes about 20

150 g butter, cubed and
  softened
1/2 cup (60 g) icing sugar
1 egg
1 teaspoon vanilla essence
1/3 cup (40 g) custard powder
2 cups (250 g) plain flour
1/4 cup (30 g) self-raising flour
200 g assorted boiled lollies
beaten egg, to glaze

1 Line 2 baking trays with baking paper. Beat the butter and icing sugar until light and creamy. Add the egg and vanilla and beat until fluffy. Beat in the custard powder. Fold in the combined sifted flours.

2 Turn onto a lightly floured surface and knead until smooth. Roll between 2 sheets of baking paper to a 3 mm thickness. Refrigerate for 15 minutes, or until firm.

3 Preheat the oven to moderately hot 200°C (400°F/Gas 6). Divide the lollies into their different colours and crush each colour separately using a rolling pin. Cut out the dough with a 9.5 cm fluted round cutter. Lay the rounds on the trays and use small cutters to cut various shapes from inside the circles.

4 Glaze the biscuits with the beaten egg and then bake for 5 minutes. Don't let the glaze drip into the cut-out sections or the stained glass will be cloudy. Fill each cut-out section with a different coloured lolly. Bake the biscuits for 5–6 minutes, or until the lollies melt. Leave for 10 minutes, then cool on a wire rack.

NUTRITION PER BISCUIT
Protein 2 g; Fat 6.5 g; Carbohydrate 22 g; Dietary Fibre 0.5 g; Cholesterol 30 mg; 635 kJ (150 cal)

Keeping the colours separate, finely crush the boiled lollies with a rolling pin.

Use small cutters to cut shapes from each of the biscuits before baking.

Fill the cut-out shapes with the different coloured crushed lollies.

SHORTBREAD BELLS

Preparation time: 30 minutes +
15 minutes refrigeration
Total cooking time:
25 minutes
Makes about 40

250 g butter
1/2 cup (125 g) caster sugar
2 cups (250 g) plain flour
1/2 cup (90 g) rice flour
1 egg white, lightly beaten
edible gold leaf, optional (see Note)

1 Preheat the oven to warm 160°C (315°F/Gas 2–3). Line two baking trays with baking paper. Place the butter and sugar in a bowl and beat with electric or handheld beaters until light and creamy.

2 Sift the plain flour and rice flour into the butter mixture, and mix together with a flat-bladed knife to make a crumbly dough. Gather the mixture together and then turn out onto a sheet of baking paper and press together gently into a rough ball. Place another sheet of baking paper on top of the dough. Roll the mixture out to a 7 mm thickness.

3 Peel off the top sheet of baking paper and cut shapes from the dough using bell-shaped cutters of varying sizes. Cut out as many biscuits as possible from the first rolling of dough, then gently press the leftovers together, re-roll and cut out more shapes. Lift the bells onto the lined baking tray, place in the refrigerator for 15 minutes, then bake for 20–25 minutes, or until golden underneath. Cool on a wire rack.

4 If you want to use gold leaf, lightly brush the top of the biscuits with egg white and lay a piece of gold leaf on top. Rub gently with your finger to transfer the gold leaf from the tissue paper to the biscuit, and lift the paper away. The gold leaf will not cover the biscuit, rather it will give an abstract, decorative effect.

NUTRITION PER BISCUIT
Protein 1 g; Fat 5 g; Carbohydrate 10 g; Dietary Fibre 0.5 g; Cholesterol 15 mg; 385 kJ (90 cal)

NOTE: Edible gold leaf is available from art supply shops and some cake decorating shops. It is expensive, but the effect is worth it.

Mix the flours into the butter using a flat-bladed knife to make a crumbly dough.

Cut shapes out of the dough using a bell-shaped cutter.

Cover small sections of the cooked biscuits with edible gold leaf.

SHORTBREAD STARS WITH LEMON GLAZE

Preparation time: 20 minutes
Total cooking time: 15 minutes
Makes 35

2 cups plain flour
2 tablespoons rice flour
200 g unsalted butter

1/3 cup icing sugar
1 teaspoon finely grated lemon rind
2 tablespoons lemon juice
silver cachous

LEMON GLAZE
1 cup pure icing sugar
2 tablespoons lemon juice, strained
yellow or orange food colouring

Preheat oven to 180°C (350°F/Gas 4). Line two 32 x 28 biscuit trays with baking paper.

1 Place flours, butter and sugar in food processor bowl. Using pulse action, press button for 30 seconds or until mixture is fine and crumbly. Add rind and juice; process for 20 seconds until mixture forms a dough.

2 Turn out onto a floured surface and knead for 20 seconds or until smooth. Roll out to 7 mm thickness; cut out 6 cm star shapes. Bake for 15 minutes. Transfer to wire rack to cool.

3 To make lemon glaze: Place icing sugar and lemon juice in a heat-proof bowl over a pan of water; stir until smooth. Dip biscuits face down in glaze, drain excess. Dip toothpick or skewer into food colouring and draw lines into icing before it sets. Decorate centre with silver cachou.

CITRUS ALMOND BISCUITS

Preparation time: 15 minutes +
    20 minutes refrigeration
Total cooking time: 12–15 minutes
Makes 30

60 g butter
½ teaspoon grated orange rind
½ teaspoon grated lime rind
¼ cup caster sugar
½ cup plain flour
2 tablespoons ground almonds
1 egg white
1 cup flaked almonds, crushed
icing sugar

Line an oven tray with baking paper.
Preheat oven to 180°C (350°F/Gas 4).

1 Place the butter, orange rind, lime rind and sugar in a small mixing bowl. Using electric beaters, beat until light and creamy.

2 Add the flour and ground almonds and mix with a flat-bladed knife to a soft dough. Press mixture with hands until it comes together.

3 Roll teaspoonsful of the mixture into 2 cm-long logs. Refrigerate for 20 minutes or until mixture is firm. Lightly whisk the egg white with a fork. Lightly crush the flaked almonds with your hands. Place in small bowl. Dip each log into egg white, roll in almonds then place on the prepared tray. Bake in a preheated oven for 12–15 minutes or until lightly golden. Dust with sifted icing sugar while still warm. Allow to cool on tray.

NOTE: These biscuits can be stored in airtight container for up to 3 weeks.
VARIATION: Use lemon rind instead of orange or lime rind if you prefer.

GINGER PECAN BISCOTTI

Preparation time: 30 minutes
+ cooling
Total cooking time:
1 hour 20 minutes
Makes about 20

1 cup (100 g) pecans
2 eggs
2/3 cup (155 g) firmly packed
    soft brown sugar
1 cup (125 g) self-raising flour
3/4 cup (90 g) plain flour
100 g glacé ginger, finely chopped

1 Preheat the oven to 160°C (315°F/
Gas 2–3). Spread the pecans onto
an oven tray and bake for 10–12 minutes, or until fragrant and toasted,
making sure they don't burn. Tip
them onto a board to cool, then chop.
Line the oven tray with baking paper.

2 Put the eggs and sugar in a clean,
dry bowl and beat with electric
beaters until pale and creamy. Sift the
self-raising flour and the plain flour
into the bowl, and add the pecans
and glacé ginger. Mix to a soft dough,
then place onto the prepared tray and
shape into a 9 x 23 cm loaf.

3 Bake the loaf for 45 minutes, or
until lightly golden. Transfer to a
wire rack to cool for 15 minutes on
either side, then carefully cut into
1 cm slices with a large serrated
bread knife. The biscotti will be
crumbly on the edges so work slowly
and if possible try to hold the sides as
you cut. Arrange the slices in a single
layer on baking trays. Bake for about
10 minutes each side. Don't worry if
they don't seem fully dry as they will
become crisp on cooling. Cool the
biscotti completely before storing in
an airtight container for 2–3 weeks.

NUTRITION PER BISCUIT
Protein 2.5 g; Fat 4 g; Carbohydrate
20 g; Dietary Fibre 1 g; Cholesterol
18 mg; 530 kJ (125 cal)

*Add the nuts and ginger to the mixture
and mix to a soft dough.*

*Place the dough on the prepared baking
tray and shape into a log shape.*

*Using a large serrated bread knife,
carefully cut the log into slices.*

GINGERBREAD HOUSE

Preparation time: 1 hour
  30 minutes + 50 minutes chilling
Total cooking time: 12 minutes per
  baking tray
Serves 30

GINGERBREAD
250 g unsalted butter, softened
2/3 cup (125 g) soft brown sugar
1/2 cup (175 ml) golden syrup
2 eggs, lightly beaten
4 cups (500 g) plain flour
1/2 cup (60 g) self-raising flour
2 tablespoons ground ginger
2 teaspoons bicarbonate of soda

ICING
50 ml lemon juice
2 cups (250 g) icing sugar, sifted
assorted sweets and sprinkles

1 Line 4 baking trays with baking paper. Place the butter, sugar and golden syrup in a bowl and beat until light and creamy. Add the eggs gradually, beating thoroughly after each addition. Sift the dry ingredients into the bowl and stir until combined. Bring the dough together with your hands and turn it out onto a well-floured work surface. Knead until the mixture is smooth. Cover the mixture with plastic wrap and refrigerate for 30 minutes. Preheat the oven to 180°C (350°F/Gas 4).

2 Cut paper patterns for the house. The sides should be 11 x 18 cm, the roof 17 x 22 cm and the front and back 14 x 24.5 cm. (measure 14.5 cm down from the centre of one of the ends and draw a line across the rectangle, draw a line from the centre point on the end to the point where the line meets each side—this will give you a triangular end to the rectangle, then cut off the corners).

3 Working quickly, divide the mixture into 6 portions and roll each out between two sheets baking paper to a 5 mm thickness. Using the templates as a guide, cut out two roof pieces, two front pieces and two sides of the house. If you would like windows or a door on your house, cut these from the gingerbread. Lift the pieces onto the baking trays and refrigerate for 20 minutes before baking. Bake for 12 minutes each and then leave to cool.

4 To make the icing, place the lemon juice in a bowl and add the icing sugar gradually until you have a smooth mixture which will stay in place when piped—if it is too runny, add more icing sugar. To assemble the house, join the front and sides of the house together with a piped line of icing and leave to dry. Add the back to the house in the same way, hold for a few minutes, then stand up to dry. Decorate the outside seam with more piped icing to strengthen it. Attach the roof pieces using more piped icing. Leave everything to dry before decorating. Attach sweets with icing or pipe decorations such as roof tiles or ivy onto the house.

NUTRITION PER SERVE
Protein 1 g; Fat 7 g; Carbohydrate 19.5 g; Dietary Fibre 0 g; Cholesterol 33 mg; 595 kJ (142 cal)

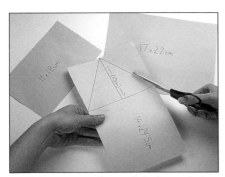

Make paper templates of the house before cutting the dough.

Join the sides of the house together, using piped icing as glue.

Carefully add the roof pieces to the house and leave to dry.

INDIVIDUAL CHRISTMAS CAKES

Preparation time: 1 hour + overnight soaking of the fruit

Total cooking time: 1 hour and 15 minutes
Makes 12

FRUIT CAKE
500 g (1 lb) sultanas
375 g (12 oz) raisins, chopped
250 g (8 oz) currants
250 g (8 oz) glacé cherries, quartered
250 ml (8 fl oz) brandy or rum, plus 1 tablespoon to glaze
250 g (8 oz) butter
230 g (7½ oz) soft dark brown sugar
2 tablespoons apricot jam
2 tablespoons treacle or syrup
1 tablespoon grated lemon or orange rind
4 eggs
350 g (11 oz) plain flour

HOLLY LEAVES AND BERRIES
60 g (2 oz) almond icing (ready-made)
green and red food colouring
pure icing sugar

FOR THE SOFT ICING-COVERED CAKES
100 g (3½ oz) apricot jam
100 g (3½ oz) soft icing (ready-made) per cake
pure icing sugar
thin ribbon

FOR THE ROYAL ICING-COVERED CAKES
1 egg white
250 g (8 oz) pure icing sugar, sifted
2–3 teaspoons lemon juice

1 Put the fruit in a bowl with the brandy and then allow it to soak in overnight.

2 Preheat the oven to slow 150°C (300°F/Gas 2). Lightly grease twelve 1 cup (250 ml/8 fl oz) muffin holes and line the bases with a circle of baking paper.

3 Beat the butter and sugar to just combine. Beat in the jam, treacle and rind. Add the eggs one at a time, beating after each addition.

4 Stir the fruit and the combined sifted flour and spices alternately into the mixture.

5 Spoon into the muffin holes and smooth the surfaces. Bake for 1¼ hours, or until a skewer inserted into the centres comes out clean. Cool in the muffin holes before turning out to decorate, so the small base becomes the top.

6 To make the holly leaves, knead 50 g (1¾ oz) of the almond icing until it is soft. Roll out on a surface lightly dusted with icing sugar, until 1 mm thick. Cut out the leaves with a cutter or template. Pinch the leaves in half, open out and press the edges gently to curl in different directions. Dry on baking paper. Brush green colouring around the edge of each leaf—don't put on too much colour or it will bleed.

7 Knead some red colouring into the remaining almond icing, and roll into it small balls to make berries. Then either paint or roll the berries in the colouring to coat thoroughly. Dry on baking paper.

8 For the soft icing-covered cakes, melt the jam until runny, strain and brush over the cakes. Roll out 100 g (3½ oz) of the soft icing at a time, on a surface lightly coated with pure icing sugar, until large enough to cover one cake. If there are any holes in the cake, use a little extra icing to plug them and make a smooth surface. Place the icing over the cake and ease over the side, pressing lightly, then trim from around the base. Mix together a little icing sugar and water into a smooth paste. Wrap ribbon around the base of the cake and seal with a little paste. Use the paste to secure two leaves and berries to the top.

9 To make the royal icing covering, lightly beat the egg white with a wooden spoon. Gradually add the icing sugar, beating to a smooth paste. Slowly add the lemon juice until slightly runny. Spread a tablespoon of icing over each cake, using a pallet knife to smooth and letting some drizzle down the sides. Secure holly leaves on top and some berries, using a little leftover icing.

Knead the almond icing until soft; cut out holly leaves with a cutter or template.

Paint the edges of the tiny leaves with colouring—not too much or it will bleed.

Roll out the soft icing until large enough to cover the cake.

Spread royal icing smoothly over the top, letting it drizzle down the side.

NOTE: These Christmas cakes can be stored in a cool, dark place for up to a month after they have been iced. This allows you to just relax and enjoy eating them at Christmas time!

LIQUEUR FRUITS

A perfectly indulgent way to finish off a holiday feast—luscious summer fruits soaked in rich, mouthwatering liqueurs.

Peaches in spiced Sauternes

Halve 4–6 kg ripe slipstone peaches, discard the stone and pack the peaches, along with 1 cinnamon stick and 1 star anise into a clean, warm 2 litre clip-top or preserving jar. Place 2 cups (500 g) sugar in a pan, add 2 cups (500 ml) water and stir over low heat until all the sugar has dissolved. Bring to the boil (at least 85°C) and boil for 5 minutes, then pour the hot syrup over the peaches and top with 1 cup (250 ml) Sauternes. Seal, invert for 2 minutes and store in a cool dry place for 2 weeks. *Fills a 2 litre jar*

Cherries in vanilla brandy

Prick the skins of 750 g cherries with a fine skewer. Heat 1½ cups (375 g) sugar with 100 ml water and 100 ml brandy in a pan, stirring until all the sugar is dissolved. Add the cherries and a vanilla bean and heat until boiling (at least 85°C). Place the cherries, syrup and 200 ml brandy in a clean, warm jar, seal and invert for 2 minutes. Store in a cool, dry place for 6 weeks, turning every couple of days for the first 2 weeks. Serve the fruit in its own liqueur. *Fills a 1 litre jar*

Drunken prunes with vanilla

Place 750 g pitted prunes in a clean, warm 1 litre clip-top or preserving jar. Cut a vanilla bean in half and place in the jar. Add 2 cups (500 ml) tawny port to cover the prunes, seal and invert for 2 minutes. Leave in a cool, dark place for at least 1 month before using. Store for up to 6 months. *Fills a 1 litre jar*

Left to right: Peaches in spiced Sauternes; Cherries in vanilla brandy; Drunken prunes with vanilla; Dried fruit salad with rum; Pears in mulled wine; Dried figs in liqueur muscat.

Dried fruit salad with rum

Place 2 cups (500 g) sugar, 1 cup (250 ml) orange juice, 2 strips orange rind and a vanilla bean in a pan and stir over low heat until all the sugar has dissolved. Bring to the boil (at least 85°C) for 5 minutes, then pour over 600 g of your choice of mixed dried fruits. Stir in 1 cup (250 ml) dark rum. Spoon the fruits into a warm, clean 1 litre clip-top or preserving jar and pour in the syrup. Tap to remove air bubbles, seal and invert for 2 minutes. Leave in a cool, dark place for at least 1 month before using. Store for up to 6 months. *Fills a 1 litre jar*

Pears in mulled wine

Place 2 cups (500 g) sugar and 3 cups (750 ml) red wine in a large pan. Stir over low heat until the sugar has dissolved. Add 1.25 kg peeled, halved and cored small pears, 1 cinnamon stick, 6 whole allspice, 6 cloves and 2 strips each of orange and lemon rind. Cover with a small plate to keep the pears submerged. Bring to the boil (at least 85°C), then reduce the heat and simmer for 10 minutes, or until just tender. Arrange the pears in a warm, clean 1 litre clip-top or preserving jar. Boil the syrup for 15 minutes, then mix ½ cup (125 ml) syrup with ½ cup (125 ml) brandy and 3 cloves. Pour over the pears to cover, seal and invert for 2 minutes. Leave in a cool, dark place for at least 1 month. Store for up to 6 months. *Fills a 1 litre jar*

Dried figs in liqueur muscat

Cut the stalks from 750 g dried figs and place in a non-metallic bowl. Heat 2 cups (500 ml) orange juice and a cinnamon stick in a small pan until just boiling. Pour over the figs and allow to stand for 10 minutes. Drain and reserve the liquid. Place the figs and cinnamon stick in a clean, warm 1 litre clip-top or preserving jar. Heat the reserved liquid to boiling (at least 85°C) and add ¾ cup (185 ml) liqueur muscat. Pour over the figs and tap to remove air bubbles. Add any remaining liquid to cover the fruit, if required, and gently shake to combine. Seal, invert for 2 minutes and leave in a cool, dark place for at least 1 month before using. Top up with liqueur muscat to ensure the fruit is always covered. Store for up to 6 months. *Fills a 1 litre jar*

CANDIED FRUIT

Candying fruit takes 8–10 days but it will keep for up to a year if stored between sheets of greaseproof paper in an airtight container in a cool, dry place. Fruits with strong flavours such as pineapple, citrus peel, apricots, peaches, pears, figs, plums and cherries are suitable for candying. Citrus peel should be cut into quarters or strips. To avoid any bitterness in the pith, blanch the peel in boiling water and refresh in cold water 2–3 times for 5 minutes each time before cooking.

DAY	FRUIT	SUGAR	METHOD	SOAKING/ DRYING TIME
1	500 g (1 lb) fresh fruit	Add 250 g (8 oz) to 1 litre (32 fl oz) water	Dissolve the sugar in the water in a large pan. Add the juice of 1 lemon, and bring to the boil. Add the fruit and poach until just tender but holding its shape (cooking times vary for the fruit used). Place in a heatproof bowl and weigh down with a saucer.	24 hours
	500 g (1 lb) canned fruit in syrup	Drain the fruit, reserving the liquid and make up to 1 litre (32 fl oz) with water. Add 250 g (8 oz) to each litre liquid.	Dissolve the sugar in the water in a large pan. Add the juice of 1 lemon and bring to the boil. Place the fruit in a heatproof bowl and pour over the boiling syrup. Weigh down.	24 hours
2	Fresh/canned	Drain the fruit, add 100 g (3¹¹⁄₂ oz) to every 1 litre (32 fl oz) liquid	Return the syrup to the pan, add the sugar and stir to dissolve. Bring to the boil and pour over the fruit. Weigh down.	24 hours
3	Fresh/canned	Drain the fruit, add 100 g (3¹¹⁄₂ oz) to every 1 litre (32 fl oz) liquid	Repeat method as above	24 hours
4	Fresh/canned	Add 150 g (5 oz) per 1 litre (32 fl oz) liquid	Repeat method as above	24 hours
5	Fresh/canned	Add 150 g (5 oz) per 1 litre (32 fl oz) liquid	Repeat method as above	24 hours
6	Fresh/canned	Add 250 g (8 oz) per 1 litre (32 fl oz) liquid	Repeat method as above	24 hours
7	Fresh/canned	No extra sugar added at this step	Put the fruit and syrup in a large pan and bring to the boil, then reduce the heat and simmer for 5 minutes. Drain the fruit on a wire rack over a tray.	24 hours drying time
8	Fresh/canned	Add 500 g (1 lb) to 150 ml (5 fl oz) water for glacé	To glacé the fruit, make up a sugar syrup and boil for 1 minute. Keep hot and cover with a lid to stop evaporation. Pour a little of the hot syrup into a bowl and dip each piece of drained fruit first in boiling water and then in the syrup, then place on a rack to drain. If the syrup becomes cloudy, start again. Place the fruit on wire racks in an oven heated to lowest temperature, with the door ajar, until dry and no longer sticky.	12 hours–3 days
		Enough to coat 500 g (1 lb) fruit	To crystallize the fruit, dip each piece of fruit in boiling water, shake off any excess and then roll in caster sugar. Place on wire racks and allow to dry.	

VINEGARS AND DRESSINGS

Unusually shaped bottles and jars quickly turn these delicious vinegars and dressings into much sought-after gifts. In fact, you may be tempted to keep them all for yourself!

Blueberry and mint vinegar

Place 2 cups (500 ml) white wine vinegar, 2 cups (310 g) fresh or frozen blueberries and 4 fresh mint sprigs in a pan. Bring to the boil, then reduce the heat and simmer for 5 minutes. Remove the mint sprigs and pour the mixture into a clean, warm jar. Add fresh mint sprigs, seal and keep in a cold place for 7 days. Line a funnel with muslin and strain the vinegar into clean, warm bottles. Seal and label. Keep for up to 1 year.
Makes 3 cups (750 ml)

Mint and teriyaki dressing

Put ¼ cup (5 g) fresh mint leaves, 1 tablespoon fresh dill sprigs, ⅓ cup (80 ml) lemon juice, 1 cup (250 ml) apple cider vinegar, 1 teaspoon honey and ½ cup (125 ml) teriyaki sauce in a food processor, and combine well. Season. Keep refrigerated for 1 week.
Makes 2 cups (500 ml)

Yoghurt and anchovy dressing

Put 800 g plain yoghurt, 180 g drained anchovy fillets and 2 teaspoons lemon juice in a food processor and combine well. Season to taste with black pepper and store in the refrigerator for up to 3 days.
Makes 3 cups (750 ml)

Left to right: Blueberry and mint vinegar; Mint and teriyaki dressing; Yoghurt and anchovy dressing; Lemon, lime and thyme vinegar; Peach and basil vinegar; Sweet orange and parsley dressing.

Lemon, lime and thyme vinegar

Put the juice and rind from 2 lemons and 2 limes in a pan with 1 litre white wine vinegar and 10 fresh thyme sprigs and bring to the boil. Reduce the heat and simmer for 5 minutes. Remove from the heat and stand at room temperature until cold. Meanwhile, place the rind of another 2 lemons in a clean, warm jar and add 10 thyme sprigs. Strain the vinegar and pour it into the jar. Seal and keep in a cool place for 7 days. Line a funnel with muslin and strain the vinegar into clean, warm bottles. Add the lime leaves, seal and label. Keep for up to 1 year.
Makes l litre

Peach and basil vinegar

Place 2 cups (430 g) drained canned peach slices, 1 cup (250 ml) white wine vinegar and 1 cup (60 g) fresh basil leaves in a pan. Bring to the boil, then reduce the heat and simmer for 5 minutes. Remove from the heat and stand at room temperature until cold. Meanwhile, put 1 cup (60 g) fresh basil leaves in a clean, warm jar. Remove the peach slices and basil leaves from the vinegar and pour the liquid into the jar. Seal and keep in a cool place for 7 days. Line a funnel with muslin and strain the vinegar into clean, warm bottles, seal and label. Keep for up to 1 year. *Makes 1¾ cups (440 ml)*

Sweet orange and parsley dressing

Combine 2 tablespoons white vinegar, 2 tablespoons cider vinegar and 2 tablespoons red wine vinegar with 2 tablespoons lemon juice. Add 1 teaspoon salt and whisk until dissolved. Slightly heat 1 cup (250 ml) orange juice with 2 tablespoons honey and stir. Pour over the vinegar mixture and add 3 tablespoons Dijon mustard, 2 tablespoons drained and finely chopped capers, 2 diced sweet gherkins, 4 tablespoons chopped fresh flat-leaf parsley and ½ cup (125 ml) olive oil. Season to taste with ground black pepper. This dressing may be served either warm or cold. Keep refrigerated for 1 week. *Makes 2½ cups (600 ml)*

HINTS AND TIPS

✳ If your attempts to roast a turkey or bake a ham are a one-off and your budget is tight, buy disposable foil baking dishes from supermarkets. Be careful though, they can bend with too much weight which can be hazardous when hot. Use two together to help strengthen the dishes under the weight of your turkey or ham.

✳ You will need plenty of fridge space for a large turkey or ham. This may require removing a shelf and some organisation to fit.

✳ Don't leave foods unrefrigerated for too long in warmer climates or heated rooms. Room temperature is the perfect environment for bacteria to breed. This can cause food poisoning, especially in chicken, duck and turkey.

✳ Think about what else you need to be cooking in the oven at the same time as your roast. For example, how are you going to fit the roast vegetables in the oven if they are being served alongside the ham? A covered kettle barbecue is ideal for cooking hams, allowing you a lot more space in your oven on the day.

✳ Don't fret if you have leftovers—you don't have to eat ham sandwiches for a week. Turkey and ham leftovers can be turned into a variety of tasty dishes. See pages 62–65 for some great ideas!

✳ It is worth paying extra for good-quality dried and glacé fruits for your cake or pudding. Look for plump, moist and glossy fruit which will help prevent your baked goods from drying out and improve the overall flavour. Soaking the fruits for two days prior to baking also enhances both flavour and moistness. For those who like their cake a little on the tipsy side, make the cake at least a few weeks ahead, and then once a week prick the top of the cake with a needle or very thin cake skewer and carefully spoon over a little alcohol of your choice (usually brandy), letting it soak in. Make sure you re-wrap it well each time.

✳ If you are making a boiled pudding, don't forget to buy some calico and string and make sure you have a pot large enough to boil it in.

✳ Christmas cakes and puddings make great gifts too, and look wonderful when packaged either with colourful wrappings or simply some brown paper, straw and a couple of holly leaves.

✳ Make ice cubes from fruit juices for additional festive colour and flavour in your drinks.

✳ Christmas is a time for people dropping in. You will save money and stress if you have some goodies on hand, such as slices, biscuits, nuts, cake or chocolates. If you are making gifts of jams or vinegars, make a couple of extra jars for those unexpected guests who arrive with a present.

INDEX

INTERNATIONAL GLOSSARY OF INGREDIENTS

capsicum	red or green pepper	tomato paste (Aus.)	tomato purée, double concentrate (UK)
coriander	cilantro		
eggplant	aubergine	tomato purée (Aus.)	sieved crushed tomatoes/ passata (UK)
English spinach	spinach		
sausage mince	sausage meat	yabbies	freshwater crayfish
thick cream	double cream	zucchini	courgette

First published 2002 by Murdoch Books UK, Erico House 6th Floor North, Upper Richmond Road,
Putney, London SW 15 2TG
This edition published 2006 for Index Books Ltd, Garrard Way, Kettering, Northants, NN16 8TD, UK

ISBN 1 897730 53 5
A catalogue record for this book is available from the British library.

Managing Editor: Anna Cheifetz **Design Manager:** Sarah Rock **Editor:** Claire Musters **Designer:** Cathy Layzell
Photographers: Craig Cranko, Reg Morrison (steps) **Food Stylist:** Mary Harris **Food Preparation:** Kerrie Mullins, Alison Adams
CEO: Juliet Rogers **Publisher:** Kay Scarlett
Colour separation by Colourscan, Singapore **Printed** by Toppan Printing Co., China

The nutritional information provided for each recipe does not include any accompaniments, such as rice, unless they are listed
in the ingredients. The values are approximations and can be affected by biological and seasonal variations in food, the
unknown composition of some manufactured foods and uncertainty in the dietary database. Nutrient data given are derived
primarily from the NUTTAB95 database produced by the Australian New Zealand Food Authority.